NO MITIGATING CIRCUMSTANCES

In preparation:
A FURTHER VOLUME OF REMINISCENCES

NO MITIGATING CIRCUMSTANCES

The Hon.
Sir Neville Faulks

One of Her Majesty's Judges

WILLIAM KIMBER · LONDON

First published in 1977 by
WILLIAM KIMBER & CO. LIMITED
Godolphin House, 22a Queen Anne's Gate,
London, SW1H 9AE

© Sir Neville Faulks, 1977
ISBN 0 7183 0325 3

Typeset by Watford Typesetters
and printed and bound in Great Britain by
The Garden City Press Limited,
Letchworth, Hertfordshire, SG6 1JS

Contents

List of Illustrations

CHAPTER ONE

Family Circle

My paternal grandfather, whom I never met, was apparently a rather successful milkman. The family lived in Bryanston Square and, after his early and untimely demise in his forties, moved to Cambridge Terrace (still with four floors and a basement).

Grandpa Faulks, I have always understood, was not a teetotaller. He was a powerfully built man with seven sons and he liked his swim in the evening at what I suppose were then the 'Public Baths'. And one day they carted him home from the baths and medicine was no good to him and he died. My father used to say that he didn't die of drink but that if he had been less fond of alcohol he would not have left us.

My paternal grandmother, his relict, I only saw once, in my pram. I must say I don't blame her. Seven sons in about ten years cannot have rendered her particularly enthusiastic when the next generation carried on the good work. She spent two months each winter in Menton, and left my unfortunate father to compete with the brood. One of her less attractive characteristics was to ring the bell in her sitting-room at the top of the house in order to summon some unfortunate 'skivvy' (as the housemaids were called in those days) from the basement to put more coal on the fire.

Her behaviour in this respect was similar to that of a character in Henri de Montherlant's *The Bachelors*. This man deliberately subscribed to a newspaper which he didn't read in order to savour the pleasure of seeing the unfortunate postman climb up a very steep hill to deliver this one copy.

I don't know when my grandmother died. It must have been at some time during the First World War. The best I can do is to remember that my grandfather was William something – my brother administers a very small trust in that name still – and she was Henrietta, known as 'Hattie'. The brood consisted first of Uncle Percy who was a year older than my Papa. He was always described as a 'good commonsense sort of chap, but not a great scholar'. He and Papa (I call him 'Papa' because over the years I called him 'Daddy' until another generation called

7

him 'Grandpa' whereupon I fell in with the prevailing practice – I used to call him 'Sir' a lot too, something that has fallen entirely into desuetude – and 'Papa' will make him more easily identifiable, particularly because he was a real 'Heavy Father') were both sent to the City of London School where Dr Abbott reigned. Papa always was very proud that he shared a headmaster with Mr Asquith, of whose politics he, being a staunch Conservative, thoroughly disapproved. Papa was born on 21st December 1876, six years after the Franco-Prussian War, was christened Major James, lived with me from the age of seventy-three, and died in November 1969, a month before his ninety-fourth birthday. He was thirty-one when I was born on 27th January 1908.

Unfortunately, as happens even in the best regulated families, Uncle Percy, although older, was not as bright as his younger brother. Papa played the piano and the piccolo, and was in all sort of teams winning the All Ages Fives Cup three years running (which is somewhere in the attic now) and poor Uncle Percy, batting along with his famous commonsense, was about two forms below his younger brother, which was obviously disastrous for his morale.

So my grandmother decided that Uncle Percy must electrify the New World with his commonsense, and at about the time that Papa had got an exhibition at St John's College, Cambridge, Uncle Percy departed for Canada. There he met and married my Aunt Kate (whom I never saw), and they started an immensely successful – for those days – store in Calgary. Their union was not blessed, which was perhaps just as well, as the commonsense did not extend to insuring the substantial wooden building, and when in due course it was burned down together with all its contents they must have found themselves in reduced circumstances. Save that they are no more, that is all that I can say about them.

The next of the brood was Papa, whom for the moment we may leave up at Cambridge, reading mathematics, stroking a rather humble boat, playing water polo for his university, a game which was in those days played in the Cam and did not even command a half-blue, going on soccer tours to Belgium with his college team, never speaking to a woman except his mother, and bicycling down to Cambridge Terrace via Ware at weekends – and back again !

Then we have Uncle Sydney who is the most engaging character. IS, mark you, for he was ninety-seven in January 1977, and never misses a rehearsal of the Sandown IOW Amateur Operatic Society, which he conducts. Quite a span for a man who went round the world conducting the orchestra for Sir Henry Irving at the turn of the century, and was the original Musical Director for *Irene* now revived in London half a century later. He is my godfather which seems faintly ridiculous. They did things in a quaint way in those days and their selection of godparents for me is especially strange considering that my parents were church-going C of E. I had two godfathers, my father and Uncle Sydney, and my godmother was my mother. Considering that Uncle Sydney was a peripatetic musician, I had no idea who in the world was to look after my spiritual welfare if my parents were run over by what, in those days, would have been a horse-bus.

Uncle Sydney is not very commercially minded. At first, he conducted the orchestra for Fred Terry and Julia Neilson, going round the country, living in digs, until he must have been sick to death of *The Scarlet Pimpernel*. Then he married one of the cast, my Aunt Ethel, of whom I remember nothing save that she had red hair. By her he had two boys, one of whom survives – a very charming retired Lloyd's underwriter. The other ran away from Cranbrook School, where they were both educated, was the naughty boy of the family, and died a long time ago.

Things always seemed to go wrong for him, poor Philip. I can remember his climbing up into the attic in about 1925, to inspect a water-softener which Mummy had proudly installed there. He managed to fall through the wooden slats, and injure himself. No one else would have done this, but he was accident prone, and to make matters worse, he had been strictly forbidden to trespass there.

Uncle Sydney went on flogging around the country because he was too loyal to the Terrys, and he failed to consider his own fortune. Typical was his arriving one day late for his appointment to consider whether he should be the conductor of the Bournemouth Symphony Orchestra. Typical, but rather endearing. Typical again, when offered the Palm Court Orchestra at the Grand Hotel, Eastbourne, he thought that Albert Sandler, the violinist, should be in charge, while he should play the piano.

And play the piano in the Palm Court (BBC, Sunday nights) he did for endless years, described in the *Radio Times* as Sydney ffoulkes. You can't blame him for endeavouring to improve our hideous, unpronounceable name, although he has reverted to it now in his old age. (We pronounce it as in 'The Old Folks at Home'.)

I was at a cocktail party a week or two ago when my hostess became temporarily flustered and introduced me as 'Sir Frederick Fooks', and for one brief moment I felt myself quite an aristocrat. Indeed, it is in a comfortable home for old Folks that Uncle Sydney lives today. But he seems very happy and there is not much point in dwelling on what might have been. He wrote some good music, notably an adaptation of 'Under the Greenwood Tree' but his old friend and rival, Ketelby, who also settled in the Isle of Wight and is dead long since, with his 'In a Monastery Garden' and 'In a Persian Market', consistently outsold him.

When my daughter Judith was married in the Temple Church on 22nd February 1975, Dr Thalben-Ball played a Wedding March instead of the usual Toccata by Vidor. The March was specially composed for the occasion by Uncle Sydney, aged ninety-five, and gave general satisfaction.

My cousin Philip, he who fell through the rafters at home, was tubby, bespectacled and looked much more like Billy Bunter than an embryo criminal when he ran away from school. But he decided that every man's hand was against him and that the life for him was a life of crime. He chose burglary. Save that he was very inefficient at it I have no details of his record nor would I ask for them if indeed the CRO of dead men is preserved by the authorities. On one occasion he jumped off a bedroom window sill into the arms of a policeman waiting below, and I cannot believe that his chosen occupation was lucrative.

Indeed the only occasion when I spoke to him after his fall in our home was just after the War. We were having a dinner-party to celebrate my demobilisation when the telephone rang :

'I'm your cousin, Philip.'

'Oh, yes.'

'Can you let me have fifty pounds?'

'I'm afraid that I'm unemployed at the moment myself. I'm very sorry.'

'Do you mean that?'

'I'm afraid so.'

'I'll put Ruby Sparks on you.'

And the telephone was slammed down. I never heard of Philip again until someone told me that he was dead.

I made enquiries and discovered that there was indeed a character called Ruby Sparks although whether he was a housebreaker or whether Philip even knew him, I am unable to say. As I had been away from England for a long time the dreaded name failed to have the expected effect. But we kept everything under lock and key for a time.

Next comes Uncle Ronald. He too had emigrated to Canada but

came to live with us in about 1915 as a Sergeant in the Canadian Pay Corps. He was with us for three years or so, until the end of the War, and was a sweet, quiet man with whom Mummy fell in love. This must have been very embarrassing for him, but Papa was pachydermatous and did not notice; and, of course, nothing happened except that (a) she insisted on calling my brother, who was born in 1917, 'Peter Ronald', and (b) there was a photograph of him in the bedroom until the day of her death.

In case this should give a hint of impropriety, there was none. Mummy was a romantic school-girl, and would insist on undressing behind a screen before she retired to bed. 'Your Mother was a prude', Papa would thunder; and I have often thought that the manner in which the four of us were conceived must have been rather dreary. There should have been a fifth (I was the eldest) but poor Mummy walked from Sydenham to Camberwell Green and back, drank half a bottle of gin, jumped off the kitchen table, and that brought about a miscarriage and did the trick. It is a much sadder story than it seems put down in cold blood here, for she did not enjoy exercise, and I should think it was the only time she took spirits in her life.

It may be that Papa had some justification for his thunderings for I remember once singing to Mummy a popular song : —

> When I brought an apple, she let me hold her hand,
> When I brought an orange, we kissed to beat the band,
> When I brought bananas, we hugged with all our might,
> I'm going to bring a water-melon to my girl tonight!

I suppose I was about thirteen, and had no idea that this ditty could have any sexual overtones. But Mummy got in a great state and forbade me ever to sing that disgusting song again. I was, being very simple, baffled. Poor, darling Mummy had had a very Victorian upbringing, couldn't boil an egg, and was never allowed into her own kitchen. She was not strong and when we went to the seaside she put on a very long bathing dress, swam four breast strokes, and then slowly sank. Meanwhile, Papa, like a porpoise, was miles out to sea.

Uncle Ronald returned to Canada when I was ten and I never saw him again. He died in Edmonton comparatively young in some industrial accident with the details of which I am not familiar. His wife, my Aunt Winifred, still resides in British Columbia and sends me Christmas cards. She is small, very devout, and eighty-five, and has been blessed with many children and grandchildren, a number of whom, as well as she herself, have stayed with us over the years. The Canadian branch of the family now calls itself 'Folks'.

I can't remember whether Uncle Victor or Uncle Claude comes next, not that it matters for both have been dead some time.

Uncle Victor was very tall and upright, and was, like Papa, an accountant. He was the great one for discovering the lineage of the Faulks family, and paid a substantial sum of money to learn from the College of Arms that we were descended from a gentleman called Fulke of Anjou who came over with William the Conqueror; what with the distance from Normandy to Anjou and one thing and another, Papa was disposed to treat this revelation with scepticism.

Uncle Victor married a parson's daughter, my Aunt Muriel, who surely still survives. She unknowingly inflicted upon me a very salutary lesson. When I was about fourteen, she came to stay for a weekend. Mummy, after luncheon, suggested that Aunt Muriel and I might like a game of lawn tennis. I patronisingly agreed, thinking myself a combination of Patterson and Tilden at that time, and ready to show old ladies the modern game. We had a good grass court, new balls, and I had a new racquet which Grandpa (of whom much more anon) had given me, while Aunt Muriel had a loosely-strung old racquet which belonged to Mummy who had given up lawn tennis because Papa was such a horrid beast to play with. So there was no excuse. I don't think I won a single point. I behaved abominably badly, slunk off to my bedroom, and sulked without even saying 'Thank you' for the game. I might have behaved better if someone had remembered to tell me before the game that Aunt Muriel had played lawn tennis and hockey for Scotland for a number of years.

Their son, Derek, had a very good war with Hurricanes; is about six feet six tall and practises dental surgery in Scotland. I cannot recollect that we ever met.

Uncle Victor also was musical and we all had to listen to some composition of his played on BBC Radio shortly before he died.

I will deal shortly with Uncle Claude and Uncle Reggie, the latter as the seventh son of course called Septimus. He died recently at about eighty-five, and I saw little of him after his wife forbade him to remain a Freemason.

The brood on the whole were very abstemious, but these two were not averse to a little occasional alcohol. Uncle Claude, whom I only vaguely remember, I recall with much pleasure as having visited us in about 1921. He was shown up into our rather vast nursery, which the previous owner of the house had used as a billiards room, and promptly put his hand in his pocket and presented me with a sovereign as a tip. I was overwhelmed and would have been more so had I realised that he almost certainly could not afford such generosity. He had the most charm of the seven, and a good deal of ability as well : but whereas Reggie got a Choral Scholarship to King's College, Cambridge and spent a worthy, but I should think tedious, life in Shell ending up as head of the Cable Department, Uncle Claude played the horses, flitted from job to job, one day the Assistant Manager of the Savoy Hotel, the next day something else, until he disappeared. I don't think I saw him after that day in 1921, although I know that he married and had a son. Mummy used to say how charming and delightful he was, with a wistful look in her eyes.

I must now devote a little space to the distaff side of my family, featuring, in particular, my mother's father, Grandpa Ginner, pronounced as in 'Gin and French'. As he was the only grandfather I ever met, I shall refer to him hereafter as Grandpa.

My father's ambition in life was to be a master at one of the great public schools, not too badly paid, plenty of fresh air, plenty of holidays, and plenty of games. But in those days, a good degree was necessary for such an appointment, and that he did not get. The poor chap was ill and only got an aegrotat in the first part of his Tripos, and somehow he scored a disastrous third in the second part. If he had been going to the Bar, which his mother could not afford, it would not have mattered so much, but obviously Messrs Gabbitas, Thring and Co would scarcely be able to find him a job at Winchester. So he started in Grantham, and, after divers other schools, moved to the Skinners School at Tunbridge Wells where he met and became friendly with a Dr Midwood of whose doctorate he was clearly envious. He used to say behind the Doctor's back, 'Midwood ! Doctor of Philosophy of Zurich ! A rubbishy piece of paper !'

He had this chip on his shoulder until the end of his life, for when he was over ninety and staying at Wittenham House with Elizabeth whom I had recently married, he rummaged about among the papers I was trying to sort out, and proclaimed triumphantly of her last husband who had been Bishop of Reading and won an MC at Gallipoli : 'Hah ! Only got a third.' I was very cross, for the papers were no business of his, and I didn't tell Elizabeth.

The Midwoods had one daughter, Eileen, who told me the facts of life at Bembridge in the Isle of Wight in August 1919. She was a year older than I was, and she swore me to secrecy. I was so astonished by it all that I couldn't keep it to myself, and unloaded it on to my eleven year old sister, Sheila, as we took our Sunday morning walk to Grandpa Ginner's. She greatly disappointed me by saying that she didn't believe a word of it, and that anyhow Eileen had a dirty mind.

It was after Papa had decided to go abroad to teach, having got a job at a school in Bermuda, where he became a Captain in the Bermuda Rifles and joined the Freemasons, that he met Mummy. This was at Hastings where Grandma Ginner had some relatives. They made up a four at auction bridge and Mummy, an only child, aged nineteen, and improving her education at some drawing school, fell madly in love with this impecunious twenty-nine year old schoolmaster who added up the figures on her bridge marker in such record time. He was five foot eleven inches tall with black hair parted down the middle, as was the custom in those days, and handsome. She was small, with a head of golden hair (this was the 'crowning glory' era) and, from her photographs, I think she was beautiful. Everybody loved her and I never heard her say an unkind word to anyone or anyone say anything unkind about her.

My first memory of her, however, dates from the age of two when, seated opposite my sister Sheila in the double pram, she then coming up to a promising one, I leaned forward and bit her big toe whereupon my mother, who wouldn't have hurt a fly, even though she endangered her life by not doing so, bent bravely forward outside Makepeace the Chemist, with all suburban Sydenham apparently operating with spy-glasses, and bit mine.

She was no fool and she could get Papa to do what she wanted even when he was bloody-minded, by making him think that he had thought of it first. And it was a joy as a small boy after she had announced proudly at home, 'I'm going down to rave at Croger', to accompany her to the fishmonger and hear her say, as he doffed his hat, 'Oh! Mr Croger, I am afraid that the plaice yesterday wasn't quite up to your usual standard.'

Mummy ruled the local Amateur Dramatic Society with a rod of iron, appointing people to the committee who would 'see her way'. She appointed the local bank manager, poor fellow, to be Honorary Secretary which involved an enormous amount of work. He was her slave and he was thrilled, considering it a step up in the world. Whether it got him any new clients, I don't know. I don't believe that he had a very happy life for he had no children and was also in thrall to his wife, who was a very tiresome little woman who served underarm and thought it unsporting to play her a drop shot. She was presumably named after the late lamented Florence Nightingale as on the rare occasions that she made a winning shot, he would tactfully exclaim: 'That was a beaut, Flo.'

He played in the third men's team with Papa, who for some reason would wear a brown homburg hat, and who berated him soundly throughout the match.

At Hastings, Papa, like a sensible chap, proposed and was warmly accepted as it was all so romantic, but her parents were a little less enthusiastic. Eventually it was agreed that they should become engaged to be married, but that Papa should serve his stint as a schoolmaster in Bermuda, returning to this country at Christmas 1906 when, if they still wanted to get married, they could; but there was to be no more nonsense about schoolmastering, and Papa was to be apprenticed to Grandpa's accountant and use his degree in mathematics that way.

Today, perhaps, those would be considered hard terms, and I am sure that they were designed to ensure 'out of sight, out of mind' for Mummy, and a disinclination to leave his career for Papa. But they did not succeed; absence made Mummy's heart grow fonder, and Papa returned to the charge as arranged.

They were married on 21st April 1907, Grandpa providing a very splendid wedding and a house. No time was lost, and I appeared nine months and six days later.

Grandpa was an East India Merchant, which is rather a grand way of saying a wholesale grocer, the senior partner in Ginner, Morton and Goddard of 10 Eastcheap, EC4. He was well-to-do, extravagant and opinionated; Papa was opinionated, careful, and, then, impecunious. They loathed each other. Papa called his in-laws 'Mr Ginner' and 'Mrs Ginner' respectively until the day they died. And for their part, my parents were addressed as 'Major' and 'Mabel' – strange names now but common enough then.

Perhaps to make up for the paucity of godparents to which I have already referred, they endowed me with their unusual forenames. Neville Major Ginner Faulks – what a name! My Great-Aunt Edith pathetically offered me money to change my name to Ginner-Faulks just before the war because she, an elderly maiden lady, was by then the last of the Ginners. But though I needed the money, I politely refused.

Grandpa was rather a formidable figure and, never having produced a son himself, doted on me, taking me up to his bedroom every Sunday before luncheon and anointing my hair with some disgusting preparation called *Pomade Parfumé à bas de Vaseline*. In consequence, Papa decided that I was likely to be spoilt, and *that* he would never tolerate. So from the start I had to watch my step as far as Papa was concerned, as he would easily get into a great rage about nothing.

Grandpa was prematurely bald, and had a Lord Kitchener moustache, only not so large. This confounded *pomade parfumé* was designed to save me from baldness. If he could see me now, he would be gravely disappointed.

Grandpa was a life-long teetotaller but, nevertheless, was always sending Mummy cases of claret which for some reason he considered good for her blood, and was a very generous host, keeping a large and well-stocked cellar. Papa, who told me in his eighties, to my astonishment, that he had never made more than a couple of thousand a year in his life, was almost a teetotaller and was never known to buy anyone a drink or to take any of us to the theatre. I used to think this meanness, but I suppose now that it was poverty. Nonetheless, we had a cook and a nursemaid. I can only surmise that Grandpa paid for them. Grandpa wouldn't give Mummy an allowance but constant streams of presents used to arrive for which my parents used to have to say 'Thank You' which Mummy didn't mind but which Papa objected to very much.

Papa left quite a few bob and could be generous about big things. For instance, he was ninety plus when I re-married and he ladled out a dollop as a wedding present to defeat the Treasury. So that, if his story was true, either Mummy, whose will I have never seen, did him proud, or, more likely, he was a shrewd investor. What made him maddening as opposed to terrifying – and he could be both – was his reaction to a tap running or a light being left on. He would rush round the house in a fury, at the slightest pretext, screaming, 'How many more lights? The system is overloaded.' And if a fuse went, as occasionally happened at Christmas, he was delighted, for he had made his point.

Grandpa was immensely proud of being a JP and a Common Councillor of the City of London. They asked him to be Alderman for the Billingsgate Ward in which Eastcheap is situated, but by the grace of God he knew that he was no after dinner speaker and refused. What would have happened to the family finances had he accepted and progressed to Lord Mayor of London, I shudder to think.

When I went to school, I always had to address my letters to him as W. P. Ginner Esq., JP, CC, and to Papa as M. J. Faulks, Esq., MA, FSAA. This was very important. Grandpa also used to bang on about his relations and, in particular, about Ruby Ginner, the now forgotten ballerina, and Dr Ginner of Monte Carlo and young Charles who had taken up painting. I have a Ginner today which Grandpa bought in 1932. Young Charles (1878–1952) has not been with us for a long time and his father in fact practised at Cannes, so that I doubt if Grandpa ever set eyes on either of these gentlemen. I have read in *Country Life*, however, that the late Edward Le Bas paid £25 for a Ginner which made 8,200 guineas for his estate. I am sure that Grandpa paid more than that for mine and I keep my fingers crossed.

Grandpa was locally considered to be very rich, and I think he could have been if he hadn't gambled on the Stock Exchange or if he had only dabbled in stocks and shares. But he would never do things by halves. His motto was always, 'the best is good enough for me', and a vague tip from an acquaintance would prompt a big gamble. In the Spring of 1914, for instance, he bought a shipload of Mauritius sugar and his partner, a shrewd, industrious man who had been one of his commercial travellers, or reps as they are now called, threw up his hands in horror, crying, 'We'll never sell it.'

Came the war, and they found themselves war profiteers on cheap Mauritius sugar. But he never lost the taste for gambling and in the long run he did not benefit. The old gentleman lived in a comparatively modest house, the only child having married, but he had his billiards room, a bit of land with two gardeners and, what was considered rather dashing by the end of the war, two motor cars – an enormous Minerva in which I was always sick unless I could sit in front with the chauffeur (but Papa always did that), and a Wolseley; and he gave his chauffeur a runabout as well.

He was very keen on the Café Royal where the head waiter, Jacques, made much of him, and we used to proceed from the suburbs in tandem in the Minerva and another large limousine hired from and driven by the local coachman, turned *garagiste*, Tom Tye. He liked a party of fourteen at the pantomime, and always got fifteen stalls so that we little ones could heap our coats on the odd seats. At the Café Royal, you could have anything you liked, but you were liable to be asked if it was good before you had had your first mouthful or spoonful, to which you prudently replied, 'Yes, thank you, Grandpa.'

After the pantomime, a flunkey would find a large tip pressed into his willing hand together with a piece of cardboard reading 'Mr Ginner's cars', and he would shout himself hoarse, and we would get away first in triumph.

But it wasn't all beer and skittles. It seems so petty now, but the way Grandpa and Papa disliked each other was very painful to me although it probably passed unnoticed by my younger sisters and brother. (Sheila is two years younger than I am, and Peter is ten. Lorna, who is dead, was born six years after me.)

Grandpa was the chairman and president and general Pooh-Bah of the Forest Hill Bowling Club and he presented a number of cups for competition. He never smoked anything but Havana cigars, and was very lavish with them. Papa for his part was the secretary of the Syden-ham Lawn Tennis Club, treasurer of the Sydenham and Forest Hill Amateur Dramatic Society, and a very prominent Freemason.

On the self-same day, each referring to the activities of the other, my father said, 'You know, the trouble with your grandfather is that he likes to be a bug among fleas', and Grandpa said, 'You know, my boy, the trouble with your father is that he likes to be cock of his own little dung-hill.' Neither remark was very attractive which I suppose is why they have stuck. But it was all very depressing, as our Sunday visits to Grandpa could have been such fun.

Grandpa had a 'thing' about Sydenham. He always used to refer to 'The Sydenham Snobs'. Whilst it is true to say that there was an astonishing amount of snobbery in Sydenham, the comment did not come very well from him, as he was the most colossal snob himself, some-thing which I could never put against my Conservative Papa. Grandpa somehow contrived to get himself presented at Court, and bought his levée dress at great expense, sword and all, and then had himself photo-graphed, showering copies upon his friends and acquaintances as well as upon his descendants.

Nowadays, both West and East Lewisham return a Socialist member of Parliament and no doubt a Communist thinks it worth while to risk his deposit, but in my boyhood there was no doubt who would be elected. West Lewisham, our constituency, was represented by Sir Edward Coates, Bart, and East Lewisham by Sir Assheton Pownall, also Bart. Grandpa, because his grandfather had supported Mr Gladstone and because he worshipped Mr Asquith, and also, I dare say, because Free Trade was better than Protection for an East India Merchant, was a last-ditch Liberal. He took the lowest view of Mr Lloyd George and Sir John Simon, and, after Mr Asquith, Sir Herbert Samuel was his favourite politician.

But that didn't stop his taking me to Conservative rallies and introducing me to the baronets, who had to be polite although they couldn't have been more bored. In the same way he used to take me to the City of London Club, of which he was very proud to be a member, and if we shared a table with a Conservative peer, he was elated. I remember his saying once, over our Derby Round, (which is what they used to call cold boiled beef in those days) 'That was Lord Faringdon who was sitting next to you.'

I had sufficient sense not to say, 'And who is Lord Faringdon?' but replied, 'Gosh! Really?' which is what he wanted, and all was sweetness and light.

Sydenham really was snoberoo land. I don't know the form now, but in those days it considered itself grander than its near neighbours Forest Hill, nearer to the City, and Penge and Anerley further therefrom. And the various strata in the suburb itself were of great social importance. Almost as if to accentuate these divisions, the railway provided three stations: Upper Sydenham, Sydenham and Lower Sydenham. Upper Sydenham served Sydenham Hill, where the very rich lived. I have a brother-in-law who lived up there with his stock-jobber father and family. We humble people of Sydenham never aspired to such heights and the only thing in our youth which I have in common with Gerald is that we used to get beaten by our fathers. Sydenham itself was a rather complicated matter: it all depended upon whether you live above or below 'the bridge'. The bridge was over the railway line which went – London Bridge, New Cross gate, Brockley, Honor Oak Park, Forest Hill, Sydenham, Penge East, Crystal Palace Lower Level. It was not altogether *comme il faut* to be below the bridge. We did not emerge from there until after the Great War and until after I had been sent to be miserable at my boarding preparatory school. Lower Sydenham was indeed below par, nearly as bad as Catford, and anyone who lived in either of these two villages in those days was out.

Grandpa was an old darling and was kind and generous beyond belief. He had a great love of anecdotes, unfortunately repeating himself rather often. A good many of them were slightly vulgar, designed to provoke Grandma to say, 'Oh! Really! Willie!', which is about all that I can ever remember her saying.

The two great favourites, harmless enough now, but considered dirty rather than amusing then, were :

> There was an old man of Madrid,
> Who went to an auction to bid :
> The first thing they showed
> Was an ancient commode,
> What ho ! when they opened the lid.

(We used to have that at least once a month and laughed dutifully.) And a rather corny piece, which had to be introduced by a certain amount of preface concerning a Doctor Humby, (a fictitious figure, I always thought), whose wife was a sort of Mrs Leo Hunter and gave parties. At one of these, a young man showed off by making rhymes about his fellow guests. To remove him from the limelight his hostess acidly observed, 'I'm sure that you couldn't make a rhyme about me.' Whereupon the young gentleman, surely conscious that he would never be asked again, volunteered :

> You make a mistake if you think I can't make
> a rhyme on your name, Mrs Humby;
> Your face is so fair
> When exposed to the air
> What can your lily-white . . . ? ? !

And there Grandpa would stop, giving Grandma an opening for, 'Oh ! Really ! Willie', which he thoroughly enjoyed, while we made appreciative noises.

It seems to me as though we went to luncheon at Grandpa's every Sunday, where we played billiards or croquet according to the season, but it cannot be so, as I know that Sheila and I, at any rate, had to go to Sunday School, under Miss Morpith, with great regularity. If you sat in the downstairs lavatory at home – that is at Peterscroft, which Grandpa gave us in 1919 and which Mummy named in a sentimental mood because she had just produced my brother Peter – you had walls to your right and left covered in stamps, one of which was issued each time you went to Sunday School, while facing you was an enormous notice announcing : 'Walk in the light of the Lord. Isaiah 2.5.' As the one thing you did not do in that little room was to walk, I often wondered who selected the text, but I was much too frightened of Papa to inquire.

I have never kept a diary, and on the whole, I think it probable that we walked over to luncheon, two or three miles, every other Sunday. When we did go to Grandpa's, it was matins at Christ Church, Forest Hill, first.

Grandpa, of course, was a sidesman, while Papa at St Bartholomew's was only allowed to take the bag round if one of the sidesmen were away. This rankled, because the husband of my mother's best friend, known in the family as 'Uncle Per', was a fully-fledged sidesman.

After the morning service at Christ Church, I used to run to Grandpa's without objection, entering by the back gate. Straight into the kitchen where Kate, the cook, would have a tin of asparagus emptied on to the plate. This was a great secret between us, not approved of by Clara, the housemaid. Having disposed of the asparagus, I would run to the front door and welcome the rest of the family.

The food was absolutely delicious for a small boy. Plenty of steak and kidney pudding, sweetbreads with pickled pork in a bechamel sauce, and, very often, saddle of mutton personally selected by Grandpa at the butchers on his way to the station in the morning, with mounds of redcurrant jelly. Papa didn't like Queen of Puddings or trifle which generally followed the main course. A special lemon jelly was prepared for him, which I thought – I am afraid with pleasure – looked rather nasty.

Grandpa, in my time at least, didn't exactly overdo it, as far as work was concerned. He would catch a train which got him to London Bridge at about 10 a.m. and walk slowly across the bridge to Eastcheap if it was fine, or take a cab if it was raining.

Apart from the train, he, like my present wife, never went on public transport. Arrived at his office – about an hour later than his partner – he would be greeted by a group of acolytes, of whom I can only remember the names Reeve, Fuller, Grant, and Samuel, but there were about half a dozen of them. These gentlemen would be despatched on various errands such as buying theatre tickets and the like while Grandpa sat down at his desk facing *Byles on Bills* and *Benjamin on Sale,* neither of which he ever opened to my knowledge, lit a very large Havana cigar, and signed a number of cheques prepared for him by some other slave.

After a while, he would stub out his half-smoked cigar, for he never finished a cigar in case he should inhale some nicotine, and the big moment of the day had arrived : his visit to the hairdresser.

The ceremony which took place five times in the week was a serious matter. Although he had almost no hair, what there was had to receive a trim and a wet shampoo, the moustache had to be curled, and the nails manicured. There was considerable concurrent conversation and the operation consumed sufficient time to make it scarcely worthwhile to go back to the office, where his partner and his partner's two sons would be working diligently. So he would move on to the club for luncheon which he greatly enjoyed. Returning to Eastcheap, he would sometimes dictate a few letters or sign a few cheques, but more often he would walk or take a cab to London Bridge. He would then call in to say 'Good Afternoon' to Grandma on his way to the Bowling Club for a cup of tea before his game. In the winter he was at home for tea.

He talked incessantly, so that Grandma must have had a very dreary time. I don't remember much about her. It was just, 'Yes, Willie', 'No, Willie', and 'Oh! Really, Willie' all the time, except that first thing in the morning and last thing at night, Grandpa would blow down the speaker (with a whistle) of an old-fashioned intercommunication system and Grandma in her bedroom would enquire, 'Are you there, Willie?' and upon receiving the reassuring news that he really was there, would say, 'Good night' or 'Good morning' as the case might be.

They were a very happy couple as, although on first acquaintance it might have been thought that he was a selfish old boy who bullied his wife, she in fact adored him, and he her.

She had a breast removed in 1931 and when told that there was cancer in the other, she refused the operation and decided to die. Grandpa took it dreadfully to heart and I used to have to go over to dine with him once or twice a week to cheer him up. Sumptuous but very embarrassing repasts marred by tears.

About six months after Grandma's death, I came back in my car from playing lawn tennis against the 'Shop' at Woolwich to be greeted by an old friend who said he had a message for me but looked miserable. I said: 'I suppose Grandpa's dead', which the assembled company considered hard-hearted and unfeeling, but the extraordinary thing is that I knew instinctively what the message was. Clara had taken up the old gentleman's morning tea on a tray and had returned in an hour as he was late for breakfast, an unheard of thing. She had found him propped upright against the pillows, the tea in the cup undrunk, and the tray as she had placed it. He was dead, and must have glided peacefully and painlessly into the next world.

Grandpa had three sisters, Emmie who disliked him, Nellie who never saw him after her marriage as far as I know, and Edith who was frightened of him. Except that Edith was the youngest, I cannot place them as to age.

When I came on the scene, Emmie and Nellie were wealthy widows, and Edith was a spinster of mature years living with her maid in a flat on Sydenham Hill overlooking the Crystal Palace. That building was her life, for she sang in the front row of the chorus of the Handel Festival, *Messiah*, Stainer's *Crucifixion*, Mendelssohn's *Elijah*, clad in white samite, mystic, wonderful, and if anyone had tried to nudge her out of the front row, there would have been hell to pay. She was a dear and had a pretty face but her figure was her handicap. She looked like a pouter-pigeon, squat with an immense bust which looked like marble. As she grew older, she became increasingly certain that she was pursued by the male sex, from the bus conductor to Sir Henry Buckland who lived opposite her, looked like a shopwalker, and managed the Crystal Palace. I imagine that she had never had any romance in her life, and towards the end – she died in 1939 – these illusions, which had been boring, became almost tear-jerking. After she had seen the Crystal Palace burnt to the ground, she seemed to lose interest in life, but, until then, she was gay enough.

Christmas was an appallingly gargantuan affair. An enormous roast turkey, Christmas pudding, and mince pie affair at Grandpa's on the day itself. On Boxing Day, their annual outing to our house, the menu was exactly repeated – Aunt Edith present at both gatherings – and the next day boiled turkey, Christmas tree, presents, and the whole shooting-match at Aunt Edith's flat all over again, with Grandpa, Grandma, Papa, Mummy, Neville, Sheila, Lorna and Peter, together with our hostess, and a few bodies whom she liked to assemble. I used to feel that I could never look a turkey in the face again. All these occasions were, of course, teetotal.

Papa didn't waste a lot of time on Aunt Edith, possibly because she was only moderately well-to-do. When she died, she did leave what there was to us, but it was encumbered with a large annuity – quite properly – to her maid Amy, who obstinately lived on for a very long time, much to Papa's annoyance, although the old villain beat her in the end.

After Mummy died in 1941, Papa got the willies and sold Peterscroft and all its contents and went liquid, that is to say, put everything in his pocket. This was not unwise of him, as certainly two houses in Lawrie Park Road, whither we had moved in 1919, had been bombed flat by that time. I don't know where he went after he had sold the house, as

I was abroad for five years during the war and neither of us was a good correspondent.

But if he didn't take much trouble about Aunt Edith, Papa positively wooed Aunt Emmie and Aunt Nellie. In vain. I knew nothing about it at the time, but today it causes me to smile.

Aunt Emmie was the widow of a gentleman called Hinchcliffe who was a man of means, although I have no idea what he did for a living, if anything. They had a son called Walter, who was head of the school at Westminster, was the apple of his mother's eye, became a clerk in the House of Commons, was all set to become the Erskine May of his generation, and died. Poor Aunt Emmie painted very well, and was also a superb copyist, a greatly underrated talent.

She spent years, unhappy years no doubt, in the National Gallery until at last she found she had cancer, a disease to which my maternal forebears seem to have been particularly susceptible. So she retired to a nursing home in Fountain Road by the Crystal Palace and on the way down to Dulwich. There in 1920 Papa instructed me to call upon her and to be pleasant to her on my way back from school. And this I did. He meanwhile was busily corresponding with her. As she was only his wife's aunt, it is perhaps not too cynical to think that all this correspondence was with an eye to the main chance, but if it was, it was a flop. For she cut up for what was in those days a great deal of money and left me a rather nice painting by herself of Dean's Yard, Westminster, and Papa a number of immense paintings of calves which would have looked superb in the V and A but dwarfed our dining-room where Mummy dutifully hung them. But the bulk of her fortune was very sensibly split in two – one half to Westminster School to endow scholarships in honour of poor Walter, and the other half to the Hospital for Incurables at Putney. Papa was particularly incensed when the Hospital, because he was Aunt Emmie's executor, made him a Vice-Patron. I was very young at the time but not too young to think that it was funny.

Aunt Nellie I only saw once but I thought her to be charming. She had married some gentleman who was very successful in trade, 'Bainbridge of Lincoln', as his second wife. He, it seems, had advanced into the county, and she had an accident while hunting, which confined her to a wheel-chair for the rest of her life. She had a large house in South Park in which a lift was installed for her convenience, a rather dashing thing for those days.

Papa was in regular communication with this wealthy widow, but it didn't come off. She left him £500 for his kindness in writing so regularly over the years, left Mummy all her jewellery, that is Ginner jewellery, and quite rightly left the rest to her huband's family. I think that Papa was a little disappointed.

I have had a few other relatives who were entertaining characters, but I think that it would be wise to leave them alone and come to a description of my early education.

CHAPTER TWO

Removed with Ignominy

I learned the dates of the Kings of England at my mother's knee. I have never forgotten them, and they are very useful to give you a background, particularly when you are reading the history of foreign parts. I had the 'tables' beaten into me by Papa, so that my mental arithmetic was not too bad, albeit entirely by rote rather than by thought. When I was 'half past four' as I termed it, I could read, and a great nuisance I must have been about the house when Mummy had a baby daughter to cope with.

So I was sent to Miss Tuck's kindergarten, a school which Mummy had attended, presided over by two maiden ladies of uncertain age, Miss Tuck and Miss Muriel Tuck. The school was of course co-educational. I was so bullied at home by Papa, that, when he was away at work or I was at my kindergarten, I was boisterous, noisy and objectionable.

The climax came when I was told to go and stand behind the screen because I had been naughty, and in a mood of derring-do, I pushed the screen forward which landed on Miss Tuck. Messages were sent to Grandpa and Papa to the effect that the Misses Tuck couldn't undertake to look after me any more, and I was removed with ignominy.

I wasn't particularly clever, which is what matters later in life, but I was quick to learn, which is what matters at the start – parrot rather than owl – so that when I was sent to the Hall, Sydenham, a large property with comfortable grounds where no doubt the squire had lived long ago, I was a little bit ahead of my contemporaries who probably had not had such strict instruction at home. And perhaps I was conscious of that and pleased always to be top of the form in the General Knowledge class, which we used to have on Friday afternoons, taken by Mr William Wallace Osborne, MA, the headmaster. Old Osborne was accustomed to addressing me publicly as 'Mr Know-all', which he enjoyed because he knew that it would make me unpopular in the form.

He had a nice wife – it is surprising how these horrible old men seem to have nice wives – who taught me the piano at which I was no good, although for about seven years I had to be downstairs at seven to practise for half an hour. He had two dreary sons, and he hated the sight of me.

What with Papa at home and Mr Osborne at school I was fairly wretched. He used to say to the class; 'N. M. G. Faulks! What does that stand for?', and when he got no reply, he would turn to me and say, 'No mortal good Faulks, of course.' This was humiliating enough but the worst occasion was when Grandpa, as the local big-wig, had been asked to give away the prizes; I went up to receive mine, a beautifully bound volume called *Book of Heroes,* chin thrust out, moving manfully, and Grandpa pushed his face forward and kissed me.

After a time, Osborne sold out and retired, and a couple of young old Harrovians bought the school, Wilkinson and Leatham. I should imagine that they were straight out of the army. They were quite nice although they beat me fairly regularly – I don't know why. They sold out quite soon to a man called Booty, and my parents decided that these changes were not good for me, and I must go to boarding school.

They knew perfectly well that, what with Papa and Osborne I still wetted the bed, or suffered from enuresis, as they say today, and that I was likely to be unhappy. My protests went unheeded and off I went in the Minerva, alone, with the chauffeur.

Before the 1914–1918 war, there was a very large German colony in Sydenham, much respected and accepted as part of the community. There were Rowold, Holthusen, Plutter, Hotopf, Blasiusz (that sounds Polish) and many others, and they had their own German church. The War made a great difference, especially among the shop-keeping classes, whose womenfolk appeared to think that all the Germans were spies whether or not they were naturalised Englishmen.

Before I went to my boarding preparatory school in January 1919, just after the end of the War, when my parents had their other children at home, it was thought wise to ask one of the German colony who was already at the school, two years older at thirteen, to come to tea and tell me something about the place. Carl, for that was how I had always known him, came to tea and was very charming, and I was greatly impressed by his height and not surprised to hear that he was in the XV. At the Hall we only played soccer, so I should have to play that game with the rabbits.

I am not going to give the name of the school, because it is still going and because I was so wretchedly unhappy there. It was the recognised preparatory school for one of the major public schools, to which I never went.

The headmaster was a very charming old gentleman with a red wig. During the short time I was there, his son appeared from Oxford to join the staff. He had won a cricket blue so everybody adored him. There were one or two pleasant female teachers, and a sadistic bachelor whose name escapes me but I think that it began with L.

I was put into the fifth form, which was high for my age, but that didn't please me greatly, for I could feel that there were breakers ahead.

The fifth form meant that I had five votes in the election of Captain of Football, and that was when I made my first mistake. The school was divided into houses or sets or something of that kind. The captain of my set was called Robert Something (Smith or Brown), and the man who was obviously going to be elected had the same surname as my man. And this Robert – he must be in his seventies by now, but I wouldn't mind having a word with him – instructed the little new boy to cast his votes for him. I thought we were all democrats, as no doubt did the headmaster, and went off and cast my five votes for another boy, simply because the matron had told me that he also had bladder trouble.

My boy came in second, and that evening Robert sent for me. 'You didn't vote for me, did you?'

'No.'

'Right, you'll have to be beaten.'

After he'd given me six with, probably, a gym shoe, he then annoyed me by turning to his sycophants and saying, 'You may give him two if you like', but I had sufficient sense not to complain.

The next thing that happened was that I made a friend. He was in my form, and, like me, a humble soccer player. We went on walks together, while the tough boys were playing Rugger. I remember his name but I won't mention it in case he is still alive. During our talks, I said what a good fellow Carl was. He said, 'Whom do you mean?', I provided the surname. End of conversation.

The next day Carl, who, I now know, liked to be known as Charles, arrived. 'I gather that you are telling people that I am a Hun', he said. I denied it, I denied everything, I lied and lied and lied. I was so frightened. It is not creditable, I know, but I was scared stiff. At last, surprisingly, he believed me and went off. I have never spoken to my 'friend' since.

The next disaster came with the sadistic Mr L. He took the view that if a child put up its hand and said, 'Please, sir, may I be excused?' or 'Please, sir, may I leave the room?', the little rabbit was trying to get off work and the proper answer was 'No'.

I had heard this ghastly man saying 'No' with enjoyment so often that when it came to my turn to want to go the lavatory it was out of the question to raise my hand and I had to try and contain myself. And, alas, I couldn't, and the urine poured down my shorts onto the floor. I was, of course, beaten. I couldn't admit to being terrified of Mr L. I often wonder what has become of him.

And then we come to point finale.

It is not a pretty story. It was a very long dormitory and I was at the far end from the steps leading down to the lavatories. I woke up at 2 a.m. on a cold February morning with no light of any kind and a bursting desire to evacuate my bowels. Under each boy's bed there was a pot. What was poor little frightened Faulks to do? He waited; he thought; he was in pain; he chose the pot.

And the stench in the dormitory was indescribable.

The next morning I was sent for to attend the gentleman with the red wig. 'I have asked your parents to remove you from the school', he said. That was all. And an hour later the enormous Minerva with chauffeur arrived and took me back to Sydenham and Papa and humiliation.

My parents were very distressed and seemed to be in trouble about what to do with me. So I suggested that perhaps I could go back to the Hall for the summer term and that then they could think. And mercifully they agreed. I went to the Hall as a day boy, no worry about wetting the bed, and Mr Booty decided that I was a good opening batsman. I went in first and very nearly broke all records. The whole side was out while I was not out 2. Eventually, poor Mr Booty was reduced to the cliché; 'all style and no runs'.

At the end of that summer term of 1919, they decided that the tiresome eldest child should go to Dulwich College. So I bicycled there in the autumn and was put in Upper IIIA where the master was old White with whom I used to play bridge later when I was an undergraduate.

I won some prize or other and was moved up into the upper school the next term. There were some other little boys in the same form who were cleverer than I was – three of them : Guthrie, who became the Master of Downing, and who was for many years the Public Orator at Cambridge which meant making recondite jokes in Latin which few understood, Griffiths and Wilson. I tried to keep up with them, and somehow managed to get into the Classical Lower Fifth with them under a splendid man called Doulton whose son has just retired from being headmaster of Highgate School.

At about this time, when there were lots of characters about, who were going to be distinguished lawyers, like Hartley Shawcross, Arthian Davies, Melford Stevenson, and so forth, whom, although they were much older than I was, I would have liked to have met, Grandpa decided to take me for two days to the Handel Festival at the Crystal Palace. Agnes Nicholls, Ben Davies, Harry Dearth, and Margaret Balfour – what a *Messiah*! And I assumed that that was all right. And bless my soul if two days later I was not called up before Mr Smith, the headmaster, who said that he had a good mind to expel me for having gone to the Handel Festival.

I was appalled; naturally I thought that Grandpa had arranged it all; but no; I had played truant unwittingly.

Accordingly the family decided to think about my going elsewhere. It was a mistake, for I used to do two and a half hours prep every night and, with Papa leaning over behind me, ready to beat my knuckles if I made a mistake, I really learned something. And, looking back on it, I think that I might have done better scholastically to have stayed at Dulwich than to have gone to the rather more upper class school to which eventually I won a scholarship.

I think that I went back to the Hall to sit my preliminary paper for Uppingham, for the idea of trying to change from one public school to another was a novelty. At any rate, Uppingham said that I was worthy of taking the final examination itself, and, in due course, I got on the train at Euston, seen off by Mummy, to do so.

Uppingham is in what used to be called Rutland, the most beautiful part of England, with the possible exception of Northumberland, and quite untouched by the Industrial Revolution. Uppingham Station has now been abolished under Beeching, and in those days it was only used for the school train to and from London. So the would-be scholars had to be deposited at Manton and proceed by taxi cab. This is the country of the Cottesmore and the Fernie Hunt. I found it very different from Dulwich when I was asked to have a game of croquet in the head-master's garden before being shown to my sleeping quarters, which were (perhaps a good omen) at the Hall, where some squire or other had lived in the distant past. It was beautiful and I was very impressed.

In the morning, I woke early, for the usual humiliating reason, and washed, dressed and crept down at the appointed moment for breakfast. I was fascinated at the row of dishes on the hot-plate, was unable to resist my curiosity, and was caught with the top of an entrée dish in each hand by the elder daughter of the house, Daphne, as I greedily inspected kidneys to the left and kedgeree to the right. Red-handed and

The author and his mother in 1908

Rule Britannia! My Parents and Grandparents in Monte Carlo in 1909

The author in 1909

red-faced, I replaced my spoils and said, 'Good morning' somewhat sheepishly, thinking it a poor start to my examination problems. But she laughed, and laughed, and laughed and all was well.

My hosts, Major and Mrs Shea – she was a Simonds of Reading and Lord Chancellor Simonds' cousin – could not have been kinder; Matron didn't mind when I wetted the bed, and much to my surprise I found awaiting me, when I got back to Sydenham, a telegram telling me that I had won a scholarship. There were two top scholarships of £85 per annum each, and I didn't win either of them but there was one of £70 per annum, which for some extraordinary reason, they gave me. When you consider that the fees for the whole year were £183 that wasn't too bad.

No doubt, Grandpa provided the rest. They gave me the scholarship for English but that didn't prevent them from putting me on the Classical side.

The standard of learning at Uppingham was much lower than it was at Dulwich. No two and a half hours prep as at the enormous day school with over 1,000 boys, but one and a half hours and that not taken too seriously. This was a games school. They used to say in the Midlands that Uppingham was the school to which you sent your boy if he was too thick to get into Rugby. And there was something in it in those days.

In my first term there (they put me into the Classical upper fifth to start with), a boy in my house called C. A. Humphrey, won a valuable scholarship to Balliol College, Oxford, and it was a non-event. On the other hand, we beat Haileybury by 59 points to 5, Tonbridge by 25 points to 5, and Rugby by 15 points to nil, and to mark that we were given a half-holiday. We were all delighted but even at that age (thirteen) I wondered if we had got our priorities right. But not for long: for, in the Christmas holidays, I bought an evening paper, while indulging in some great feast at the Café Royal at Grandpa's expense, and read that England had beaten Wales by 7 points to 6, all seven scored by assistant masters at Uppingham, a try by H. L. Price and a dropped goal by A. M. Smallwood, and I was in heaven.

The great Percy Chapman had left the term before I arrived, and had led the school to victory in all sorts of games, as indeed he later led his country when they regained the Ashes from Australia. The last time I saw him was on a Boxing Day at Twickenham watching the Harlequins play Richmond when he took his drunkard's face down to the bar at half-time. He died soon after – very sad.

The headmaster who led all this games mania was the Reverend Reginald Herbert Owen MA, who afterwards became Archbishop of New Zealand. At this time, however, he was *persona non grata* with a lot of OU's who couldn't understand how he had obtained a rowing blue at Oxford, joined Uppingham School as Headmaster in his twenties, taken Holy Orders almost immediately thereafter, and had been unable to spare any time for hostilities. I didn't agree with these criticisms and thought it a good idea to have a young man (who to me was a very old man) as headmaster. This was the fashion in those days and Reggie was succeeded by the present Lord Wolfenden when he too was in his twenties.

Reggie was a very strict disciplinarian and I admired him for that. He played full back for the headmaster's XV against the school, and I admired him for that, but he was, although a very persuasive speaker for which I admired him again, not much of a scholar, which was a pity.

In my fourth term at the age of fourteen, I found myself in the Classical upper sixth having taken my School Certificate (today known as 'O' levels) the previous summer. This all sounds very precocious but there was a boy called O'Hagan who was even more precocious, always came first, and left, as I did, in the summer of 1926, so that during my five years at Uppingham I did not win a single prize.

I spent my first year in the choir, shouting very loudly in unison, but scared absolutely stiff when called upon to utter a solo. I found it rather enchanting that we had a little printed slip in the summer term signed 'T. C. Sterndale-Bennett', who was our very talented music master, to the effect that on Founder's Day we should sing 'Summer suns are glowing over land and sea' unless, of course, it was raining when we should sing 'Fight the good fight with all thy might, Christ is thy strength, and Christ thy right' etc.

My first term wasn't too bad. Matron was so kind that it was not long before I ceased to be ashamed of my lack of bladder-control, and although, of course, I had to refuse invitations to go and stay with other boys in the holidays, I began to acquire confidence so that in the end it ceased to trouble me and never has done since.

The house had two Rugby Football teams, the Unders and the Overs. I was a scrum half and they put me in the under XVI side. For some reason, they couldn't find a scrum half for the over XVI side and I was put in that as well. We beat somebody or other in the first round, but in the second played a house called Highfield where the scrum half was, to me, an enormous boy of eighteen called Martineau. He duly pounced on me when I was rather slow in getting out the ball to my fly half, and I was carted off to the Sanatorium with what was apparently a twisted bottom. There I was looked after very kindly by the Matron under the supervision of the senior school doctor, a dear old Irishman known affectionately as 'Daddy Dunn'.

My second term had brought me promotion to the Classical lower sixth (where we were taught more or less what we had learned in the Classical lower fifth at Dulwich), and also brought about my undoing.

The various school houses were spread about the village of Uppingham, and Brooklands, where the master of the Classical lower sixth – a splendid man whose readings of the Old Testament lessons in chapel were an inspiration – resided, was over a mile from the Hall, involving going up and down a steep hill; while the main classrooms were about half a mile on the return journey involving the same hill.

In January 1922, a sensitive little man, whom even I, a quasi-Cockney, could sum up, was appointed to teach mathematics. Five minutes were allowed between the end of the lesson at Brooklands and the mathematics lesson in the main building. This was achieved at the double, no doubt for our physical benefit. But my well-known twisted bottom did not permit me to run, and I arrived late. The teacher, very red in the face, demanded to know the reason. I replied, 'I'm very sorry sir, but I hurt myself playing Rugger last term, before you came, and I can't run.'

I think the words 'before you came' were ill-chosen for he shouted, 'This is a piece of gross impertinence and you will go and see the headmaster.'

The headmaster being a muscular Christian – he had no children – was only too anxious to thrash me when I called upon him unwillingly in his study at 12.30 that morning. But I managed to put across the story of my twisted bottom as indicating that I was not at that time a suitable recipient for corporal punishment. Foiled, he told me to go and get the school doctor's opinion. Alas! Darling Daddy Dunn was away and I had to go and see his assistant, Dr Wallace, a down-to-earth Scotsman who investigated my posterior with care and announced that it was in extremely good trim for receiving a few strokes of the cane. The headmaster was delighted and I was duly executed.

I never forgave the mathematics master and I refused to attend some dinner for the Archbishop of New Zealand when I had become a High Court Judge. Not very creditable of me, as a man who professes Christianity, but perhaps, also, understandable.

I learned to my surprise in my fourth term that if you had arrived at the upper sixth, you were entitled to be let off fagging. I immediately put in a plea to be allowed to be excused from my menial duties in order to pursue my esoteric studies. If this had happened the year before, I might have got away with it, as the head of the house was a 'slow-starter' who would probably have thought that I was up to some tremendous research work in the top form, to which he had not aspired. Unhappily, the head of the house in 1922 was a charming and delightful young gentleman, who is now a Royal Academician, and was also in the Classical upper sixth. He knew the form and, as a result, said no, but very sweetly let me off the next term, so that I only fagged for four instead of the normal six terms.

The form was this. The upper sixth was presided over by a dear old thing, Doctor Arnold Taylor. Doctor in this case meant D.Litt. which is something rather senior. He was a Wykehamist, a bachelor, well-to-do, the housemaster of West Deyne, and bored with and too old for the job. No one did any work at all unless (and in adolescents this is unusual) they felt like it. Every Thursday (early school 7.30 a.m.) we had a syntax paper of astonishing complexity, but as the same paper had been set for about thirty years, the questions were procurable in advance, you memorised the answers by heart, satisfied Dr Taylor, and didn't learn a thing. Looking back on it, I am really dispirited to think how I wasted those valuable years. Every Friday afternoon, we had to write a 'Critical Paper' of even more apparent difficulty, but the secret was out. If you learned some book by Professor Mackail, you were home and dry. I can remember getting 'alpha minus' for my splendid criticisms of the works of Propertius and Catullus without having ever read a word of either of them.

I shall never forget those four years in the same form. I suppose that I must have moved up as people left and I became more senior, but in my mind it is as if I was throughout those years at the same desk. I retain a mental photograph of it.

Two rows ahead and two places to the left was C. H. M. Waldock, the marvellous fly half and hockey player. I never dared to speak to him. Indeed, it was only last year when he was Treasurer of Gray's Inn that I was bold enough to do so. By this time, he had become Sir Humphrey Waldock, Acting Warden of All Souls, Chichele Professor, and was about to be the nation's representative at the International Court of Justice at the Hague, which is the best job a lawyer can get. We didn't see into the future, and when he got a Heath Harrison exhibition to

BNC, Oxford 'for all round merit' we thought that so to reward our heroic fly half, who got a hockey blue, really was an event.

And staring up at me from my desk were three initials cut in the wood – J.E.F. How I learned that they stood for James Elroy Flecker I know not. I think I must have been to see *Hassan* first, for Grandpa took me to it, and I could recite the cast by heart today were it not boring and I am not quite sure who played Jafar. I suppose that they are all dead now except Cathleen Nesbitt and Basil Dean himself to whose son I gave a 'red bag' in 1960. (This esoteric expression will be explained later.)

But going to see Henry Ainley and the rest of that marvellous cast did something to me. I had read *Man's Inhumanity to Man* on the beach at Wimereux in my summer holiday in 1922 and had been profoundly moved by it. The book was really a potted history of the world and when I learned the next term that I was to go into the Classical upper sixth, I asked if I could transfer and read history. No. I could not, and no reasons were given.

I had to do something to show my independence and it must have been in 1924 when I was sixteen – the first night was on 20th September, 1923 – that I obtained a copy of *Hassan*. It used to sit on top of J.E.F. with my other school books, and when we were supposed to be preparing for something or other, I would open it and intone to myself, unhappily without a lute :

> How splendid in the morning glows the lily;
>   With what grace he throws
> His supplication to the rose :
>   Do roses nod the head, Yasmin ?
> But when the silver dove descends
>   I find the little flower of friends,
> Whose very name that sweetly ends,
>   I say when I have said, Yasmin.
> The morning light is clear and cold;
>   I dare not in that light behold
> A whiter light, a deeper gold,
>   A glory too far shed, Yasmin.
> But when the deep red eye of day
>   Is level with the lone highway,
> And some to Meccah turn to pray,
>   And I toward thy bed, Yasmin.

Or when the wind beneath the moon
  Is drifting like a soul aswoon,
And harping planets talk love's tune
  With milky wings outspread, Yasmin,
Shower down thy love, O burning bright !
  For one night or the other night
Will come the Gardener in white,
  And gathered flowers are dead, Yasmin !

I thought and still think that that was magic. Little boys readily become enthusiastic, but that Old Uppinghamian who died in 1915 at the age of thirty-one would have been a great dramatic poet. As Basil Dean wrote in 1951, 'He had had no time to do more than spread the wings of his poetic fancy. Yet he left behind him a play of lasting memory.'

In 1951, the Festival of Britain production of this play took place and Ian Baillieu who was my best man at my first wedding and my old friend Leslie Allwood organised a party of about thirty of us to go. But the stage was too small, the wonderful Delius score was missing, and the German actor who played Hassan wasn't up to it. There was a feeling of anti-climax for me who had looked forward to it so much, although the others seemed to enjoy themselves.

I took the Higher Certificate ('A' levels) four times, getting less and less enthusiastic, until my marks at the age of eighteen were worse than they were at fifteen. I was a keen but not very good games player and never got anywhere, possibly because the school at that time was producing blues and internationals by the dozen.

Perhaps I should have mentioned that in addition to getting myself beaten for nothing, I distinguished myself by bringing back German measles to the school in my third term which made me greatly hated because, although I was free to play ping-pong in the Sanatorium, the Shrewsbury match was cancelled.

In a way, I do not regret my dreadful indolence at Uppingham. I became a house praepostor at the age of sixteen which was much too young, but Major Shea liked and was kind to me in a manner far different from that of the headmaster and the common little man. I was horrid to all the younger boys, I think, and would only like to ask their understanding if any of them has read this far.

The gallant Major and his wife were darlings and I was so lucky to be their house scholar. He played the flute and she the viola in the school orchestra. She was a very keen musician and I remember with awe her telling me that she had been to Leicester the previous night and that Galli-Curci sang flat. Brave words, for the Prima Donna (*'Ah fors e lui'* on one side and *'Caro nome'* on the other) was very much the ideal of *bel canto* in the early Twenties.

There was a full sized billiards table as well as a tennis court available, and the Sheas used to ask me to play bridge with them in the evenings. All very civilised, and the house itself from without was beautiful. It is true that the boys had earth closets, which were unbelievably smelly, but on the whole I was very lucky.

The Sheas were well-to-do and did not need to make a profit out of the food. I gather that it was not the same in other houses. Ma Shea (as she was called) once turned to me and said, 'Macalister-Hall's father has sent us an enormous haunch of venison. What shall I do? I am sure they won't eat it.'

I said, 'Red-currant jelly.'

And she bought an enormous quantity and it was a triumph.

She was also a little absent-minded. Once an old boy came down to visit the house while I was a praepostor. He entered – his name was Elliman – and she said, 'How lovely to see you again, Eno.'

The boredom of the Classics – which have done nothing for me except to make me rather good at the Crossword Puzzle – was such that one summer I was able to get through Hugo's Anglo-German and German-English Conversation Book in my classroom without being discovered. This was in preparation for a walking tour in the Black Forest which was to be my first holiday away from parental sway.

When I was sixteen, I had come back from an O.T.C. Camp at Strensall, which I had hated, to our lodgings in the Isle of Wight and was impertinent to Papa. He, standing at the top of the stairs, swung a leg at me, caught me on the chin, and knocked me down. I didn't hold it against him because I knew how quick his temper was, but the idea of a 'free' holiday was enchanting.

My companions were Geoff Gee who was head of the school, and is now Stead and Simpson's Shoes, and has a well-known daughter called Prunella who was at Benenden with my offspring, a delightful fellow called Teddy Clarke who had streak of white in his black hair which used to be known as a *mousse blanche*, and was the Sketchley Cleaners, and a brother, Geoff, of whom I remember nothing save that like General Dayan he had a patch over one eye. We had a very good time but were rather flabbergasted to find how many people in Stuttgart begged us to join in the next war on their side against the French.

The gallant Major Shea is dead, and his charming wife predeceased him, and the only connection I now have with Uppingham, apart from the fact that I sent two boys there, is that Daphne Shea (now Saunders) still resides there, and I was an usher at her wedding.

The time came to see if Faulks could get up to the University. He had become extremely religious after being confirmed and contemplated taking Holy Orders. That this was inconsistent with beating all the little boys unmercifully, didn't worry him. He even tried to take an interest in the Headmaster's Greek Testament lessons about some screaming bores called the Essenes concerning whom the headmaster had a 'thing'. The Essenes and the rather easy Odyssey were the only things which he taught us – two divinity and two Homer periods a week – Doctor (prematurely mummified) Taylor taking on the rest.

Then, just before trying to break into the University, the scales fell from my eyes. I realised, one early morning, that I was bogus, and that the only reason that I wanted the Church was because I was only too fond of the sound of my own voice, and that I was really destined for the Bar. I had sufficient intelligence to realise that, bored though I was with the Classics, I must try to scramble up to Oxford or Cambridge on the Classics and change, if allowed, to read the Final Honours School of Jurisprudence or the second part of the Law Tripos as the case might be.

So we started off. One Dickson, now dead, and I, both from the Hall. We had a bash at Oxford first with very bad results. We used to drink vast quantities of Bovril every night which we thought to be rather avant garde, but it didn't seem to help our performances at the examinations. We ended up with Wadham offering me the princely sum of £30 p.a. and Dickson being offered nothing at all.

So we returned to Rutland. Dickson was advised to retire from the chase, and I was told to have a go at Cambridge, where there were some closed exhibitions available. I didn't do any better there, for five years at a philistine school, as it was in those days, scarcely improves the adolescent mind, but they offered me £50 p.a. as a closed Archdeacon Johnson Exhibition at Sidney Sussex College, together with £25 p.a. as a leaving Scholarship. This was better than Wadham's little offer and I accepted it. Both my boys have done the same.

CHAPTER THREE

Cambridge and Chambers

Sidney Sussex sounds pretty grim today from reports (no doubt exaggerated) of students screaming for the right to have women in their bedrooms, and banging their forks on the table because they disapprove of the menu. In my time, it was the greatest possible fun, and I annoyed my first wife by saying that the most enjoyable years of my life were spent at Sidney Sussex. I did in fact enjoy those years so much that I managed to persuade my family that it would be rather a good thing to stay up for a fourth year to take an LL B, which was very dishonest of me as I knew quite well that whether you had an LL B or not didn't matter a row of beans.

It was the smallest college at Cambridge with the possible exception of Peterhouse and Downing (in those days, Fitzwilliam House was not a college) and, although it had a very large number of Fellows of the Royal Society among its Ruling Body, it was not nationally well known. So much so that a few years ago a young lady at a cocktail party asked me at which college I was educated, and when I answered, 'Sidney Sussex', she replied, 'Oh! how divine. One of the new colleges, like Churchill!'

I could not resist saying that it was in fact comparatively new, but that Oliver Cromwell had been educated there, to which she replied, 'Oh! how divine!'

On reflection, I think that I lost.

I did no work at all during my first two years at Cambridge – that meant the best part of seven years of idleness, a wicked waste of time and opportunity – for I didn't care whether I got a first or not, and I knew that I could get a second without any trouble, as I in fact did.

I ran a poker club, as well as playing a good deal of bridge. As Sidney Sussex was a small college, my moderate athletic prowess enabled me to flourish as I never had at Uppingham. I played Rugby Football, lawn tennis, squash racquets, and hockey for the college, and they very kindly let me captain the cricket team on its tour of the Kentish villages during the summer vacation. Times have changed, for on one occasion Staplehurst or Ashford couldn't find a team and I was able, my parents being debenture holders at Wimbledon, to take the entire team there in comfort to watch the Championships.

I was the president of the JCR (Junior Combination Room), which I suppose nowadays might mean that I was a Maoist-Trotskyist. In those days we didn't have any politics. I was also chairman of the May Week ball which may have been abolished. Grandpa made me a life member of the Union, but I only went there once and decided that everyone was so clever and talented that it was not for me. The present Lord Caradon was in the chair, before the Feet had stepped out to the Left away from their Cromwellian Liberal father.

Charles Ziegler of Pembroke was the tutor under whom I was sent to study when, after my second year, I became emancipated from the Classics and was allowed to read law.

I spent the Long Vacation reading Cheshire's *Modern Law of Real Property* and it was bliss. I worked hard the next year and Ziegler told me I was a certainty for a first. He told me this so often that I began to believe it. As a result, the disappointment when I found that I had got a 2 (1) was the greater. Two of my friends got 1 (1) and I was very jealous. One was Joe Molony, now Sir Joseph Molony QC and the other, Harvey Hackman, one of my oldest friends, lately the senior partner in Royds, Rawstorne and Co.

I was so cross about this that I decided to have a try at the LL B, and stayed up for a fourth year, idly but enjoyably, to do it. The subjects, like Bills of Exchange, were very boring but I worked at them and there is no excuse. I got a 2 (1) again, and Joe Molony, who hadn't even bothered to stop up at Cambridge, and had done it by correspondence, got a first. Faulks bit his nails. However, I had managed to pass my exams and get called to the Bar while still up at Cambridge so that a career of a kind lay ahead.

Perhaps one of the reasons why my career at the University was not too successful was because for three of those years I had a car, VB 887, a Morris-Oxford coupé with a dickey. I acquired it in rather an odd manner. At Christmas 1926, when I was rising nineteen, and had had one term at Cambridge, we had the usual enormous luncheon at Grandpa's after which he banished the women and children from the dining-room, and, the crackers having been pulled and the dessert dealt with, said, 'You're a man now', producing two decanters of vintage port.

Grandpa continued with his Malvern Water. Papa reluctantly had a glass, of port and Grandpa kept pressing this sugary stuff upon me, which I enjoyed. The result was that I drank a great deal too much and eventually vomited on the drawing-room floor to everyone's consternation and my disgrace. Papa and I walked home to Sydenham that evening in silence.

There was no alcohol at home for the second 'Turkey Roast' on Boxing Day, and not only did Papa but Grandpa, who had pressed the demon alcohol upon me, pitch into me, so that I finally said, 'Well, if you treat me like your chauffeur, Grandpa, I'll be prepared to play.'

Lewin, the chauffeur, had become intemperate on the occasion of the annual outing to the Tunbridge Wells Bowling Club and had deposited the Minerva, carrying six old gentlemen besides himself, in the ditch. He was not sacked but was given his own little car in exchange for a promise of teetotalism. The upshot was that I was given a car on a promise to be a teetotaller till the age of 25. Cider did not count as alcohol; beer did. How I did it, particularly as I ran my poker club at Cambridge, I don't know – but I did, and received a second car, in due course, for being a good boy.

Pupillage was the first necessary step, but neither the accountant nor the East India Merchant knew anyone who could help. I should probably have been sunk, but for the fact that I had won the singles at the Sydenham Lawn Tennis Club, and a new member had joined with whom I played a lot. His name was Slade and it transpired that he was a busy barrister. He very kindly took an interest in me, modestly did not suggest that I should become his pupil, and offered to find me a pupillage elswhere.

He did this, and I became one of three pupils to Wilfrid Lewis, just appointed the Treasury Devil, allowed to carry on his own private practice, married to the daughter of Lord Justice Bankes, and eventually to become the Hon Mr Justice Lewis.

I should say here that poor Ziegler never lost faith in me and arranged for me to become a pupil of Walter Monckton, later Lord Monckton of Brenchley, but when I arrived at Harcourt Buildings, the great man said how sorry he was and how much he would have liked me as a pupil and so forth, but that the Lord Chancellor had just offered him a silk gown so that he couldn't take any more pupils. I didn't understand what he meant, but I thanked him as he was so charming and went away crestfallen.

When he led me in later years, I noticed how many photographs of the Royal Family he had in his chambers. The play *Crown Matrimonial* had a scene in which Walter, as the emissary for King Edward VIII, begged Queen Mary, wonderfully played by Wendy Hiller, to permit a morganatic marriage. I don't know who the actor was, but he was made up to look exactly like this very popular figure who had such a good war for Churchill in Cairo, and became a very successful Minister of Labour later. He always had a smile for everybody and never forgot a face.

Well, hardly ever, for Peter Rawlinson has a story of how the two of them were walking down Whitehall when off came someone's hat, off came Sir Walter's, 'How do you do? my dear fellow?', until it was realised that the hat was in fact being raised to the Cenotaph.

My two co-pupils were Paul de Laszlo, the painter's son, and Glanville Brown, whom I have scarcely seen since, but who is a distinguished linguist. During my year's pupillage, for which we paid one hundred guineas, I entered Wilfrid Lewis's room once, when he told me, quite rightly, that I had incorrectly pleaded a defence under the Sale of Goods Act. He asked me once to dinner and to take his daughter to a dance (they lived in an enormous house in Eaton Square, well above my station) and he was prepared to let me sit in his place as junior to some KC when he was away earning more money on his own. In that manner, I sat through a number of exciting trials and was content. Paul de Laszlo was not so content, and asked for his money back. He got fifty guineas, after having had to resort to solicitors' letters.

The other youths who were about at that time were my dear friend Gerry de Winton (of whom more later) and Jack Ashworth, lately the Senior and greatly admired Queen's Bench judge, who came back after I had been thrown out, to devil for and be the best man at the wedding of Sir Wilfrid Lewis.

When I arrived as a pupil, I was shown in to a room where a gentleman in a tail coat and butterfly collar presided. I naturally thought that he was Mr Wilfrid Lewis and called him 'sir' with diligence. After a time, it transpired that he was Townsend, the clerk, and I realised that I had not been very clever, but he seemed to be pleased. As my pupilmaster was always too busy to see me, and as my life consisted of collecting his briefs from the clerk's room and taking them up to the fourth floor, where I was allowed to kindle a fire and write my solution, (which no doubt went into the wastepaper basket), hurrying down later to compare my effort with the authorised version, and thus learn, I spent quite a time in the clerk's room pretending not to be there, but hoping that something would happen.

And one day something did. The second clerk looked at Townsend in dismay.

'What is it?' the great man said.

'Simon's coming back to the Bar,' was the answer. Gloom for minutes.

Sir Thomas Inskip, who had been the Attorney-General in the Conservative Government, was the Head of Chambers. Sir William Jowitt had left the Liberals to be Ramsay Macdonald's Attorney-General, and that would normally leave the ex-Attorney-General as the most desirable and highly paid advocate at the Bar. But the fact was that Sir John Simon, who had been Attorney-General years ago, Home Secretary in the First War and the man who decided what to do about India, was now apparently out of a job, and was 'coming back to the Bar'. Everybody knew that he would sweep the board, although, oddly enough, nobody liked him. So there was much gloom when his return was made known.

As a result, I was lucky enough to attend the whole of the trial of Lord Kylsant, on whose behalf Sir John Simon and Wilfrid Lewis had been briefed. Lewis, of course, was earning more money elsewhere, and I sat behind the great man.

It was all about a prospectus which the Royal Mail Steamship Company had produced and which was said to be dishonest. The only two who were prosecuted were Lord Kylsant (who looked like a very tired and rather stupid old horse, and for whom I was very sorry) and a man called Morland who was a partner in Peat, Marwick and Mitchell, the accountants who drafted the prospectus.

Lord Wright (as he afterwards became) was the judge. I, being young and stupid, thought that either both or neither would be convicted. But no. It was my first experience of the jury system : the peer went down and the accountant was acquitted. Perhaps Sir Patrick Hastings was a better advocate with a common jury than the great Sir John Simon, although I cannot remember all the details.

The whole case depended upon the alleged suppression of the amount due for EPT, or excess profits tax, and there was a lot of cynical amusement at the Bar at the fact that Sir Leslie Scott, who was also a director and had signed the prospectus, was not prosecuted. After all, he had been Solicitor-General and was shortly to be in the Court of Appeal. The gossip was that he had taken the brief for the Indian Princes which Simon had turned down, received an enormous brief fee, invested all in the Company without making any provision for tax, would be in the hands of the taxman for the rest of his life, and that was punishment enough for him.

Other gossip said that Mr Morland was a Quaker who obviously could not tell a lie, while his Lordship was a Welshman, and. . . .

Hugh Quennell of Slaughter and May, who used to drink a bottle of Kummel after dinner every night, and fell down dead in a New York Street, perhaps in consequence, was a very charming personality with whom I spent a lot of time in Florence in the war.

He acted for Mr Morland and had a very good story about Lord Plender of Deloitte's, one of the 'big five' accountants, who was the chief prosecution witness. He was expected to say, as he had in the Police Court, that what Mr Morland had done was very dreadful, and Hugh had a great pile of prospectuses under Pat Hasting's hand for all the world and Lord Plender to see, where, Hugh said, Lord Plender's firm had done the same thing. And, he said, Lord Plender did not come up to proof.*

Now I hope that no one will take this too seriously. It is an entertaining story, and is not intended to lower the reputation of either very distinguished firm in the estimation of right-thinking people.

Poor Lord K lost his appeal to the Court of Criminal Appeal and went to prison.

During my year as a pupil, I had the chance to follow my pupil-master, like a keen little puppy, to the House of Lords and to the Privy Council and in particular to the Divisional Court where as Treasury Devil he was so often engaged. I once heard Sir Stafford Cripps stand up and say, 'My Lords, I have a motion . . .' which seemed to be very well received by the Bench, whereas I did not understand what he was talking about.

I also had my first lesson in mastering the intricacies of the law of libel – later to become my 'thing' – in puzzling over the pleadings in the case of Chapman against Lord Ellesmere and others, where the stewards of the Jockey Club, Messrs Wetherbys, and *The Times* Newspaper, were all sued about allegations of the doping of a horse called 'Don Pat'.

Sir Patrick Hastings got £16,000 from a mesmerised jury, and if my memory is accurate – and I am away from my books – Wetherby's and the Stewards succeeded in the Court of Appeal but poor old Auntie *Times,* for whom Wilfrid Lewis was instructed, did not. He was led by Stuart Bevan who was a wonderfully impressive advocate as well as a member of Parliament, making Patrick Hastings and Norman Birkett

*A lawyer's expression for not repeating in court what he had said to the solicitors.

seem slightly, very slightly, vulgar, for he was so urbane. It was said that he had some matrimonial trouble which impeded his preferment.

The reference to Stuart Bevan KC calls to mind an event many years later when Mr Justice Stable (The Rt Hon Sir Wintringham Stable) was approaching eighty (and he is happily still alive, as I write, at eighty-nine having got his driving licence back at the age of eighty-three). He told us that Stuart Bevan had told him in 1913 or some far off time, 'My boy, the best breakfast in the world is a brace of snipe and a bottle of Moselle.'

And so, at the lodgings in Birmingham, we set out to satisfy his whim on his birthday. The Moselle was no trouble and his two boys came to breakfast bearing the most enormous bottle I have ever seen, inscribed 'To Methusaleh on his 80th birthday from Lamech and his brother – a Stable of Whisky'. Mr Commissioner Norman Richards QC produced a vast bottle of brandy also, but the trouble had been the brace of snipe, it not being the time of year for snipe. As we, Owlie (so called as his Nurse used to call him Master Howlie without an aspirate, because he screamed) Stable, Arthur James and I, had to dispense justice during the day, Elizabeth, my wife, was delegated the job. On the night before the birthday, she located a brace of snipe in the deep-freeze of a friend of a friend of the High Sheriff at Stratford-on-Avon, and all was well.

On that circuit, the veteran, who lives at Llanbrynmair in Montgomeryshire, arrived at Birmingham first and had to answer many telephone calls for the very popular Arthur James, just made a judge, and originally a Birmingham local, and when the latter arrived, the old gentleman said, 'I've heard so many people saying, "Is that you Jimmy" or "Is that you Arthur" that I propose to call you Frederick for the term of the assizes.' And, by George, he did, and the, alas! late, Lord Justice James loved it.

Owlie, who is a great countryman, nearly won the Bar Heavyweight, as a judge, at the Pegasus Point-to-Point. He was disappointed but nearly to have done so is remarkable enough.

He never went to the Court of Appeal: he was never asked. But he wouldn't have gone because, as he used to say, 'It's chaps I like, not hypotheses.'

There was nothing he didn't know about Kipling; there was little he didn't know about military history.

To be out on circuit with him and his delightful wife, Lucy, who rode down to Petra on a mule when over seventy, was a privilege we would have been sad to have missed.

One of the few remaining things I remember about my year of pupillage was George Bankes, one of Wilfrid's devils, coming back from the House of Lords and saying, 'That damned fellow Pritt has done us.' This was a reference to a case called Bell and Snelling against Lever Brothers. These two gentlemen had been speculating in Cocoa futures in Nigeria, which Mr Justice Wright had thought naughty, and the Court of Appeal presided over by the redoubtable Lord Justice Scrutton, who never shaved in his life, had unanimously thought naughty also. And when Mr A. T. Miller QC asked for leave to appeal to the House of Lords, Lord Justice Scrutton said, 'Do you really mean that, Mr Miller, when you have four judges against you already?'

And dear old Miller, who led me in the only case I made any money out of before the war, said, 'Well, my Lord, there is sometimes a good case for changing horses in mid-stream, and I expect my clients will want a new leader in the House of Lords.'

And in the House of Lords, they briefed an elderly silk called Schiller, who left a lot of silver to the Inner Temple, to lead, instead of Miller. Schiller cut very little ice, but Pritt, followed him and stormed home by three Lords to two. Levers had had six judges in their favour and had lost, three only being against them. Gerald Slade always said that he couldn't understand what it was that the case decided, and I have seldom heard it quoted. Pritt was 'that damned fellow' because both he and Bankes were at Winchester, but whereas the latter was a staunch Conservative, Mr D. N. Pritt KC MP was so far to the left that even the Labour Party withdrew the whip from him.

George Bankes was a remote relative of Wilfrid Lewis by marriage, and when I came back from the War he was still there. He was a bachelor and a dear man living with his mother in a vast house in St George's Drive, Pimlico. He was a 'professional' Old Wykemamist, jumping up and down on the touchline at all games, and working self-lessly for the Working Men's Club. He died on the cricket field, playing for that institution, having made 33, reported to be his highest-ever score.

The other devil for Wilfrid Lewis was Geoffrey Rose who spoke in a treble voice, said to have been the result of a wound in the first war in which he won a Military Cross. He used to deal with Wilfrid Lewis's vast practice before the Mixed Arbitral Tribunal, which I thought must have been very boring, and eventually he became a Metropolitan Magistrate at Lambeth, in the course of which duty he fined me £2 for leaving my car in Waterloo Place while I went to the theatre. He died suddenly just after some unkind criticisms about a sentence he had imposed. There may or may not be any connection between the two events.

Jack Ashworth, who eventually became the principal personal devil to Wilfrid Lewis, seems to have been the junior of the Northern Circuit at the time, for I remember, in addition to admiring his lack of nervousness when doing a case before the Privy Council, that he had to prosecute some woman for abortion, which, again, although a bachelor, he did with unruffled demeanour. For my part, I knew that it had something to do with bodkins in back streets, but then I was a very simple young man, and I was glad no one had offered me such a brief.

The chambers were great religious pluralists, which means that Wilfrid Lewis was Chancellor of about five dioceses, George Bankes had two, and later on Jack Ashworth inherited a number. There is money to be made in being a Chancellor of a Diocese. The duties are interesting and varied but a detailed description of them would be out of place in this book. When eventually such an appointment was suggested to me, I said that unhappily I could not honestly subscribe to the Thirty-Nine Articles which seemed to me to be unnecessarily anti-Semitic. I dare say I was stupid.

CHAPTER FOUR

Devil for Gerald

When the end of the year came, I, of course, hoped to be asked to stay on in chambers. I had been keen and had stopped in chambers every night until 7 o'clock before driving back to the suburbs, but I wasn't good enough, and when I reported on 10th October 1931 (the Long Vacation was longer in those days) the great Townsend took me down to Crown Office Row, dumped me at the ground floor of Number Five and told me that this was to be my future abode, and walked off. That was my pupil-master's way of performing his moral obligation to find me somewhere to practise.

The chambers consisted of a charming old bachelor, called Robert Gething, a gentleman who specialised in licensing, and myself. There was no doubt that Gething, who had come down from Liverpool to set the Thames on fire, was not going to do so, and the specialist shortly departed to become a deputy-clerk of the peace.

Gloom : no prospects at all. In those days, there was no Legal Aid and little boys were very lucky to get little briefs. I used sometimes to sit in for a man named Lawrence Vine, when he wanted to be somewhere else, but the idea of his paying me anything for this would have been unheard of. It was wonderful experience for me ! He eventually became a Deputy Chairman of London Sessions. So I did the Index for the Encyclopaedia of Forms and Precedents for Butterworth's for a ludicrous payment, reported Income Tax Cases for some periodical at £2 a time, and did my best to keep the wolf from the door by drudgery, never admitting that I was a failure.

To indicate what sort of Grub Street performer I had become, and what we used to get paid, I spent two whole years before the war producing under the aegis of Gerald Slade a new edition of *Fraser on Libel*. It was hard work in the Library for me, and every Sunday was taken up with discussing the results of my researches with Gerald at his house at Beckenham. Result : because it would be such an advantage to me professionally to have my name on the back of the book, I was paid £25 for 2 years work, while Gerald managed to extract a copy of *Halsbury's*

Laws of England, on which he didn't have to pay tax, and which cost the publishers very little.

The only thing in those dreary years which saved me from giving up the Bar and becoming an assistant master at a preparatory school, teaching the Classics, (for the idea of commerce, trying to get the better of someone else all the time, revolted my immature mind – I had declined Grandpa's offer to become, perhaps, a prosperous East India Merchant) was a piece of good fortune. In my suburb I had a friend called Jim Swanton (now known to millions as E. W. Swanton of the *Daily Telegraph*) who has been reporting cricket and rugby football for many years. He was one of three people I took to the theatre on my twenty-first birthday. My parents allowed me to throw an expensive dinner party for my chums at Cambridge but I had said that I ought to entertain my chums who had not gone to the University, and they said, 'All right. Dinner and the theatre on us, but not more than three.'

I asked my friends what they wanted to see and they all agreed that they wanted to see Stanley Lupino in something or other at the Gaiety. I said that I would guarantee them a good dinner but they would have to see something else. They reluctantly agreed and we saw the second night of *Journey's End* and I sat next to Gerald du Maurier. It was a wonderful play and its recent revival has shown that it has stood the test of time.

Jim was a very determined character and had got himself an assignment with the *Evening Standard* to write about public school cricket under the name of 'Juventus', and he was offered a job which he was too busy to accept so he passed it on to me.

It was to ghost the autobiography of a man called Jim Mollison who was the first man to fly from Australia to England, and from England to America, (Lindbergh having flown from America to Paris) and had married Amy Johnson who was the first woman to fly from England to Australia, and it was all very sensational and topical and romantic. The only time I saw the lady was when she was sitting in the lavatory with the door open which I found somewhat embarrassing.

I used to drive to the Dorchester – or was it Grosvenor House? – (no trouble in parking the car in those days), go to the Mollison apartment and cross-examine him about his life. Question and answer were taken down and transcribed by the beautiful Miss Pickering who I suppose was supplied by some agency and upon whom I gazed lustfully without ever doing anything about it, and then I went to work on the material and made a lengthy document out of it.

Then we had to sell it and of course neither Mollison nor I had the slightest idea what to do. Somehow I got in touch with a freelance journalist. He claimed to be brother-in-law to D. N. Pritt, KC, to whom I have just referred, who, he said, disapproved of him. I thought Pritt was probably right, for this was a slightly boozy chap, and I was either still or only just not a teetotaller, and somewhat of a prig. However, he engineered an interview with the great Mr Beverley Baxter MP, then the editor of the *Daily Express* who offered us £750 for the serial rights. I nearly fell through the floor and didn't realise that we were being had for suckers when we agreed to split the money three ways with the freelance journalist.

But at any rate I was proud of myself when I could say on my summer holiday to some young friend who was reading the *Daily Express*, 'I wrote that.' Disbelief followed by admiration was as good as a lot of money.

Then came the question of whether we could find a publisher. The journalist found us Hutchinson's. They made a bad bargain for they offered us an advance on royalties – not very much but better than nothing – and the book entitled *Death Cometh Soon or Late* did not sell and there weren't any royalties.

I am sure it was appallingly badly written and I have never opened it since publication although there is a copy on my shelves in the Law Courts.

I didn't know any solicitors nor did Papa or Grandpa, and business was very poor. I had a few licensing briefs but they were purely formal and, after Mollison, I could see little hope. Then came my first real piece of luck, and without luck it was in those days impossible to suceed at the Bar.

Gerald Slade asked me if I would like to go into his chambers at 1 Brick Court. He told me he was earning £4,000 a year which was a lot for a junior at that time and that although there would be many people between him and me I might be able to do some devilling for him, at half-fees for the paper work, and might occasionally be able to get into Court. This seemed thrilling to me, and I asked for time to think it over. I spoke to my clerk, who pooh-poohed the whole idea and was sceptical about Gerald's earnings.

I had come to admire Gerald very much both at our tennis club and when playing bridge with him, in spite of his teetotal bigotry which played a large part in his outlook. (We used to play singles together on

Saturday mornings, and then drive down in his Rolls-Royce to have a soda and milk at the Express Dairy : and he wouldn't allow alcohol at his daughters' weddings.)

So I decided to take advice and drove off to Stowmarket to see Judge Hildersley KC who had been the head of my chambers before his appointment.

His reaction was instant : Gething would never do anything very much, and Slade would. He was right : dear old Bob Gething, without ever talking silk, died before he was seventy, as did Wilfrid Lewis, (by then a High Court Judge) and married his housekeeper just before he died, while Gerald Slade built himself up an enormous practice and became Chairman of the Bar Council before he went on the Bench. He died before he had done his fifteen years; he was a very conscientous and fair man, which meant that cases before him took longer than before most judges. But however expensive this may have made it, the parties always knew that they had had a thorough and absolutely fair trial. He was my eldest boy's godfather.

He made what to most people would seem the idiotic mistake of not putting his fortune in his wife's name before he died. But you can be too clever : I put my very valuable house, about all I then possessed, in my first wife's name, and when she died, fourteen years younger than I was, I had to pay substantial death duties to get my own house back again.

I gave my clerk Grandpa's gold hunter watch, which he had left me, and ran for cover to 1 Brick Court where I was to spend the rest of my life until I became a judge.

Arriving there was very like being a pupil again with the difference that you had a chance of being paid for such paper work as you did. There were a lot of us only too anxious to devil for Gerald and it was consequently rather important to be at chambers early in the morning to bear off any papers which had just arrived. It was also very important to be on the spot when he was paid for any paper work you had done. If you were, you got your half-fees willingly and with a smile. If you applied forty-eight hours later, you were told frostily, 'I am sorry, but I have already made up my books.' It wasn't meanness but meticulousness, but it kept you on your toes. He was, like Papa, generous in big things as evinced by the fact that when I came back from the War, more or less penniless, he let me live rent free for two years at 1 Brick Court until I was lucky enough to be able to support myself.

Judges in the 1930's seemed very terrifying. I doubt if they are today.

Hill-Kelly and Crawford in the County Court were frightening, although there were many of a kindly disposition like Snagge, Konstam, Clements, and old Tobin, who was always said to be homosexually inclined although I know of no evidence of it. He had a junior brief in the trial of Crippen, as his chief claim to fame, and when he was put on the County Court Bench by Lord Birkenhead, the then Lord Chancellor, who had defended Miss Le Neve in that trial, he was determined to do as little work as possible. 'Can't you two gentlemen put your heads together?' was the cry as soon as the case was called on, and if you showed any signs of fight, so much the worse for you. The most entertaining of them all was Judge Cluer at Shoreditch and White-chapel. He once delivered judgment in eight words. After the Defendant had put his hat on and taken the oath, he said : 'As God is my Judge, I do not owe that thirty pounds.' Cluer : 'He's not : I am : you do' : pause 'with costs'.

The High Court Judges could be petrifying. One of my first per-formances was in a Divisional Court case on appeal from Sir Ernest Wild, Recorder of London, exercising civil jurisdiction, a closed book to him. Wild had behaved very unfairly, and Martin Jukes (now Director-General of the Engineering Employers' Federation) had beaten me, both briefs marked two guineas. I managed to persuade Mr Bate-man, of whom more anon, to let me take the case to the Divisional Court which consisted of two judges from whom lay an appeal to three judges of the Court of Appeal. I opened the case from memory, having rehearsed it for about a week, and didn't know what to do with my hands. 'Take your hands out of your pockets,' thundered Mr Justice Talbot, the great ecclesiastical expert, who was sitting with Mr Justice Macnaghten, who was sweet. I was struck dumb and lost the appeal.

Again, I appeared before a common jury (now, like that Divisional Court, abolished) presided over by Mr Justice Swift. My client was called Abrahams, and Hitler was just in power. Facetiously, I said to the jury in my opening speech that the fact that my client was non-Aryan would, I knew, not weigh with them.

Old Rigby Swift, who knew perfectly well what I meant, thumped the desk with his pencil for silence, 'What, Mr Forks, is non-Aryan?' 'Oh! oh! my Lord, it is an expression in use by anti-semites in Central Europe.'

'You mean he's a Jew then?'

'Yes, indeed.'

'Well, why not say so.' Terrifying for a little boy, and all this was in a thick Lancashire accent.

This case I won because after luncheon he came back full of whisky and pointed his remarks at my opponent whom he disliked. He was a very very entertaining judge, although naughty of course, and he had a way with a jury, so all was well. My opponent was the late Robert Fortune, known as 'Frothy Bob' as he would foam at the mouth when excited in argument. He used to live near me in Surrey in the early 1950's and I remember his telling me once that he would retire and enjoy himself one day, and not 'fall down dead in the Strand outside the Law Courts, like poor MacKinnon'. I had no idea that Lord Justice Mac-Kinnon had perished in that manner, but the story came back to mind when I read that poor old Bob had fallen down dead outside the Temple Underground station.

And finally a case before the inevitable Common Jury, Mr Justice Hawke presiding. My client, a bearded lady, sued Boots Cash Chemists for having sold her a preparation which was said to have given her acute eczema. Not a very difficult case, as my woman was a nasty sight, with her face covered, apart from the beard, with skin eruptions of a repellent kind. She attracted sympathy and the shop assistant had to admit that she dealt with many customers daily, while to my client this was a solitary occasion.

'Whose memory, members of the jury, would be likely to be the better?' Then I went too far. 'And, members of the jury, you will remember the look of compassion on his Lordship's face when. . . .'

A banging on the desk, and his handsome old face was raised, 'You leave me out of this.'

I sat down almost at once, but we won. Mummy and her friend Mrs Killby thought that the judge had been unkind, but I didn't.

That case took three days during the whole of which the other side's brief marked, 'Mr Norman Birkett, QC, with you Sir John Forster,' lay in the row in front of me to my right and during the whole of which the great man did not appear. And I had to do battle with his junior. I can even remember the name of the solicitors at the bottom of the brief: Messrs Seaton, Taylor and Co. I wonder what they thought about that, for Birkett's amazing charm with a jury should surely have won them the case.

On the whole, my dull little practice in the Police Courts and the County Courts is not worth recounting but thanks to Gerald I did take part in two interesting cases before the War and thanks to Providence in another which I shall never forget.

The latter I shall come to in my next chapter; the two with Gerald were (1) *Stretch* v. *Sim* which was in the House of Lords and which gave rise to a declaration by Lord Atkin as to how to define defamation, a matter which has caused the Committee on Defamation over which I presided 1970–1975, a lot of trouble recently, as two members dissented, and (2) a case where a Mr Hayley Morris sued some journalist for whom Gerald and I appeared, and Victor Gollancz, the publishers, who were represented by my dear friend Harry Leon, alias Henry Cecil, the author.

In this latter case, the Plaintiff, the squire of Pippingford Park in Sussex, had struck the headlines when he was charged and convicted at Lewes Assizes with unlawful sexual intercourse with a number of young ladies. He also had a mistress called Madeleine Roberts. Our client had thought it worth while writing a book about this and in it he said that Morris had raped one of the girls. An action followed, which for some reason we fought. It wasn't very easy to defend because Mr Justice Humphreys who had tried the case sent a note to say that there had been no question of rape and Roland Oliver QC who had prosecuted went into the witness box and was cross-examined at great length and very unsuccessfully by Gerald. These two disliked each other very much. Gerald, the teetotaller, was far removed from Roland (later Mr Justice) Oliver, much married, keen violinist, addict to gin and creme de menthe and as Owlie calls him 'Jekyll and Hyde who ought to have left his liver to the nation'.

In those days, a busy barrister, leader or junior, would be in two or three cases at once, and in this case, just as we were obviously losing the sympathy of the jury and the mistress, Miss Roberts, was called, Gerald was summoned away and I was left alone in the field. It was my duty to cross-examine this woman to the effect that she had had a miscarriage and had slipped the result down the lavatory, although what on earth that had to do with the case, I cannot remember. Very embarrassed, I blundered away getting the wrong answer to every question, and then Mr Oswald Hickson, our solicitor, turned round and said, 'Hurry up, the insurance money has run out.' A few more questions and I sat down red-faced. The Plaintiff, of course, won but did not get very large damages.

Oswald Hickson built himself up a substantial practice in defamation; so much so that in 1937 he was appointed a member of the Committee on Defamation presided over by Lord Porter on which Gerald also sat. I never had a very high opinion of his judgement, and when he invited me to write a book on libel and slander for nothing, to be published under his name, the quid pro quo being that he would send me his defamation work, I refused. His successor in the firm, Peter Carter-Ruck, has written a book on the subject which is absolutely first class.

CHAPTER FIVE

By God and My Peers

On 15th August 1935, a young man about my age became involved in a collision between two motor cars on the Kingston by-pass, opposite number 6 Malden Way at three o'clock in the morning. He was driving a twelve horse-power Lancia saloon; and the other car was a twelve horse-power Frazer Nash open touring car, with three passengers on the front seat, which had been observed passing the Coombe Lane traffic lights at 45 to 50 mph, after which it was reasonable to assume that it would have accelerated. The result of the collision was the death of the driver of the Frazer Nash and the position of the Lancia at the point of collision was astride the crown of the road somewhat to the wrong side. The Lancia stopped in a few feet and the Frazer Nash went on for 88 feet.

The young man in charge of the Lancia said at once to the police constable who came to the scene, 'I was doing about 40 miles an hour, when, coming towards me, I saw a car which was driving along at a tremendous speed, and I thought the car was out of control. I went over to my off-side to avoid him, then crossed to my near side, but collided.'

There was, of course, a coroner's inquest with a jury, and the other two occupants of the Frazer Nash gave evidence as did the young man. For some reason the jury didn't care for the young man and before he knew where he was he found himself committed for trial at the Central Criminal Court for manslaughter. This might seem grave enough when there was little to disprove what he had said to the police. Really, there was only the fact that he was over the crown of the road at the moment of impact.

But it was much worse for him than that, for his name was Edward Southwell Russell, 26th Lord de Clifford, created 1299:— manslaughter was a felony, and the poor young man had to be tried by his peers. After this case, this antiquated nonsense, for nonsense it was, although everyone there, except the unfortunate prisoner, appeared to enjoy it enormously, was abolished, and there will never again be such an occasion.

The poor young man had to pay his own costs which must have been considerable. He went to an excellent solicitor, the late Tommy Halsall, who retained the great Sir Henry Curtis-Bennett to lead Teddy Ryder-Richardson in my chambers (he had recently appeared with Dick Levy QC for the Rector of Stiffkey who sadly ended his career in a barrel), and somehow a brief marked five guineas descended on me to help and there was a fourth counsel caled J. C. Tait who got two guineas. I have not heard of him since and unless he is still alive, Judge Christmas (Toby) Humphreys, our only Buddhist judge, and I, are the only two advocates alive who took part in that trial.

Sir Henry was a well-known figure at the Bar who had a very large practice in motor manslaughter and in licensing, which in those days was much more lucrative than it is now when no one opposes anything.

His law library was said to consist of *Ruff's Guide to the Turf* and a case called the King against Bateman. It was probably the latter which he was quoting when he addressed their Lordships of whom Lord Hewart, the Lord Chief Justice, was one, 'May I just respectfully remind your Lordships as to what the law is about this matter. In a judgment of my Lord Hewart, the Lord Chief Justice, which was delivered as the judgment of the Court of Criminal Appeal (of which there were five members), a judgment which was delivered by my Lord, a considered judgment, the argument having taken place in February of the particular year, the judgment being given at the end of May, when a number of cases bearing on the matter had been before that Court, the Lord Chief Justice said : "In order to establish criminal liability, the facts must be such that in the opinion of the jury the negligence of the accused went beyond a mere matter of compensation between subjects, and showed such disregard for the life and safety of others as to amount to a crime against the State." Later the Lord Chief Justice said, "It is most desirable that in trials for manslaughter by negligence, it should be impressed on the jury that the issue that they have to try is not negligence or no negligence but felony or no felony. It is desirable that, as far as possible, the explanation of criminal negligence to a jury should not be a mere question of epithets. It is in a sense a question of degree. It is for the jury to draw the line, but there is a difference in kind between the negligence which gives a right to compensate and the negligence which is a crime." '

I don't know, being a Family Division Judge, whether that is the law today, but I do know that in those days you couldn't get a conviction for motor manslaughter unless the offender was shown to be drunk. Then he got eighteen months.

Now this poor fellow whom nobody suggested was drunk had to endure what was really a marvellous pantomime, such as only England could put on, with the undertones in the Commission which cannot have been very amusing to him . . . (the Monarch speaking) 'We, considering that Justice is an excellent virtue and pleasing to the Most High, and being willing that the said Edward Southwell, Baron de Clifford of and for the felony whereby he is indicted as aforesaid before us in our present Parliament, according to the Law and Custom of England, may be heard, examined, condemned and adjudged . . . etc. etc.' And he must have felt that the scales were loaded against him. It was the most remarkable event.

Four judges of the High Court were present :

> The Honourable Mr Justice Swift
> The Honourable Mr Justice Branson
> The Honourable Mr Justice Charles
> The Honourable Mr Justice Goddard.

The Lord Chancellor (Viscount Hailsham) was on the Woolsack. The names of their lordships present beginning with the Junior Baron were called over.

I can understand the Law Lords being there but there were a great many others present to see this poor boy butchered to make a Roman holiday. It seemed like a party and there were a lot of peeresses there, too.

After it was all over and the poor man had been acquitted I heard one of these ladies say to another, 'Darling, I can go home and tell Harry it's all right to drive on the wrong side of the road.' And this was meant to be a serious criminal proceeding. Evelyn Waugh would have loved it.

The company of their lordships present was called over, they standing and answering 'here' as follows :

Lord Roche	Lord Thankerton
Lord Maugham	Lord Atkin
Lord Alness	Lord Blanesburgh
Lord Rockley	Lord Hewart
Lord Brocket	Lord Swinfen
Lord Wright	Lord Ruthven of Gowrie

Lord Rhayader
Lord Rochester
Lord Macmillan
Lord Russell of Killowen
Lord Faringdon
Lord Charnwood
Lord Ilkeston
Lord Kilbracken
Lord Fisher
Lord Holden
Lord Waleran
Lord Killanin
Lord Loch
Lord Monkswell
Lord Tweedale (Tweedale M)
Lord Sandhurst
Lord Wolverton
Lord Lawrence
Lord Stanley of Alderley
Lord Denman
Lord Clements (Leitrim E.)
Lord Clanwilliam
   (Clanwilliam E.)
Lord Ker (Lothian M)
Lord Ellenborough
Lord Fisherwick (Donegall M)
Lord Berwick
Lord Middleton
Lord Sempill
Lord Teynham
Lord Cromwell
Lord Darcy (de Knayth)
Lord Strabolgi
Lord Hastings
The Bishop of Sheffield

Lord Morris
Lord Annesley (Valentia V)
Lord Doverdale
Lord Carnock
Viscount Wakefield
Viscount Chelmsford
Viscount Finlay
Viscount Bertie of Thame
Viscount Mersey
Viscount Goschen
Viscount Esher
Viscount Portman
Viscount Exmouth
Viscount Hereford
Earl St. Aldwyn
Earl of Liverpool
Earl of Halsbury
Earl of Iddesleigh
Earl of Lytton
Earl of Cottenham
Earl of Onslow
Earl of Lucan
Earl of Drogheda
Earl of Malmesbury
Earl of Mansfield
Earl Fitzwilliam
Earl Stanhope
Earl of Airlie
Earl Poulett
Marquess of Aberdeen and Temair
Marquess of Dufferin and Ava
Marquess of Salisbury
Duke of Argyll
Duke of Rutland
Duke of Richmond and Gordon
Viscount Halifax (Lord Privy Seal).

Lord Leigh, Viscount Brentford, and the Earl of Birkenhead arrived late and joined the number – 86 in all, including the Lord Chancellor.

The party then adjourned from the House of Lords, into the Royal Gallery. There their Lordships all in full fig sat, and the judges in their full-bottomed wigs were deployed somewhere in front of the Lord Chancellor, also dressed in his most colourful garments, on a throne. We then discovered that the Lord Chancellor was to be Lord High Steward for the occasion. The Clerk of the Crown in Chancery, who became Lord Schuster, and was unfortunately not as tall as his three distinguished and dignified successors, Napier, Coldstream and Dobson, made three reverences and presented the Commission under the Great Seal appointing the Lord High Steward, on his knee, to the Lord Chancellor who delivered it back to him to read.

Then after three more reverences, Schuster went back to his table and the Sergeant at Arms said, 'Oyez, oyez, oyez! Our Sovereign Lord the King (that was George V) strictly charges and commands all manner of persons to keep silence under pain of imprisonment.'

Everyone at the Lord Chancellor's instruction stood and uncovered. Schuster then read the Commission which was very long, at the end of which the Sergeant at Arms loyally cried, 'God save the King!'

Other members of the dramatis personae then suddenly appeared when (and this must have taken some practice) Garter King of Arms and the Gentleman Usher of the Black Rod made three simultaneous reverences, both of course magnificently dressed, and kneeling before the Lord High Steward, jointly presented to him his White Staff of Office, which was delivered to Black Rod on the right, while the Purse Bearer holding the Purse was on the left of the Lord High Steward.

Then the Writ of Certiorari, the Return, the Caption of the Indictment, the Indictment, the Caption of the Inquisition, and the Inquisition were all read involving much repetition and consuming much time, while the unfortunate accused waited and waited.

Then the Lord High Steward asked if it was their lordships' pleasure that the judges have leave to be covered. Their lordships somewhat improbably rejoined, 'Aye, Aye' and four full-bottomed wigs were replaced.

The Clerk of the Parliaments who had previously called the roll of those present then said, in the most terrifying terms, 'Sergeant at Arms make proclamation for the Gentleman Usher of the Black Rod to bring his prisoner to the Bar.' And the Sergeant at Arms said, 'Oyez, oyez, oyez! Edward Southwell, Lord de Clifford, come forth and save you and your bail or else you forfeit your recognizance.'

Lord de Clifford, who must have felt that he had been found guilty before the trial had even started, was brought to the Bar, made three reverences, and was told that he might be seated.

It all seemed part of the Middle Ages.

Next the Lord High Steward said, 'Lord de Clifford, you are indicted for the crime of manslaughter, committed at the time and place and under the circumstances disclosed in the indictment which has just been read. If you have anything to offer you may have an opportunity of saying it. I say to you, as to all others who may have occasion to speak in the course of this trial, you are to address their Lordships generally and not any one Lord in particular.

'My Lord, your Lordship will do well to give attention while you are arraigned upon your indictment.'

And then the Clerk of the Parliaments read out a shortened form of the Indictment again, ending, 'How say you, my Lord, are you Guilty of the Felony with which you are charged or Not Guilty?'

And the answer came, 'Not Guilty.'

'How will you be tried?'

The dramatic answer, 'By God and my peers.'

To which the Clerk replied, 'God send your Lordship a good deliverance.'

And the Sergeant at Arms cried once more, 'Oyez, oyez, oyez! All manner of persons who will give evidence on behalf of Our Sovereign Lord the King against Edward Southwell, Lord de Clifford, the Prisoner at the Bar, let them come forth and they shall be heard, for now he stands at the Bar upon his deliverance.'

And after all that, and the poor pale peer must have been thinking about 'cutting the cackle and coming to the horses', the trial began. It was only a trivial little road accident which ended unfortunately in death, but the Prosecution consisted of Sir Thomas Inskip CBE KC MP, who had become Attorney-General in the new Tory government, the Solicitor-General, Sir Donald B. Somervell OBE KC MP as well as Mr Eustace Fulton and Mr Christmas Humphreys, Old Bailey experts to whom this sort of case was run of the mill. Inskip later became Minister of Defence, Lord Chancellor, Lord Chief Justice, and Viscount Caldecote. There is a most unflattering portrait of him in my Inn, the Inner Temple, by Augustus John, from which I can only assume that the two men did not like each other. Which, when one comes to think of it, is probable, as Tom Inskip was low church and devout, and we all know about Augustus John. Donald Somervell was much loved and ended up as Lord Somervell of Harrow. Neither of these gentlemen could be described as a specialist criminal lawyer.

On our side, Tait and I were just luggage, but Ryder Richardson was very, very good and the very fat old man who led us, who was only outmatched in girth by Walter Frampton, his gigantic junior in criminal and licensing cases, was the man for the job.

The evidence was not very exciting, as it had all been given at the Coroner's inquest.

At the end of the Prosecution's case, Curtis-Bennett turned to Ryder Richardson and said, 'I think I shall make a submission that there is no case to answer.' Ryder Richardson like a sensible person looked pensive and said nothing. I, like a fool, said, 'Oh! Do you think you should?' whereupon the old gentleman said, 'Be quiet, you impertinent young puppy.' And quite right too. Actually he wasn't really an old gentleman because he died soon afterwards in his fifties while making a speech at a city dinner, an exercise which he greatly enjoyed and at which he was very talented.

So he made his speech, in the course of which he referred to Lord Hewart's judgment which I have already mentioned and also to the statement to the police constable by Lord de Clifford which I have also set out, only to meet with this rather tart interruption from the Lord High Steward, 'Sir Henry, you have repeatedly, in your submission, referred to the statement of Lord de Clifford as if it were evidence of the fact. Of course, if and when Lord de Clifford gives evidence to the effect which he stated to the Police, that will be most cogent evidence to be taken into account by their Lordships' House, but, at present, there is no evidence before the House, so far as I am aware, that the statements made by Lord de Clifford are accurate, that he either saw a car out of control or that it was on the wrong side of the road. He can give evidence of those facts, and, of course, their Lordships will bear it in mind, but, at present, you are submitting that there is no case. As I understand your submission, you are basing it largely upon the assumption that their Lordships have to take, as being evidence of the fact, the statement which Lord de Clifford has deposed to as being true.'

Shivers ran down my back. How were we going to get out of that? There was no doubt what the Lord High Steward felt.

Poor Sir Henry didn't seem to me to do very well when he said in answer, 'My Lords, I am submitting to your Lordships' House that the fact that the statement was made by Lord de Clifford at the earliest possible moment is evidence of what is contained in the statement; and I am submitting that that is a very important matter to consider upon the question as to whether or not there is a case.' Then he added some remarks to the effect that his client was not afraid and was indeed anxious to go into the witness box.

Grandpa and Neville, 1926

Mummy 1937

Bespectacled dog-lover, 1938

Wengen 1938

Sisters, nieces, and washing 1943

Fancy dress ball, Wengen 1938

Then the Attorney General asked what he should do and the Lord High Steward again made his view plain enough. 'Mr Attorney, you appreciate that in this trial every one of their Lordships is a Judge of law as well as fact. If it were a matter for me to rule upon I should be quite prepared to give a ruling, but that is not my function . . .' etc. etc. Further shivers down my back.

The Attorney General accordingly made rather a good speech in which he pointed out that the fact that the Frazer Nash had gone on for 88 feet didn't establish its excessive speed as probably the driver was unconscious after impact.

And the Lord High Steward injected some further shivers by saying, 'My Lords, if your Lordships wish to consider this point, it will probably be convenient to adjourn into the Chamber and after that to disperse for the necessary luncheon adjournment. I do not think we ought to take very long in discussing this particular submission. Possibly the Court might adjourn till half past two.'

Alarm and despondency. A rather depressing luncheon.

But at half past two the House was adjourned into the Royal Gallery, the submission by Sir Henry Curtis-Bennett having been considered.

After a number of oyezs and calls for silence by the indefatigable Sergeant at Arms, the Lord High Steward, with great dignity, for it must have hurt him to say this, observed, 'Sir Henry Curtis-Bennett, their Lordships have thought it right to submit the question of law which you have propounded, to His Majesty's Judges who are here for the purpose of advising their Lordships' House upon questions of law which may arise during the course of the trial. The Judges have unanimously advised their Lordships that your submission is well founded and that there is no case to answer. (So much for all that about the Bishop of Sheffield being a judge of law as well as of fact.) Their Lordships, in pursuance of that advice, have resolved to uphold your submission.' He continued, 'My Lords, the question for your Lordships is: Is the prisoner Guilty of the felony whereof he stands indicted, or Not Guilty?'

And then, and it was very moving, the Clerk of the Parliaments, standing up, called every Peer by his name, whereupon they put their hands on their hearts and cried, 'Not Guilty, upon my honour', and it was very difficult not to weep. There seemed to have been 84 of them: perhaps two were lost over luncheon.

And the Lord High Steward cried, 'My Lords, I declare that Edward Southwell, Lord de Clifford, is acquitted of the felony whereof he stands indicted, by the unanimous verdict of your Lordships' House. Let the Prisoner be brought to the Bar.'

Lord de Clifford was brought to the Bar by the Yeoman Usher of the Black Rod (possibly because the Gentleman Usher had been baulked of his 'prisoner'). The Lord High Steward declared that he had been found 'Not Guilty' unanimously and Lord de Clifford retired.

Then came the only entertaining part of the occasion. The Lord High Steward, if I may so call him as he was soon to be Lord Chancellor again, said, 'My Lords, this trial being at an end, nothing remains here but to determine the Commission. Let proclamation be made for dissolving the Commission of High Steward.'

And our old friend the Sergeant at Arms said, 'Oyez, oyez, oyez!' and after some preliminary observations announced that his Lordship, The Lord High Steward of the United Kingdom, intended now to dissolve his Commission. Then the Gentleman Usher of the Black Rod (the Yeoman still presumably still filing off the fetters) knelt before the Lord High Steward and handed him the White Staff of Office.

This was the moment critique. The Lord High Steward stood up uncovered and holding the staff in both hands, *failed* to break it in two. It was a pity. But with great dignity again he declared the Commission dissolved and adjourned the House to the Chamber of Parliament.

I know that my brother judge, Cumming-Bruce, who was present as a younger son of a peer will corroborate me as to this and I would expect the ex-Lord Chancellor, the second Lord Hailsham, to have been there and to remember it also.

Envoi : I think it must have been in 1942 when I came across the Lord de Clifford somewhere in the Western Desert, then a Colonel in REME, who were the chaps who actually knew how the tanks which we drove, worked.

Having been introduced to him, I was seized with a desire to know how he pronounced his second name for during the trial he had been called both Southwell in a straightforward way and as Sutthle as in the 'Bishop of Southwell'. But I never found out. I said that I had acted for him at the trial in a humble way, and he said, 'Don't let us talk about that.' I understood : we talked of something else, and I have never seen him since.

It is because of that conversation that I have hesitated long and taken much advice before deciding to describe this trial, for after all if Lord de Clifford had been convicted and fined or given six months, or something of the kind, I should have been liable to be fined and sued for defamation for telling the truth under The Rehabilitation of Offenders Act, and it would seem hard to write about a trial where a man was acquitted when it is a crime to do so if he was convicted.

My advisers tell me that this trial is history and my doubts are absurd. All the same he is still alive and might take umbrage, and it is only the fact that I see that he made a speech to his Peers in the House of Lords on 11th June 1974 against the proposal in the new Road Traffic Bill that it should be compulsory to wear seat belts, that has resolved my doubts and convinced me that he must have forgotten all the horrors of forty years ago.

CHAPTER SIX

Trooper Faulks

I think it was Bernard Shaw who said, 'He who can, does. He who cannot, teaches,' and I struggled along after that great trial on 12th December 1935, wondering how I could last out until someone decided that I was worth briefing or whether I should become an assistant master at a preparatory school.

At about this time I began to get interested in politics and pursued my unfortunate member round his meetings, to enquire why he preferred Mr Baldwin, or, later, Mr Chamberlain to Mr Churchill. I even took Socialist voters to the poll as a mark of esteem to Mr Churchill and of hatred to Mr Chamberlain.

I had not bothered to understand the Socialist party's attitude to rearmament.

Then it dawned on me that I might as well do something as well as just talk, although in fact all my life I have been much better at talking than at doing, I am sorry to say.

My talking had made me Public Bore Number One at my table at the Inner Temple at lunch. So much so that one day in 1937, Guy Aldous already an acknowledged expert in patent law, said to me, 'Where is this Casko Slavonika that you keep on belly-aching about?' It is hard to believe, but in June 1974 a young man asked me at a cocktail party where was Czecho-Slovakia.

And five of us from 1 Brick Court, Temple, EC4, joined the Territorial Army, the Inns of Court Regiment, to show our disapproval of Mr Adolf Hitler.

Charlie Cahn was the oldest at about forty; he must be well over seventy-five by now. After the war he went into the Judge-Advocate General's Department, and became No. 2, but they thought he was too old to be the Judge-Advocate General and threw him out with a CBE and a pension. Bill Behrens was next. He ended up as a full colonel in AMGOT after having been in the Desert with the Bays. He won the St Leger last year with his horse Peleid. It was the first time I had backed a horse for many years. Then came Kenneth Barraclough who is now the Chief Magistrate at Bow Street, and who was much the most military of any of us. He saluted beautifully, had lots of commonsense and was a lance-corporal before you could say knife. He also ended up as a full colonel.

Trooper Faulks was full of ideals, but not very efficient. We were all a decade older than most of the Regiment and my fellow-troopers used to annoy me by calling me 'Daddy'. Going to camp was a burden. Issued with 15 cwt trucks which we had to pretend to be armoured cars, we had to put bootblacking on the tyres so that they looked smart for 'stables'. And as a humble trooper I used to have to arise to take a cup of tea to some useless major who was allowed a camp bed, confound him. Eventually, Bertie Bingley who was the regular adjutant – he was an 11th Hussar – said one day, 'Well, Faulks, it's a pity you can't salute, but all your friends are Lance-Corporals, so I suppose I'd better make you one also.'

I was madly keen and I remember that when Hitler marched into Prague, I was up in some drill hall in North London on a Bren gun course trying to dismantle and reassemble the weapon in record time, and coming in last of the class with unfailing regularity. I was determined to carry on, inefficient as I was, when, at luncheon, I was offered a commission in the Middlesex Yeomanry, the second line of which was being formed by a fellow barrister named Pat Doyle, a well known gentleman rider who, no doubt, had joined the Territorial Army, as had most young people, for the riding.

I accepted and took along with me the fifth member of our number from chambers, Christopher Smuts, a South African, who had been president of the Oxford Union, who was younger than I was, had stood three times as a Liberal candidate for Parliament, and was very handsome. My younger sister thought very highly of him.

This unit had lost its horses in the '14–'18 war and was now Armoured Divisional Signals, and we all rushed up and down the Duke of York's Barracks, being drilled by a character called Corporal of the Horse Ring, with great enthusiasm. I had to learn the Morse Code and to tap away, and I was rather better at that, having been a Signal Sergeant in my corps at school, until in 1926 I was reduced to the ranks for having done the Charleston on parade.

At any rate, messing about with morse seemed to me to be more worth while than bending one's knees in Lincoln's Inn Fields pretending to be on a horse crying, 'Infantry to the right, bonk' and 'Infantry to the left, bonk' while the public looked on and laughed.

However, we still went on with the old tricks, and at just about the start of the war I recruited Judge Geoffrey Howard as an unpaid sergeant-major to teach some of my young gentlemen signalling by flag and lamp which was, although quite useless, very well received.

Camp with the Middlesex Yeomanry as an officer was a different world from the camps I had attended with the Inns of Court as an other rank. But even so I was a lot older than most of the other officers and it seemed to me that with the war so obviously soon to come upon us there was a lack of a sense of purpose about it all. There was too much changing of uniform and then there was cock-fighting after dinner in the mess. It was all too much like that wonderful play, *Conduct Unbecoming*. I kept my mouth shut, but Christopher Smuts, who being a Liberal was madly idealistic (in those days), used to express his views in his cups which didn't make him too popular. He decided one evening to be very democratic and tell one of our number who was a Viscount what he thought of the ari-something-stocracy, which was poorly received.

When we came back from our summer camp in 1939, it was pretty clear that war was upon us. I had spent most of 1938 (which was the first year in which I earned £2,000 a year, mostly out of one commercial case) digging a shelter in the tennis lawn, and telling my mother to buy enormous quantities of tinned food. She did that, and it was good advice. But after some months digging and putting in steps and pit props, the shelter was a failure and I came across water. All I had done was to reduce the value of the property.

I was the duty officer at the Duke of York's Barracks when I switched on the radio to hear Neville Chamberlain tell us that we were at war.

I do not propose to be prolix about my war. In fact I was a major in 1940, and after some two years as a half-colonel, I was demobilised as a major again in 1945. Not very grand. And so these matters will be dealt with delicately.

The high spot of my war was being lucky enough to be present as the Signals officer of the Brigade when the sixty tanks of the 22nd Armoured Brigade, known to General Horrocks as ELH, 'Egypt's Last Hope', took on and defeated Rommel at point 102 on the Alam Halfa ridge. The newly arrived 10th Armoured Division with 66 Grants were dug in in a defensive position to block the wide encircling movement, the alternative which Rommel might have adopted. We had several rehearsals of this battle, and most of us had no idea what it was all about. But

Field-Marshal Auchinleck, at the age of ninety, described it rightly, on television, as 'the first battle of Alamein,' and 'the one that turned the scales.'

By then, of course, 'The Auk' had gone and General Montgomery was in charge. We thought that Monty had the most marvellous intuition. It never occurred to us that, thanks to 'Ultra', the marvellous cipher-reading device which enabled us to read the enemy's airborne messages, he actually knew Rommel's intentions. It is that experience with which I shall probably bore my grandchildren. It was very good for our morale, for at last it really was a 'bloody good win,' but 'bloody' because too many people were killed later on at Alamein.

But there were a great many low spots in my war as well.

When the War came I moved into Number 18 Draycott Place which belonged to my old friend, Ian Baillieu, who is best known for having rewritten the laws of croquet, and less well known for having been my best man. Draycott Place was within spitting distance of the Duke of York's barracks where we were still situated, and the Pheasantry in the King's Road was equally happily poised.

However, we had a hurried signal to the effect that our Divisional Commander, of whom I had never heard, but who bore the tremend-ously military name of General Hotblack, had fallen to his death down the Duke of York's steps (sabotage not suspected) and we were pre-cipitately removed to the outer suburbs, to Cockfosters, Herts, at the end of the Underground Line.

There the man Baillieu and the man Faulks and a little sweet man called Murdoch, who alas was killed at the battle of Sidi Rezegh, took up their warlike stations at No 38 Belmont Avenue. The man Faulks pored over his Signals Manuals, but the other two were more relaxed and went off to some dance or other at Barnet.

I was a heavy cigar smoker in those days; indeed Grandpa had fur-nished me with vast numbers of boxes of Partagas when I was an under-graduate. (Partagas to him were number two; number one were Henry Clays. Times have entirely changed, for the Monte Christos which I used to buy as a boy at the Bar from a little shop by the Old Bailey in Newgate, are now so much grander than either Partagas or Henry Clay.)

Late in the evening when I was still perusing my dreary manual and on my second cigar, these two characters returned with a very young and very attractive ATS. Both of them had apparently taken a fancy to her – Ian was married so perhaps I shouldn't have said that. I wasn't interested, and Murdoch took her home.

Two days later I was bidden to have a drink with Captain and Mrs Andrew who lived at Barnet where he, aged over fifty, had volunteered to take a job in the Pay Corps. And who should be the fourth but little Miss who was apparently attached to the Pay Corps too.

The well-known bachelor was bowled over, the bowling possibly being added to by the fact that he felt that he was going to be killed anyway, and we met for the eighth time at the altar.

The affair was on the dreary side. As I was stationed in Cockfosters, the church had to be nearby. We obtained an Archbishop's licence, £25, and were married at St James The Less, Lower Barnet, on the coldest day of the century, 20.1.40. Of course most of the people who had been asked didn't come, and those who did come said that the war would be over soon, and then they would send a present.

However, two things were good about the wedding. One was that the Baillieus very kindly paid for the reception, which was a splendid occasion in the Officers' Mess – and, two, that my friend, Bobbie Milburn, now the Master of the Temple, having been Dean of Worcester, and all sorts of things before, was kind enough to marry us as he has my son and daughter and also assisted at my step-children's weddings.

We nipped off in the snow and ice to Draycott Place, which Ian and Jo had lent to us for our honeymoon, only to find that the pipes had burst owing to the cold and that we had to find solace elsewhere. After three very pleasant days at the Cumberland Hotel, we went to Draycott Place when the climate was better. It was one of those houses which has four floors and a basement, and Mrs Dyer, a worthy 'treasure' as they used to be called in those days, would send the food up from the basement on a service lift. On our second night there, we were ready to go to some musical or other, I think called *Up and Doing* with Cyril Ritchard, where my mother-in-law had been responsible for all the costumes, when the service lift came up bearing a vast quantity of smoked salmon which kind Jo Baillieu had bought for us. Mrs Dyer had found it her duty to fry it !

The honeymoon over, we went back to Cockfosters.

Bridget soon became pregnant and we obtained leave to go home and tell my parents our great news.

I remember being smartly saluted by one of my oldest friends who was at an OCTU and feeling rather stupid, but the whole visit, and we hadn't been home for months, was very sad. Dunkirk was 29th May – 4th June 1940, and my young brother Peter was there, with the first battalion of the Duke of Wellington's Regiment, having gone straight down from Cambridge into his OCTU. There was, of course, no news of him, and there we sat, in the morning room with Mummy looking like Cassandra and all our happy tidings of no account.

Peter turned up later in a small boat at Lulworth Cove or somewhere like that and the next time we saw Mummy was in an hotel in Sheffield – by this time we were stationed near Whitwell in Nottinghamshire – where he was to be sent to re-equip, the Duke's being a Yorkshire Regiment.

We didn't see him, but she looked like a tragedy queen, and I was worried.

My next leave was in September 1940 when I was under canvas at Skellingthorpe in Lincolnshire, the only fully equipped, but by no means fully trained, Armoured Division in England, ready to do our incompetent best in case the Hun should invade. I forget where Bridget was; at home, I assume. In those days the authorities hadn't got round to providing us with proper transport, and I drove home in my Delage coupé, a 'cad's car', which I had bought in 1937 or 1938, and which had four gears in forward and four gears in reverse which used to thrill the girls immensely. (This was, of course, going down to Glynde-bourne before the war.)

Arrived at home, we had two dramas. The lesser was that London was bombed, and we could see the smoke coming up from the docks many miles away, and houses were levelled nearby. But we were young, we declined to accompany my parents into the cellar which had been made into an air-raid shelter, (much better than my effort in the tennis lawn) and we found it all rather exciting.

The major drama was that Mummy, who was only fifty-four, had been stung by a wasp. She made nothing of it, but I said that she looked dreadful and I must send for Dr Barnes. She was against it, saying that in war time he had too much to do. But I won; Dr Barnes came and to our consternation told us that she had cancer of the bowel. This was too much for Papa, and I was left to deal with the situation. Dr Barnes said that she could have a colostomy but that would only prolong her life in pain and he advised me to let her die peacefully.

What would you have done? I did the wrong thing; I said that I couldn't let her die. She must have the operation, and the Almighty would see to the rest.

The doctor was unhappily right. She saw my eldest child once after her operation, and said, very nearly unable to speak, that she was 'better'. She died in July 1941 when I was about to go abroad. Poor

Papa had to spend a year in digs at Oxted, where she was in the Cottage Hospital, and commute, and I was unable to attend her funeral. I loved her very much, and shall never forget her.

At the end of my visit home in September 1940, the telephone rang. A mysterious voice said, 'Cromwell'. That was the pre-arranged code-word for an invasion by Corporal Hitler. I kissed everyone goodbye, thinking that I should never see them again, started up the Delage, which was a very fast car, and set off hot-foot for Skellingthorpe.

Up the Luton-Dunstable road I went, which was then the road to Lincolnshire. I passed through the village of Markyate at about 30 mph as it was a narrow village street. But no; the limit was 20 mph, and I was stopped by a police constable. I was in uniform and I endeavoured to tell him that my return to duty was a matter of urgency. No good. And I received a summons a month or two later, by which time, Cromwell having proved a non-starter, we were protecting England in Surrey, where Brigade Headquarters were at Park Hatch, the Duke of Westminster's property near Hascombe, itself near Godalming.

I wrote a tremendously legal and marvellously appealing document to the magistrates at Markyate. Tear-jerking, I thought. Result : 30 shillings fine and licence endorsed. (I took a low view of that, although other events put it into the background.)

The next time I fell foul of the police was in 1971 when I had to go to the Judges' Clerks Annual Dinner at the Waldorf Hotel where my clerk, who had had a stroke and was retiring, was to make a speech. I parked, as there was nowhere else available, just on the Bush House pedestrian crossing, and got to the dinner in time. At that time of night, no one could possibly have been using the pedestrian crossing. Result : Conviction at Bow Street, 31.1.72. Fined seven pounds and licence endorsed.

Those three, Waterloo Place, Markyate, and Bush House, have been my only troubles with the law in a long life, and I have not felt entirely happy about any of them.

But then I blush to think how many people have been dissatisfied with my judgments in two years of presiding over Courts-Martial and, at the date of writing, over fourteen years as a High Court Judge.

The fact is that we are all human : none of us is infallible; we do our best : and there is no more that we can do.

*   *   *

Late in 1940 we were in Surrey. Bridget was heavily pregnant, and I took a very nice house in Chiddingfold. The Brigadier who disliked me and whom I disliked, tried to make me live under canvas, and then, when the weather grew more inclement, in Park Hatch itself. He had ditched his wife somewhere, but I wasn't going to ditch mine and somehow I managed to get permission to live out. He had commanded the 4th Hussars in India before the war, and, as a High Sheriff has recently told me, the regiment was dreadfully split between the Pig-stickers and the Polo Players. I didn't know this at the time, but now I understand what at the time I thought to be a most mysterious occasion.

I had made a number of records at Decca studios which were designed to teach operators how to speak over the wireless to others also in tanks. When I say 'I', the idea was not mine but that of two distinguished characters at Cambridge University, when we were stationed nearby, and we had much help from Pye Limited.

For some extraordinary reason, it was decided to use these records at OCTU's and Brigadier Scott-Cockburn was even more pleased about this than I was. I suppose that he realised dimly that his was a pig-sticking coterie rather than the Bloomsbury set. Mark you, if I had to choose between the two, give me the cavalry every time. I drove over to Dorking on the Brigadier's instructions, to fetch the Divisional Commander to come and listen to these records to which the 22nd Armoured Brigade had given birth.

The Divisional Commander honoured me by coming to Park Hatch in my staff car.

As a humble major, I waited until he spoke.

When he did he said, 'You know, you're very lucky to be the signals officer of this brigade – finest brigade staff in the Army.'

I said, 'Oh! Sir, why?' which I supposed I ought to say in order to feed him, although I rather suspected what, as he was an extremely brave and distinguished Cavalry Officer, was to follow.

'Your Brigadier won the Khadir Cup twice – your Brigade major, Bunny Head, won it once, and Jack Archdale, your intelligence officer (a most delightful, sweet man) won it once also, and Bunny Hewitt who commands your Headquarters Squadron, edited the Pig Stickers' Annual in Calcutta.'

I said, 'Yes, sir', and wondered how on earth we were going to beat Corporal Hitler.

I need not have worried because, although none of the pig-stickers rose above their then ranks, the Divisional Commander became not only a Corps Commander, but Governor-General of New Zealand and a peer of the realm.

In early 1940, I had been summoned to 2nd Armoured Divisional HQ to be told that my squadron and I had been selected to go to Norway. I said, 'Very good, sir', or something equally oily, but mercifully it was all cancelled. (The only other occasion when I can remember my Adam's apple coming up into my mouth while attempting to appear nonchalant was when, somewhere in the desert, the Ghurkas came under command. My brigadier said that the foe were about a mile away and the Ghurkas would take them by surprise at night, kukris to do their work in slitting throats, but that they must have communication back to Brigade and that Faulks was the man to go down the hill and up the hill laden with wireless sets to achieve that object. Faulks, feeling extremely unwell, expressed his entire approval of the project.

But he felt much better, when, just before the attack was due to start, we had a little signal putting the Ghurkas under the command of someone else.)

My infant was born on 26th January 1941, a month late, during which time we had had the trained nurse, who insisted upon being waited upon, Clara, our housemaid, and Moore, my marvellous batman, all ready to lend a hand. It was not really an enjoyable time and when, meaning to cheer her up, I used to sing 'Roll out the Barrel', then the popular hit, it was not well received. Finally the poor girl had her birth pains at the Godalming cinema when the nurse had her day off. All, however, was well.

Six months later saw us in a rather scruffy lodging in Trowbridge, with my squadron at Upton Scudamore, and the Brigade near Warminster. My little boy was jumping up and down in his cot, and when we heard that we were to go abroad, there was a terrible scene. We shared these digs with another couple, with whom we had shared a caravan a year before, with cows peering into the windows in the early morning, and both the women worked themselves up into a state. Christopher Smuts had to march my boys to the station because I was in tears. Not very military, I am afraid, but I caught the train. The other chap, whose name was Tatton, and was one of the best people I have ever known, was killed during the hugger mugger after Sidi Rezegh. She, I am glad to say, married again later, happily. When we got on the train, we had absolutely no idea where we were going.

We were in fact in for the most tremendous treat. We arrived at the Clyde, embarked in three luxury P & O cruising ships, the *Orion*, the *Strathmore* and the *Strathnaver*. My young gentlemen who were only about 130 strong were aboard with the 2nd Royal Gloucestershire Hussars, and a more delightful batch of companions I could not have desired. The other ranks had a wonderful time playing Housey-Housey, now known as Bingo, while the officers indulged in a little innocent poker or bridge. We made for the middle of the Atlantic and then turned south to fox the foe, attended by three ships from His Majesty's Royal Navy. First stop Freetown, second stop Cape Town. The food was fantastic compared with what people were eating at home. Each of these ships had stocked up in Canada and we might have been in peace time. No enemy submarine was observed, and the only thing that brought the realities of war at all near was when one of His Majesty's ships rammed the *Orion*, no doubt with admirable intentions, which caused her to have a little refit in Cape Town.

Christopher Smuts was able to secure us hospitality for the week-end, and, anxious though we were for battle, another day or two at Cape Town would not have been frowned upon.

When eventually we arrived in Egypt, I had had a rattling good holiday, and had only justified my existence by teaching my squadron the use of the sun compass in which I was scarcely proficient myself.

We were all issued with tropical kit, always too small, so that my squadron from the back looked like a collection of sausages. The Brigadier very sensibly banned the consumption of alcohol before the sun was over the yard-arm which was arbitrarily fixed at 1800 hours, and we did a certain amount of desultory training.

Then I was told to go up to the wire (ie, between Egypt and Libya) with my Brigadier and the Brigade Major. They didn't tell me what was afoot : why they asked me to go, I don't know. I was always known in the desert as 'Nosey' because I did want to know the form. When anyone teased me with this soubriquet I was always happy to reply that a nick-name which was good enough for the great Duke of Wellington was good enough for me. When we came back from the wire I was not much the wiser, but I knew that there had been a battle there the year before, (Operation Battleaxe), and suspected, correctly, that compara-tively untrained as we were, we were to take part in a major contest of arms.

Our first engagement was at Gubi, where the 2 RGH lost many tanks and Tom Elder-Jones (now His Honour Judge Elder-Jones) lost his arm. From there we proceeded to Sidi Rezegh where the Brigadier, forgetting perhaps that he was supposed to be in command, but bravely scenting the enemy's blood, disappeared in an armoured car of the 11th Hussars, and was out of touch with me throughout the battle. Esmond Baring, who was the G3, and I, had to cope with communications forward to the regiments and back to Division without any spectacular results. I got a very small piece of shrapnel indeed in my right shoulder and insisted on going to the Field Dressing Station where I was told politely to go away as they had a great many more serious cases on their hands.

At the end of this battle, I came across Gerry de Winton, once of 3 Hare Court, Temple, who had broken out of the garrison at Tobruk. It has always been a point of debate between us as to whether we rescued them, as we were always given to understand, or whether they saved us, as they were taught. At any rate, the enemy disappeared and we followed them to Agedabbia. Poor Gerry had been in the Greek disaster while I was travelling round the Cape.

I didn't see him again until late in 1943 when he burst into my room at San Severo in the south of Italy, having walked half way down the country from his POW camp.

One of his many stories, told in his own words, is as follows: 'At some time towards the end of February 1943, it was announced that a Legate of the Pope would visit the camp at Easter in the interests of humanity and goodwill. As most prisoners had found the Papal machinery for reporting their survival as prisoners of war more efficient and more rapid than the official Italian and British military channels, they were well disposed towards the Holy See and very ready to welcome the Emissary.

'As the day approached, the authorities began to suggest with all the tact at their disposal that the prisoners should for the occasion lay aside the blankets that were their usual covering and put on their uniforms and that those who like myself went habitually barefoot should put on their boots.

'The negotiations reached a personal stage. For myself, I had to admit that I owned a pair of boots. They were, however, suffering from the effects of a 150 mile walk from Tobruk after its fall and I had for some time been wondering how, if the chance came, I could ever escape in boots that could not possibly last another 20 miles without disintegrating. The Legate's visit seemed to present a possibility of remedying the situation.

'I presented myself at the office of the Commandante and regretted that my boots were in so disgraceful a condition that it would constitute an affront to the Legate and an unbearable humiliation to myself were I to wear them. The authority disagreed. I persisted, saluted and left.

'Some days elapsed and I was again summoned to the office. I was reminded that I was subject to military discipline and told that it was an order emanating from the highest possible source that I should put on my boots. I refused. I was told that if I did not put on my boots, they would be put on by force. This was going a bit far, and I could see that this particular suggestion did not emanate very high up. However, it provided an opportunity, always valuable in negotiation, for displaying offended dignity. Who was going to put on my boots for me, I asked. If an Italian soldier, the violence offered to a British officer would constitute an insult to the entire British corps of officers; if on the other hand an Italian officer should be ordered to put on my boots, this would constitute an insult to the entire Italian corps of officers. I saluted and left before the more sensible Italians, most of whom were concealing grins, could propose the obvious course which was to put me in solitary confinement for impertinence for the duration of the visit. I then managed to suggest through sympathetic, if unofficial channels, that everybody's dignity would be saved if my boots were to be repaired.

'The next day an Italian corporal appeared, cigarettes changed hands and he took away my boots. They were taken to the village bootmaker in Poppi. The boots were a large 12 in size. The bootmaker had never seen such boots. He re-soled them with soles of vast thickness. He inserted in the soles clumps of huge nail apt for climbing the Alps. He exhibited them in his window for 24 hours to the astonishment of all. The enormous major's enormous boots. The corporal brought them back. "Fit for the Alpini", he said.

'So I wore the boots for the Pope's Legate and he gave to every Catholic a medal and to every heretic a postcard. "Fair enough", we all said. And when the time came I walked from Fontenallato to Isernia, seven hundred miles along the tops of the Appennines in my boots. They just lasted. They were the keys to freedom.

'Late on the second day after leaving the camp at Fontenellato, I found myself having to cross a broad expanse of shingle, the dry bed of a small river. It meant that one would be exposed to the view of all for a mile in every direction. It should be understood that I was well disguised. Dirty blue linen trousers nine inches too short, a black jacket, much too small, a Chico Marx hat. I scrambled down the bank and set out across the shingle. When I had gone about three hundred yards there came a shrill cry from behind me. "Ullo", it cried. I stamped on, not looking around. "Ullo", came again, "Ullo, *Englishman*". I stopped. It was no good going on like this. I turned round. A small figure leant over the wall of an orchard waving genially. I walked towards him in a huffy silence. When I was within about ten yards, the little man raised his hand in a welcoming manner, "I am Cook's man", he said.

'He invited me to supper and to spend the night in his house. It was late, I had no idea where I was going, he appeared to be a nice little man and well disposed, so I accepted with thanks. We walked up the road about half a mile to his village. He had a little house with a stable in the main street. Over the stable was a loft; in front of the stable was a large water trough. He took me up into the loft. "Keep very quiet", he said. "Soon, the Germans will come, but they will soon go again". I did not like this much but thought him trustworthy and stayed in my loft. Soon the Germans did come. They came in order to water their horses at my trough. This was all right and interesting; the drawback was that the Cook's man, though trustworthy, was overcome by the realisation of his own heroism and the drama of the situation. He walked up and down the street telling the citizens to keep quiet. "What about?" one could see them asking. "The *prigioniere* in my loft", he was obviously replying. Soon the whole street was sick with suspicion and apprehension. The Germans of course noticed nothing and in due course left. The Cook's man came up with my supper accompanied by half the village. They were now brave and I was very nervous. "What if they come back to fetch something left behind?" I asked. "Nonsense", they said, "Germans never leave anything behind". This faith proved justified. Afterwards, the Cook's man showed me his official hat. "Thos. Cook" it read. He was indeed a Cook's man – that great firm's local guide. He took the clients fishing. He would take me fishing he said. I said, "No, thank you, I must get on".'

Gerry now lives happily in his castle in Wales. He never came back to the Bar.

CHAPTER SEVEN

The Old Girl

I rushed up and down the desert until the beginning of 1943, sometimes under 1st Armoured Division but generally as a Desert Rat. The inspired choice of the Jerboa as an emblem for the 7th Armoured Division by Major-General Sir M. O'Moore Creagh long before I came upon the scene gave that Division a feeling of superiority over the rhinoceros of the other. It was as Desert Rats that we fought at Alam Halfa.

By the time of Alamein, my original Territorial Brigade existed only in name, so many men had been killed. The 2nd RGH had been disbanded owing to their tremendous casualties at Knightsbridge, and the 3rd and 4th County of London Yeomanry had had to be amalgamated.

I see from my Strength Return (by trades) that on 4.10.42 my little squadron had grown from 130 or so to an establishment of 271 with a strength 233, troops under command being 3/4th CLY, 1 RTR, Derby Yeomanry, 44 Div. Recce Regiment, and 1 RB. Quite a brigade!

The poor 44 Div. Recce Regiment were largely blown up on a minefield when the 7th Armoured Division of which we were part were told to create a diversion against the Italians at the South end of the line. By this time, we had shed our cavalry brigadiers and had acquired Pip Roberts of the RTR, a little man whom everyone adored and who ran the brigade single-handed. At Alamein, the brigade major and the G.3 were away ill with jaundice and in theory I took over both their jobs. In practice, I did nothing that I was unaccustomed to, and Pip carried the day.

When Winston Churchill came out to see us he kept calling Pip 'General Roberts' because all brigadiers were brigadier generals in the First War, but it was intelligent anticipation because Pip ended up the War as a Corps Commander in Germany and he would certainly have been a Field Marshal had he not left the army to provide for his numerous children, and gone into biscuits.

So much has been written about the desert by distinguished generals, by military historians, and by humble soldiers, that a mere civilian in uniform has nothing useful or entertaining to add.

Arthur Cranley, later Lord Onslow, wrote a book about the brigade which I should have liked to have read. In those days, however, I was too busy at the bar to read books. Arthur had a wonderful war and it was sad when he died so young.

Except when dug in at night in a trench, I spent my life in an ACV, an Armoured Command Vehicle, inhabited by brigadiers and above which was principally a signals centre full of various sets which communicated forwards, backwards and sideways, and, theoretically, into the air, to our supporting aircraft, except that there never seemed to be any. Indeed we got bombed by our own side at Knightsbridge when my poor Corporal Haydon got killed and the Earl Haig, then the G3, got 'put in the bag', that is, taken prisoner. He was called Dawyck, very difficult to pronounce. The staff captain, who was away behind with Michael Lubbock, was Tony Tichborne who also is no more. It wasn't done to say so but Tony looked very like the old daguerrotypes of 'the claimant'.

On the whole, however, signal communications in the flat desert were easy enough, and once we got the American tanks and ditched the Crusaders we didn't have to spend most of our time getting batteries re-charged.

The ACV also had a glass window in the top to let in a little light. In the summer of 1942 it was rather jolly to sit on the roof. On one lovely afternoon, I was sitting there with the G3 when we were Stuka'ed and the poor fellow fell through the window and cut his bottom so badly that he had to go back to Cairo for a re-fit. I didn't see him again until 1973 and he is now a VIP. I will not reveal his name lest it might occasion a loss of dignity, particularly as my daughter has married his grandchild's godfather.

I was fortunately hurled off into the sand and came to no harm. That was my second desert ACV.

My first Armoured Command Vehicle in the desert was a splendid machine of which I grew very fond. In 1940 and up to the summer of 1941 we had had a prototype model which never ceased to give trouble and was known as 'It'. In June 1941 I took it upon myself to instruct the driver how to manoeuvre the vehicle with dash and élan over difficult terrain at Larkhill, in anticipation of trouble which we might expect to encounter in foreign parts.

The demonstration greatly impressed my driver but proved that the vehicle was unsuitable to hard going and it may still be at Larkhill for all I know.

It was a blessing in disguise, for we received notice of embarkation shortly afterwards and another ACV appeared which had been especially prepared to the demands of the Divisional Commander of the First Armoured Division. She survived the battle of Sidi Rezegh in spite of becoming temporarily stuck in a bog when within range of the enemy's tanks. That was a very nasty moment and it was a great relief when they ignored us and stopped to refuel for long enough to enable us to escape, and join up with the Support Group commanded by Brigadier Jock Campbell VC, who lost his life shortly afterwards. I had really very little idea of what was going on in that battle, although, wearing my earphones and being permanently tuned in to Divisional Head-quarters, I probably knew more than most of the Brigade. I knew for example that Rommel was making a vast encircling movement to our south and coming up behind us to strike us in the rear, but there was nothing I could do about it. The battle went on for a very long time, it seemed, during which the batteries in all the Crusader tanks ran down and my squadron had a very unpleasant time driving about the battle-field replacing them. Eventually it appeared that we had won through, how, I could not imagine, and we went back to refit. A number of my friends in our Rear Echelon had been taken prisoner by the enemy in his daring movement and then set free again presumably because he had failed to find our petrol dumps and was forced to retreat. Having been at the centre of things throughout with very little understanding of what was going on, I was surprised to receive from Bridget in England some months later a document which reads as follows :

Extract from a letter from Brigadier J. Scott Cockburn, Commanding 22nd Armoured Brigade, consisting of:— 3rd and 4th City of London Yeomanry, and 2nd Royal Gloucester Hussars.

1941

Nov. 18   Advanced 70 miles into Libya and saw no enemy.

19   Attacked enemy position. Tank versus tank action. Destroyed 50 enemy tanks.

20   Moved to help another Brigade. Destroyed 4 enemy tanks.

21   Fought on same ground in morning. In the afternoon another tank versus tank engagement, and destroyed 15 enemy tanks.

22   Fought on same ground in morning. In the afternoon another tank versus tank engagement. Losses about equal. Our losses 20 tanks. Two of my staff wounded.

23 Counter-attacked enemy tanks with help of artillery and destroyed 45.

24–26 Protected flank of our infantry. Destroyed each day a number of enemy transport and took prisoners.

27 Attacked enemy column advancing on our infantry. Stopped it and destroyed about 8 enemy tanks.

28 Small action in morning. A warmer one in evening but no main engagement.

29 Afternoon battle. Shot a lot of enemy infantry.

30 Went back to refit.

Dec. 1 *General Auchinleck* arrives and says, 'Tell your men the whole Army is proud of them.'

General Norrie says, 'Scotty, I must shake your hand. I *always* said you had the best Brigade in the Army. The 11th Hussars who have been through all the campaigns out here, say they have never seen men fight like yours.'

Scott Cockburn himself then says, 'They really have been astounding, fighting on till their tanks were in flames. Many have had as many as five of their tanks knocked out under them. We have been fighting most of the time a few miles south of Tobruk. Bill Carr has proved himself a great soldier and as brave as they are made.' In 10 days continuous fighting, the Brigade destroyed over 140 enemy tanks.

I was one of 'two of my staff wounded', and it wasn't much of a wound, although it is true that the other one, the CRA who was standing beside me, lost his leg, and I wondered if there was just a dash of hyperbole in this dramatic report.

After that the 4th Armoured Brigade's ACV was captured and Jock Campbell's machine had its tyres shot up. We had to lend my 'Old Girl', as she had come to be called, to the 4th, crew and all, and I thought that I had seen the last of her. But no; the crew returned with their pockets full of sweets given them by the Brigadier and bearing a note of thanks extolling her virtues.

After the relief of Tobruk we pushed on after Rommel towards Agedabbia where we ran out of petrol in our turn at a spot called Saunnu. It was Christmas Eve, we were limited to two cups of tea a day, and when it transpired that we had missed our rendezvous by twelve miles, tempers became frayed at Brigade Headquarters. The situation was only saved by my· producing a Fortnum and Mason parcel which had mysteriously arrived on the previous day with sixteen letters and had caused some jealousy. The Christmas pudding was well received, but one of those who enjoyed it was killed next day, Christmas Day.

At last the petrol arrived at Saunnu and the battles of Belandak and Chor es Sugan took place where a lot of Crusader tanks were lost. But the 'Old Girl' navigated the steep Wadi Faregh under an alarming amount of fire with little difficulty and on the morning of New Year's Eve she was proceeding along the Antelat-Agedabbia track in the direction of the latter place.

The Column came to a halt and the Brigadier got out and asked if he could borrow my Staff Car in order to go to Corps to see General Lumsden whose 1st Armoured Division was about to relieve us. Five minutes after he had gone the General arrived to see the Brigadier, unannounced. I got a message in code and told the others. 'Six Stukas landed Agedabbia Aeorodrome'. No one was very interested. A few minutes later there was an explosion quite near and I was thrown out of my seat on to the floor. The Old Girl stopped. 'Drive on, Chappell', shouted Charles (Dick) Spencer, the Brigade Major, but she didn't move.

There was another bang and she was full of smoke from a number of small incendiary bombs which had been intended for the destruction of secret documents if ever we looked like being captured. I went for the door. The General and the Brigade Major were outside, both wounded, and Driver Chappell clambered out holding his arm. Hawkins, my forward-tank operator, and I were all right but there was no sign of Corporal Barton, my rear-link operator, who had been sitting immediately behind me. It was very hot when I climbed back but it was a waste of time for when he was pulled to the door the poor fellow was dead with a hole in the head.

The Old Girl burned for most of the day and when the bodies had been buried, she was still burning. She had meant a lot to me and I was very sad. Esmond Baring, the G3 after whom I named my second son, and I both escaped with singed hair, which is said to promote growth, but Herbert Lumsden was in hospital for some time and I don't think I saw the Brigade Major again during the War. The General commanded Monty's *Corps de Chasse* at Alamein as a lieutenant-general but fell out with him afterwards and died in the Far East when advising Chiang-Kai-Shek. Esmond is dead, as is Sandy Scratchley who was in the armoured car in front of us. Those behind us were blown to bits.

After Alamein we raced ahead to try and cut off the enemy at Agedabbia and in early December 1942 we went down the track again. Hawkins was still in an ACV and Chappell could only drive a 15 cwt truck and everyone else who had been in the Old Girl had gone. I went on ahead with two operators and tidied up the graves. She was a fine upstanding landmark, still bearing the rhinoceros sign she had worn in England. It was quite moving to see her and when her successor came past with a hole in the front from Knightsbridge and a dent or two from Alam Halfa, we felt that she would have dipped her ensign if she had had one.

Unfortunately I was to see her once more. It was three weeks later, when, after a refit, Brigade Headquarters passed along that track for the last time on the way to Tripoli and Tunis. They had turned her over on her side, had thrown her down and painted 'HD' (Highland Division – or as we used to call them, 'Highway Decorators') on her as she lay.

I was not amused.

In between Knightsbridge and Alamein I was asked if I would like to go to the Staff College at Haifa. I took the view that they would find me out if I did. Neither of my two courses in England had been much of a success. The Internal Combustion Engine and the Otto Cycle proved very difficult to comprehend and a course on hygiene, where I learned all about what flies get up to, was so revolting that I decided to eschew all complicated courses in future. So I refused it.

Looking back, I am sure that I was wrong and unduly modest. But there it is: I recommended Christopher for the nomination and he went, but not because of that. His first job after he came out was GI (ops) 8th Army, and when eventually he didn't see eye to eye with General Sir Oliver Leese – he very rarely saw eye to eye with anyone, except me – he became first of all Governor of Gorizia and then Governor of Trieste at a time when the Yugoslavs and the New Zealanders were striving for that valuable prize. When the war ended, he didn't come back to the Bar, because he didn't want to tie himself to people's petty little quarrels. That was silly of him.

The poor fellow has since had two cataract operations, two strokes and new hips, and when I last asked him to dinner he wrote from Osborne House where he was convalescing after a prostrate operation. All very sad.

But I took the view that there was no harm in going on a simple course. And Sam Maxwell and I went on a course on Signals Administration or something equally woolly for a fortnight where we were regarded as the belles of the ball being the only two who had been at the 'sharp end'. That was of course a lot of nonsense because anyone anywhere was equally vulnerable to attack by air, and at a Brigade or Divisional HQ you were usually (not always) as safe as if you were in Cairo.

Sam had not been at the sharp end very long as he had only just been appointed to command 7 Armd. Div. Sigs. under whom came my 22 Armoured Brigade Group. Up till then, he had been with the 1st line of the Middlesex Yeomanry who were having an old-fashioned war doing the signals for the Cavalry Division in Palestine, Syria and Iraq. Although no doubt he had joined the Middlesex Yeomanry for the riding and the fun and games, he was no playboy, and his was an excellent appointment. He was a Member of Parliament, young for the position, and was the heir to Lord Farnham. We got on very well together. He was a gentle creature, unlike most of the aristocracy whom I came across who seemed to become more foul-mouthed the more noble they were. This is of course only a, perhaps foolish, generalisation and certainly doesn't apply to Gerald Grosvenor who had been my Brigade Major for a time in the previous year and who afterwards became Duke of Westminster.

The only reason I am mentioning Sam Maxwell is because one day we had a conversation in which he said that he would not survive the war. I was embarrassed and made the appropriate noises. He said, 'No, I know.' All that I could say was that I was sure that I should, and we left it at that. It was nearly a week or so after we got back to the desert that there was a dot of smoke behind us at Divisional HQ – those damn Stukas again – and poor Sam was carted off to Tobruk where he died. So we were both right.

It was after we had passed Mussolini's 'Marble Arch' that I became browned off or far above myself, according to which way you look at it. I made it known that I had been in command of this superb squadron (and it was) for two and a half years and it was time that I had a change, if not a promotion. I suppose that it was my marvellous Brigadier who was responsible, but before you could say 'knife', I was flown straight back to Cairo to see the Top Brass. Pathetic, when I think that only the week before, the mess truck which had driven all the way to Alexandria and back and had returned laden with goodies was dive-bombed and destroyed before our very eyes, our rather greedy and thirsty eyes, and poor Corporal Hemming met his Maker.

In Cairo, General Penny who later commanded the First Infantry Division when my brother got his fractured skull at Anzio, and Major General Nickalls who had been the Army Heavyweight Champion, which made one wonder whether he was a bit thick or not, received me with much courtesy. Old Nickalls became Chairman of Cables and Wireless after the war so that he was obviously much more intelligent than he looked.

First of all they offered me 2 i/c of a Base Depot Signals. I said that I should feel ashamed at being so far from the sharp end and anyhow I didn't know what a 2 i/c did. That was very pompous. Nickalls, bless him, said, 'No trouble at all : all you have to do is to order supplies, and the Quartermaster will tell you what to order.' I thanked them and said that I wasn't interested, and went back to Tunisia.

There, within twenty-four hours, I got two offers, almost as though I was a parti, instead of a tired old incompetent.

One was to be 2 i/c First Armoured Division Signals to take the place of a gentleman called 'Cheesy' Rhind. This I thought flattering, but the idea of a 'B' echelon mess with a lot of regular signallers talking shop which I should not understand was not a very attractive prospect. And the Colonel, a nice enough man, was much too bright not to find me out and expose me in no time. He had climbed Mount Everest or at any rate tried to, and was obviously a serious character who would not approve of a rather light-hearted man like me.

The other offer came unexpectedly. Would I like to be a lieutenant-colonel presiding over Courts Martial? I would lose my signals pay, but I would be up quite a bit on balance financially.

I made the wrong choice, which led to much unhappiness for me.

I opted to become a half-colonel dealing with courts-martial. I can't think why : I had always been against joining the non-combatant Judge Advocate's Department. But something made me do this thing. I can only think that I thought that it was high time that I was a lieutenant-colonel.

Dear me, those were sad days, solely because it was my ridiculous idea that I ought to go out and get killed for my country. In fact, I ought to look back on them with pleasure – Cairo, at first, where a nice fellow in the JAG's Department taught me about the burden of proof; Beirut, from which I used to fly to Nicosia to deal with naughty Cypriot boys;

Tripoli – (all my money was stolen by a Safraghi at Mahdi en route); Sicily, where an old friend of mine was killed at Centuripe and where we were all injected with mepacrine against malaria – which I believe may be the reason for my dreadful psoriasis and arthritis today – and where I eventually landed at Catania. Superb billet, birthplace of Bellini, but I found some of my staff raiding the place. Very embarrassing. I think we got round it somehow. I've never seen the difference between stealing, winning, and looting, myself. I was unpopular.

I go too fast, for Beirut really deserves more than half a sentence. The weather was marvellous, my parish extended from Cyprus to Deir-ez-Sor in what used to be called Mesopotamia, so that you could take in Palmyra (rather disappointing) and Baalbek (marvellous) en route. Up the mountains from Beirut was 9th Army HQ to which I was supposed to be attached, all biting their nails with frustration because they still hadn't been allowed to hear a shot fired in action. From Aley in the snow you could see the brilliance of the sun reflected in the water at Beirut. Over Aley the road went down to Damascus or to Baalbek. And wonderful food in Beirut at the Lucullus Restaurant where Tom Mitford and I dined together. I never saw him again. He was killed in Italy. The two great hotels were the Saint-Georges and the Normandie, on the sea. I couldn't afford them, but after some not very comfortable nights in the Officers' Club where the trams went past on the way to the American University and the French Officers' beach (the French knew about class distinction in those days), I ended up with a nice man called Campbell, who took up riding, at the Hotel Regent, where the red mullet was unforgettable.

The French, because they were Vichy French, hated us, and the Spears Military Mission was much resented. But I enjoyed myself enormously and Beirut, after Florence, was the best port of call I had.

After Catania I had a signal asking me to go to Bari. This was bliss. My driver was Corporal Hose, who wore Mutt and Jeff from the first world war, and was a dear old gentleman. He was a madly keen territorial and for a living drove a horse and cart in Liverpool. He and I drove in my staff car to Messina. Over to Reggio Calabria on the boat and we spent two nights – because our movements naturally had to be very secret – in a fig grove.

Figs have always been something that I adore. Papa used to say, 'You can't adore figs; you can enjoy them.' Twelve years later I was to live in a house with an abundance of figs, but I was not to know that.

Old Hose wasn't so keen on figs but I had a marvellous two days.

Figs and the dreaded dysentery of course go together, but so what! Then across Calabria to Barletta and Bari, and off to Foggia and eventually to Campobasso.

While I was there up in the snow, I was summoned down to see my brother who was said to be on the DI (dangerously ill) list. Cyril (now Lord) Salmon had received a similar message.

We drove down to Naples – not all that far, yet the oranges were starting on the trees – and then to the hospital at Castellamare. I was lucky – my brother, who had a fractured skull, went to the opera with me that night – Cyril's poor cousin died muttering brave orders to his platoon.

We were rather a long time in Campobasso where nothing particular happened except that it was very cold and the thing to do was to sing 'Lili Marlene' in Italian. For by this time the Italians were our chums. When I was in Sicily the King appointed Badoglio in place of Mussolini. And in the south, the Mezzogiorno, they were genuinely pleased. *'Benito finito'* and *'abbasso il duce'* were written up on all the walls. And I remember the wife of the piano teacher in Campobasso telling me how they were always bound to lose the war because, and she threw her hands up to the heavens expressively, of *la flotta Inglese*. I imagine that she had not heard of what happened to the old *flotta* in Singapore, and was relying on what she had learned at school.

Snobbery seems to be the same all over the world. The Signora had been born in Turin, and regarded herself as having married beneath herself as she had come to the South, while the excitement when the boy of another family was ordered by the Army to help shovel the snow away was astonishing. The boy shouted, *'Io studente, spalare la neve, no'*. I can remember it all after so many years, and the parents supported him to the full, for with the Italians it is tremendously important not 'to lose face'. I tried to get a job as a postman when I came home from the war to possible penury, but your middle-class Italian wouldn't do that because of the loss of face involved. So silly.

After Campobasso to Presenzano, near Monte Cassino. There were lots of swifts and swallows, the Mayor could actually understand my Italian provided I spoke *'adagio, adagio'*, and the present Lord Chancellor, then Major Elwyn-Jones descended upon us, and made us happy with his charm and his anecdotes.

I have obviously left out one or two ports of call, but I don't know that it matters. San Severo, for instance, where I discovered the most superb white wine which people were kind enough to call the 'Château Faulks', and which when later I was at Castel Duino near Trieste was procured by a three ton lorry for the mess, hundreds of miles away. In San Severo, I bought and sent home to England a number of felt hats, *coni di feltro*, but Bridget wasn't very thrilled with them. Like many men, I have no taste where female apparel is concerned.

From Presenzano, the outfit moved to Rome, in fact to a charming village north of the capital which had featured in Garibaldi's famous march, called Monte Rotondo. I learned how to pronounce the hero's name which I had always innocently imagined to be Garry-bald-y. But I was not overworked. We used to go for long walks in the afternoon heat and the villagers would tap their foreheads and cry, *'Pazzi'*. And of course we got pink and not brown like them.

This 'we', I should explain. A Field General Court Martial consisted of a President and two other officers junior in rank to him, and, if the matter involved any law, a Judge Advocate. Either because I was by now well-known not to be 'gruntled' or because I was known to be legally qualified, the authorities seldom inflicted a Judge Advocate on me. Indeed, they sometimes used to ask me to sit as a Judge Advocate to help out, which I did reluctantly.

When I was in Rome I had the opportunity to go to an open audience with the Pope, the diplomat Pacelli. I found the invitation attractive, what with the Swiss Guards and Michael Angelo although I wasn't sure that, being Church of England, I ought to accept it. However, I should probably never see a Pope again and he was a man whom I greatly admired, so I went. The place was crammed and the atmosphere scarcely ecclesiastical when the Pope entered and addressed us from a dais. He told us that he was the father of us all, which made me feel that I had no business there, and proceeded with his speech which was suddenly interrupted by a stentorian voice from behind me crying, 'Hold it, Pope', as one of our American Allies knelt on one knee and took a snapshot of His Holiness. The latter, initially startled, continued talking, quite unruffled. It was very impressive.

After Rome, we went to Arezzo. There we managed to impose ourselves on Conte Scolari, whose son has recently written to me to say that he is changing the place into a motel. The Count played the usual game when my outriders appeared. He would love to have us, as we were now allies, but alas, the Swiss Minister or Ambassador at the Vatican would be arriving at any moment so that there would be no room for us.

I am afraid that when this was reported to me, I said, 'Swiss Minister, my foot,' and we moved in.

His wife was in fact Swiss, and was very sensibly at that time in Switzerland, so that there was some, if not much, support for his story. But no Swiss Minister ever appeared.

The Count had a sister who challenged me to lawn tennis on their hard court. I very stupidly beat her 6–1, 6–1 thinking that if she got a game in each set she would be happy, but not at all! It was just like Aunt Muriel when I was a boy and she went off and sulked and we never played again.

The Count (Count of Malta, which I think you can buy) was a character. He had made a vast fortune out of zip fasteners which were a novelty in those days. He even gave me a brief case with a zip fastener when we left which lasted until 1950 at least. His right hand trembled but that was because, I was fascinated to know, he had been for years the world champion at a type of billiards which we don't play here but which is popular on the Continent, where there are no pockets and the game depends on cannons.

While I was there he gave me some advice. I don't know what it was that I wanted to buy, but he said, 'Never say *d'accordo*; always *molto bene*'. I suppose that you are bound by the former, while the latter is like 'subject to contract'.

From Arezzo, where there was quite a lot of crime, to Perugia, where I had to deal with the boys who were running away, as well as the uniformed thieves and rapists. Perugia is a beautiful city which houses a university to which many young Englishmen, of whom my brother, Mr Justice Cusack, is one, have been sent to acquire a little culture.

It is no way from Assisi, and there we lived in great comfort among the very rich. It was very interesting as an experience to tread the grapes at the 'Vendemmia'. Most of my team lived with the Fanis. Signor Fani had been Minister of Justice in Mussolini's government and was trying very hard to forget it. He had a most delightful and charming wife called Elvira (and she might have come out of *Don Giovanni*, so splendid was she).

Roddy Romain who is now a stipendiary magistrate and sent me one of my most entertaining cases when he was a solicitor, was billeted on the other grand family in Perugia, the Buitonis. The family is now a household word for all kinds of pasta. If you buy anything in a tin for an Italian meal it is sure to come from Buitoni. She, Alma Buitoni, was charming and hospitable. I don't remember him. (Rather like

Danny Kaye: 'How did you like the Himalayas?' 'Liked him; didn't like her.')

And from Perugia, where you could sit in an expensive hotel, and actually see the smoke from the guns below, I went to Florence.

I don't know who got the billet, but I am very grateful to him.

It was in the Piazza Savonarola, and belonged to a most charming couple, the Conte Giulluci, and his wife. He was an old dear, always known as 'Nello', his Christian name being 'Donatello', and the facto-tum, really Giovanni, was always known as 'Nanni'. It was an enormous house, of which the owners only retained a small part, but the cries of 'Nello' and 'Nanni' reverberating round the walls were quite a joy. Nanni had a wife who made *pasta asciuta* which was out of this world; she did a jolly good minestrone, and her escalope Milanese was in-comparable. We all put on weight.

This, of course, was bad for the conscience. Marvellous food, com-fortable living, excellent opera, and poor frightened little boys going to prison. I knew that there would be an amnesty and that the sentences imposed were principally *'pour encourager les autres'*, but it was no fun.

The Countessa was an Englishwoman from Guernsey, probably a Carey. The Count had a sister, Buona, who was much in evidence. The old boy, bless him, used to say, 'Buona by name, and Buona by nature' which is rather nicer than 'Horridge by name, and horrid by nature', which as small boys we used to say of the old judge who fined the High Sheriff for going to Ascot.

I went to Vallambrosa, and in Florence we had demi-johns of chianti, and chestnuts roasting on the fire, but it wasn't war. I had misunderstood what I was offered when they asked me to take this job. I thought that this was a legal job which required legal experience. I found that it was for dead-beats, of whom I must naturally be considered one.

To give some idea of the opinion in which one of my brethren was held, let me quote the only two verses I can remember of the 'Ballad of the Permanent President', the tune of which escapes me:

> I'm exceptionally partial to Field General
> Courts-Martial,
> The justice I administer is rough:
> I inspire my Courts with awe as a
> Substitute for law
> And cover up my ignorance with bluff.

I take a solemn view
Of Moslem, Turk and Jew :
You never know the oaths these chaps will take :
They speak a foreign tongue and their colour
Is all wrong,
And anyhow the interpreter's a fake.

However, I felt that there was no point in making a fuss about it, and Florence was beautiful. What you could see of it, that is, for the Uffizi was not open.

While I was in Firenze, my brother Peter came to call. I was very proud of him. He had been wounded three times, led the army into Rome, and had an MC for bravery in Tunisia.

Now he had been sent to look after the invalids from his regiment in some remote part of the Tuscan hills. I dined with him, and I think he dined with us, and it was a splendid reunion.

I taught myself to type on a Olivetti in Florence but got ticked off by Bridget because air mail letters in type were so impersonal. I took the machine back to England at the end of the war, but never used it and I have no idea where it is now. I am writing in longhand at the moment and my writing is not readily legible, and it may be that I shall have to learn to type all over again.

One of my young gentlemen in Florence was even older than I was. A delightful modest unassuming chap, Captain Kingsley had been one of the four musketeers who had won the Davis Cup for us in the Thirties; Perry, Austin, Kingsley and Hughes – they were headlines in their time. Charles Kingsley was primarily a great doubles player, but he interested me by telling me how he used to have good practice matches with Helen Wills, later Helen Wills Moody, who was un-disputed champion for years, *but* the rule was that he was not allowed to go up to the net.

Perhaps I ought to have gone up to the net against Aunt Muriel, but I think that she would just have lobbed me.

One day, Master Kingsley came back to Piazza Savonarola bearing with him an astonishingly good likeness of himself, painted in tempera. I genuinely admired it and asked him how he had come by it, and, in a conspiratorial undertone, how much it had cost.

He had got on to the painter through his boss, Michael Noble, wearing his hat as Town Major. The Germans had left Florence immediately before we entered it, and the occupying power was having meetings with the citizens about this and that, and the painter had been appointed to represent the arts. Charles had seen some murals which he had painted in a small church and was impressed. I too was impressed, and said that I would be amused to be painted also. He warned me that it had to be very early in the morning, as that was the only time of day that the light was right in the studio, and there being no fuel available it would be very cold and I would be well advised to wear an overcoat. It was good advice because Pietro Annigoni, who afterwards came to fame by his portrait of the Queen, made a marvellous job of the overcoat but gave me a head a great deal smaller than it really is. I had to borrow from a Florentine banker to pay for this, but it wasn't very much, considering what he charges today, and I am glad to say that I did repay the banker his loan after the war.

After the war, Annigoni came to see us when we were living in Pembroke Gardens – four floors and a basement, a cook, and two young Scottish girls, all very grand and quite beyond my pocket; people used to think I was very successful and that I owned the freehold, both of which were entirely untrue, as in fact I had it on a short lease at a low rental from the Prudential who were for some reason or other very generous to me. One evening I came back – this was about 1948 – from chambers to find a conversation taking place in French with which neither he nor Bridget appeared to be familiar. My French is poor, but my arrival was greeted with relief, and we conversed in Italian, Bridget looking intelligent and understanding nothing. He did say of my portrait that it was, '*Abbastanza bene per quell' epoca,*' so that if the painter approved of it, it may be worth a few shillings one day, and he was interested in a portrait of Savonarola in wax which I had bought in Exeter. I think I only bought it because of sentimental recollection of the Piazza, but I had grown very fond of it and would not sell it. A quarter of a century later, I am even fonder of it.

When I was in Florence, the Army was beastly to me. They decided to down-grade the job of Permanent President to the rank of major.

That that was morally a gross breach of contract was obvious enough. However, having been a lieutenant-colonel for only eighteen months or so, I was in army terms major, (temporary lieutenant-colonel) Faulks, and I suppose they were within their rights. The job, as I see it now, had been invented as a convenient way of placing elderly misfits who had already reached the rank of lieutenant-colonel. It didn't matter if they knew no law. If there was any law in a case, you could always have a Judge Advocate. No doubt, the job was only worth a major's appointment, but then they should have sold it to me on the basis that it would have a chance of being reduced in rank. And I wouldn't have taken it. But I would have missed my marvellous tour of Italy. And pro and con ad infinitum. Anyway, having been so stupid as to refuse the Staff College, who was I to complain?

So off I had to go, all the way down to Caserta Palace, where the King of Naples and the Two Sicilies used to reside, whom Nelson whisked away from Napoleon to Palermo in the nick of time, to be told that I was down to major, and with no specialist pay, so that I was worse off financially than I had been back in England in 1940 as a major with extra signals pay.

But the most astonishing thing about this demotion is that when I arrived at Caserta I found that the chap who was designated to give me the chop was George Baker who is now my master as the President of the Family Division. We didn't know each other very well then, but it must have been as embarrassing for him as it was infuriating for me.

My signals squadron, which I had visited in Sorrento after the Salerno landing, was now in Germany so that it was no use saying that I'd go back to 'the dear boys' where at least I'd be better paid, and I motored back to Florence with my tail between my legs.

While I was in Florence I was sent over to Algiers, as a half-colonel, to decide in some point about the treatment of refugee Yugoslavs. Before Tito consolidated the country, there were the most frightful schisms between the various races, but I cannot recall the details. I took evidence for about a fortnight but the work cannot have been unduly onerous because my only recollection is that of lying in the sun on the roof of the Officers' Club in Algiers re-reading Philip Guedella's *The Iron Duke*.

Returned to Florence, I wrote what Hugh Quennell thought was rather a good report and sent it in after getting the two other members of the Court to sign it.

And I was sent for to Caserta Palace once again to meet General Clark and Air Marshal Slessor. It appeared that Clark thought the report was all right, and Slessor, very loud-voiced and a more powerful character, thought it was all wrong. I don't know why: I had found in favour of his man, but I imagine that I had been too temperate in my criticism of the other side.

I think he hadn't realised that lawyers see both sides of the question, while military men often do not. Neither of these distinguished gentle-

Some of the 'Dear Boys', 1942

Batman Martin, Alamein 1942

'Dear boys' at the Pyramids   Batman Moore *mit* Jerrican

Driver Wood and Another, Desert 1942

men had any legal qualifications. I heard no more of that matter.

Then the gallant Major and his coterie moved to Forli from Florence. Not a change for the better although the asparagus was the best I have ever eaten. There wasn't much to do either, as the war in Italy was coming to an end. The locals were still vociferous in their hatred of the late B. Mussolini, and I believed them, although my knowledge of their tongue was not enough to prevent my being fooled.

From Forli we moved out of Italy into Pfortsach (I have probably spelt that wrongly); it is where they now have international tennis tournaments) in Austria on the Wertersee and finally to Klagenfurt. Here the work was quite different. Whereas in Florence I used to try twenty deserters in a day, and get letters from angry Brigadiers because I had only given little Tommy three years, instead of twenty-five years and twice privately whipped as I should have done if I understood what war was : — in Forli and Klagenfurt we were back to civilian-type crime, principally rape. Now this, although disgusting, was more interesting from a lawyer's point of view. In rape, it is necessary to have what lawyer's call 'corrobbers' – that is corroboration because, as defending counsel always says, 'No charge is easier to prefer and no charge is more difficult to refute.' And what constitutes corroboration is a difficult subject, in those days not very well covered in the Manual of Military Law. After the war, the law got itself into a dreadful state with regard to characters who are charged with offences against numbers of young boys and one had to hold one's head very firmly to understand what was the form : now, happily, the law seems to be clear enough again.

In all this time, I think that I only sentenced three people to death.

What was so awful about that was that you had to call them back and say that you had actually sentenced them to death, but that in fact the sentence was subject to the review of the confirming officer, (almost certainly someone without legal qualifications). The worst of these was when I was sitting as Judge Advocate at Trieste on the case of a boy in the Signals who had taken the view that his Captain was intercepting his mail from home, and had shot him dead. He was obviously potty but not so potty as to come within the McNaughten Rules. I won't say what they are for if you are a lawyer you will know, and if you are not, it will bore you stiff.

So he had to be sentenced to death and I wrote to General Alexander (as he then was) and suggested that this sentence be commuted, as it in fact was.

The most odd sentence that I have ever passed was in a case at

Tripoli, where the proceedings took place in Swahili. I forget what the accused had done, although I think he had been responsible for a riot : all that I can remember was that the only words that I could understand before the interpreter went to work were 'Sergeant-Major Keelibeele' who turned out to be the principal prosecution witness.

I had been furnished with two officers to assist me, one of whom was a young lieutenant from the particular brigade in which the accused was serving. This young black man was obviously guilty, and the only question was what to do with him. The practice was to ask the junior member first, then the next senior, and then I said what I thought, with which they generally agreed as I was very ancient and a lieutenant-colonel.

(As I write this I am staying with a son-in-law aged 34 – I then was 35 or 36 – who has been through the Staff College, is a major, and upon whom I look as an infant. *Tempora mutantur nos et mutamur in illis.* Monkish Latin, says Sir Ashton Roskill with scorn, but it has its point.)

So I asked the lieutenant.

'This man needs twelve on the bottom,' he answered.

I could scarcely believe my ears. 'Do you mean that seriously ?' I said. 'I don't think you'll find that in the Manual of Military Law.'

He said, 'Oh ! that's the usual thing in our brigade. They understand it and it works. The unit would like it, and they don't want to lose him. He works very well when he is sober, and what's more, I am sure that he expects it.'

The other member was very taken with the idea. I didn't think that I had the power to make such an order but after all there was a Confirming Officer and all these sentences went back to England to be considered by legal boffins. (I am not sure about that; perhaps it was only when there was a Judge Advocate sitting who sent in a report of his summing up. That, I suspect, was generally what he knew that he ought to have said rather than what he had actually said, as there was no shorthand writer.)

So I allowed myself to be persuaded to sentence this young man to twelve strokes on the bottom. I don't remember with what implement. Nobody seemed surprised, neither the villain, nor the escort and Sergeant-Major Keelibeele showed his teeth with satisfaction. I never heard any more of the matter and concluded that all African matters were not dealt with in the Manual of Military Law. I think what made me give in was a story that had been told me by one of my own co-presidents, an elderly man (or so he seemed to me then) called Colonel Sir Somebody Brocklehurst. He was an old dear who had done frightfully well for himself by being polite to an ancient lady in an hotel in Worthing. She being touched by his beautiful manners and impressed by the fact that he was a baronet, did the right thing, cut up shortly afterwards, and left him the lot, which was quite considerable. His story was that he once commanded a company of Sudanese based at Khartoum. When someone had offended greatly it seems that he was placed flat on the ground and beaten by the Sergeant-Major.

'But how did they take it?' I said.

'Oh! They didn't mind; they used to rush away into the lines and have a woman. That's what it did for them.'

What it did for my young gentleman in Tripoli, we shall never know.

Now that we have abolished capital punishment and corporal punishment and are continually having reports from working parties who wish to limit the population of the prisons, and now that the militant students seemed to be allowed to make as much a nuisance of themselves as they like in the name of democracy, and at the expense of the taxpayer, I feel that we may be getting near to the point where the average man and woman who quite naturally only think of the cost of living, the telly, and the World Cup, will demand discipline in the nation once again.

At the beginning of 1945, when I was at Trieste I was caught up in the coils of a scheme called 'Python' and told at 24 hours notice that as I had been abroad for three and a half years, I could fly home for a week's leave.

As I got to the flat on the corner of Kensington Square, I met Bridget getting into a taxi to go a dentist in Maida Vale. Why Maida Vale I never understood. I accompanied her. She was clearly unwell when she came back into the waiting-room. We returned by taxi. I was shown my boy who had been six months old when I last saw him, now aged four, howling his head off, in bed with measles.

I had left Bridget at the age of twenty with a baby and a roof over her head with friends not of hers but of mine, where the husband was a man with a heart of gold but an impossibly quick temper.

She quarrelled with him after three years, stayed with friends of both of ours and finally got this flat with the money she had saved from her marriage allowance while she was living in Devonshire. Incidentally, the gentleman with the heart of gold thought he was doing me the best turn in the world by selling my 1939 Delage with its famous four gears front and back to a dealer for £400 without consulting me. We saw it after the war in a window of Jack Barclay's for sale at £1,200.

This flat, the address of which was Abbott's Court, Thackeray Street, on the corner of Kensington Square, belonged to Barkers' of Kensington. She got it, during the Blitz, with V bombs dropping all around for £275 p.a., they, I think, paying the rates. It was a very large, commodious, and comfortable flat with two double, one single, and one miniscule bedroom, and so forth. I wonder what it is letting for now!

To see your own country again after so long was very agreeable. We were able, somehow, to hire a car and drove out into the country to see my sisters. My elder sister, Sheila, seeing me in a pair of navy blue trousers which I had just bought, and which I thought very smart, sensibly said, 'What's the matter with you? You look as though you've just come out of a convalescent home'. This was amusing but I didn't think so. Stupid of me, for if I had not been at the receiving end, I would probably have laughed.

After a day or two, the health of the family began to improve and I flew back to Florence Airport happily.

Back to Klagenfurt, Trieste, Udine, Venice, etc. One bottle of whisky a month doesn't go a very long way, but these various trips were fun. And really I was very idle : only champing at the bit to get home.

I was in my cottage at Castel Duino when I heard Winston Churchill's unfortunate speech saying that if meek and mild little Major Attlee, whose portrait by Laurence Gowing is in my view the best we have in the Inner Temple of which he was an Honorary Bencher, got in, the Gestapo would be in Britain. That made even me vote Liberal and I have no doubt it must have made any number of decent middle-of-the-road people vote Socialist.

I only knew Attlee late in life but I thought that he was both shrewd and sweet. He must have been both because he used to take Elizabeth's mother (whom I never met) to dances.

It was really rather jolly if you had to try a case in Venice. You travelled by air from Trieste landing at the Lido Airport which probably no longer exists. To see Venice from the air on a fine day is an unforgettable experience.

And from the Lido by vaporetto to your hotel wasn't too bad. The New Zealanders under General Freyberg had pinched the Danielli, and who shall say that they didn't deserve it, but we had the Europa which I found splendid.

In Trieste also these magnificent New Zealanders had got Castel

Miramar which I think was meant to be first prize but Castel Duino where General Harding (now Lord Harding of Petherton) reigned wasn't half bad. Marvellous swimming pool, down a lot of steps, and when the previous owners, the Prince and Princess of Thurn and Taxis went away they very kindly left a splendid collection of light music on gramophone records behind them. I had a little lawn tennis at Monfalcone as well as at Trieste, and had an idle, suntanning time. The war was nearly over.

At last the process of demobilisation began. As far as I can remember, the form was 'first in, first out', and some respect was paid to age. I'd been in for six years all but a month, was rising thirty-eight, and had been abroad for four years non-stop except for that week which I have described. It was decreed that I was in Group 6 of Group 8 or something very high indeed. And in August – I could hardly believe it – we wheeled off in a truck from Klagenfurt to Innsbruck, and eventually to Calais, my family having been notified of my impending arrival. Two of my companions I knew but I can't remember their names : one was a rugged Scotsman who was a Staff Captain 'A' and the other, a Major D, A, Q, M, G, was in civil life an apiarist in Cumberland or somewhere equally wild, who could not wait to get back to his bees. Uncomfortable, but deliriously happy, it was. And then the white cliffs of Dover. I'm the sort of chap who cries in church, which is very embarrassing for everyone else : so you may imagine how the cliffs killed me.

Home : well received, and my next infant appeared in June 1946.

Although I was allowed to go home, there were still two important matters to be dealt with. One was to be demobilised. (I thought that an unhappy word in the circumstances : after all on the 1st of September 1939 I had as a Territorial been embodied into His Majesty's Army; why shouldn't I now be disembodied ?)

I had to go all the way up to Catterick to undergo this sea-change. I read *Brideshead Revisited* on the way there and back. It's one of the few books that I have read three times, and I never thought that I should one day be involved in three libel actions on behalf of the author and spend an enjoyable fortnight in Dar-es-Salaam with Evelyn Waugh.

At Catterick I met dear Sergeant Byers, my old standfast when he was in charge of the RGH troop. It was really rather moving. I think that he'd become a Major by then, but I've never seen him since. The saddest thing is that I've never seen my old Jackaman, my marvellous Sergeant-Major; he went to an OCTU, of course, but I only know that letters to him are marked 'Gone Away'.

One of my boys became a Full Colonel, and last year a Major-General wrote to me thanking me for my discernment in sending him to an OCTU. In case this sounds rather like line-shooting, his name was Corporal Carroll, and I expect that he is in *Who's Who*.

The next thing, before I was entirely free, was to get my demobilisation suit, etc., at some place near Shepherd's Bush. (The only time I ever heard Shepherd's Bush mentioned in Court was at Middlesex Sessions. When I was very young indeed at the Bar I used to go there in the vague hope of picking up a brief but really, knowing that there was no chance of that, to listen to the experts – there are not so many today – and try to learn to model myself upon them.

One day, a young man pleaded 'Guilty' to something or other, and the point made in mitigation was that he was not very bright.

'Why do you say that, doctor?'

'Well, I asked him which were the three principal cities in England and he replied at once, "London, Chiswick and the Bush".'

CHAPTER EIGHT

Back to the Bar

When I went back to the Bar, it was without much hope. Gerald Slade was very generous with regard to my rent, but one had to make a living. And I didn't. A number of barristers whom obviously I shall not mention had, like Norman Birkett and Bill Jowitt in their day, been unable to take part in hostilities, and had cornered the market. Buster Milmo went into MI5. Rodger Winn, stricken with polio, who could perfectly well have stopped at the Bar, went and saved the Navy in an underground shelter by Admiralty Arch. But there were others for whom those of us who had been away for a long time felt bitterness.

I tried to leave 1 Brick Court and go to some Local Government Chambers where I had been told that you made immense sums of money, had to know nothing, but to have lots of charm. Exactly like licensing, I thought: marvellous. But they wouldn't have me (in retrospect, thank heaven) and I crawled back on my knees to 1 Brick Court. Bridget used to make sandwiches every day, for I couldn't afford to go into Hall for luncheon. Before the war a fried Dover Sole was 1/6d, a couple of lamb cutlets with tomato was 1/4d, and the best bet for a small boy was Thick Winter Pea Soup at 6d with a roll and butter at 2d. And that was the lot: You had had a very good luncheon for 8d and if you were so rash as to have a small black coffee (1d) there was always the danger that you had to visit the lavatory immediately afterwards.

After the war, it was sandwiches and I put on weight.

Before the war, my principal practice had been in the Southwark County Court before a dear old fellow called His Honour Judge Moore who wore a beard and was never known to say any unkind word to anybody. As he never interrupted, cases before him were liable to take rather a long time. The same clients also had a lot of work in the Lambeth County Court where the County Court Judge was a character called Judge Spencer Hogg whose principal objective was to finish the day's list by midday, so that he could have a round of golf. With this desirable end in view, immediately a case was called on, the usher would collect the Plaintiff and the Defendant, march them up the Court, and place one in a witness box to the right of the learned judge and the other to the left. The Judge would then cross-examine them both at once leaving very little for Counsel to do. At two guineas a time, which I did not despise (for if you were lucky enough to be on the list of an insurance company's solicitors, you started at being despatched to a coroner's inquest for one guinea where you rose to your feet trembling to ask if the tribunal would kindly allow you to ask a question as strictly speaking you had no right of audience), I ran up over the years a sum of about £250 which was owed to me by a Mr Bateman, the solicitor in question.

I could never understand why he had decided to brief me and was genuinely grateful for being paid for what I enjoyed doing. His firm was quite efficient compared with some which I have encountered after the war. For instance, on two occasions they saved my bacon.

The trouble was that the batteries of my Morris Oxford VB 887 always seemed to be run down, so that I had to push her out of the garage on to a slope, jump in, try to start her in gear down the slope, turn her to the right down the road where the buses ran, if she still hadn't started, down a steep slope, and if she was too cold by then to start, which was very seldom, I had had it. Walk home and ring up the garage. Very expensive and I could be late. Once I was off, all was well because I used to park her in King's Bench Walk where there was quite a good slope and she always started there on my way home over Blackfriars Bridge.

It wasn't always so easy to find a good slope at the County Court or at the Police Court as it was then called. Often I had to be pushed.

I used to put my little blue bag with my wig and robes in it inside the car before I started to push. I then jumped in, holding the steering wheel, and it was only when I had read the brief over breakfast, having been out the night before, that I failed to put it in the bag, but opened the gate at the bottom of the slope, placed the brief on the garden wall, threw the blue bag into VB 887 without thinking and after many vicissitudes arrived at the County Court with the brief still on the garden wall. On each of these occasions, there was a young clerk sitting behind me, who understood the position perfectly and handed me a carbon copy of the brief, no doubt designed to deal with such a contingency.

It was only when Mr Bateman went bankrupt – and I didn't get paid a penny – that I realised that he'd summed me up as a poor little Twittle-berry Watkins who would be prepared to work just for experience.

It was on the instructions of Mr Bateman that I did my first case on my own in the Court of Appeal before Lord Merriman and another, an appeal from the Westminster County Court in a matter where I thought I had succeeded wrongly. The Appellants took in Lord Erleigh QC, afterwards Lord Reading, as a leader, a most delightful and urbane performer in the Stuart Bevan, Dick Levy, Cyril Salmon, style, but Lord Merriman, who was a beastly tribunal to appear before, was so rude to him that when he had finished after many interruptions, he said, 'That, my Lords, concludes my argument', bowed, and without resuming his seat, turned and walked out of Court without any look of embarrassment or loss of dignity.

(It was a great deal more impressive than the behaviour of a leader in a case which my brother Ashworth would have remembered where I was suing the P. and O. for wrongful dismissal and, upon the Judge apparently taking a favourable view of the Plaintiff in the witness-box, the silk sulked and sat in his seat speechless for the rest of the case, leaving the entire matter to Ashworth, his junior, who won it after a hard fight.)

Well, it was really very valuable experience, petrol was cheap in those days, I lived at home paying nothing for my keep, and all I did was to pay for such sherry or whisky as was consumed, which was very little indeed.

But then, in the thirties I was a bachelor. It wasn't so funny just after the war. Gerald Slade did his level best to help me apart from freeing me from liability for rent but, to start with, there wasn't a lot that he could do. He was very busy defending 'Lord Haw-Haw', alias William Joyce, who had made himself greatly hated by broadcasting from Germany during the war and often telling us of disasters such as the sinking of a battleship which the authorities were reluctant to communicate to us but which they eventually had to admit to be correct. And my principal form of support came from doing what were called 'greater hardship' cases in the Brentford County Court, at, as you will probably have guessed, £2.2.0 a case. Sometimes they added a guinea for a conference.

I was pleased to have the work, and occasionally there were three cases a day, but with one child in hand and another on the way, it wasn't exactly thrilling. That was when I had to be discouraged by Bridget from applying to be an auxiliary postman at Christmas to help with finance. And all the time there was the spectre of Mr Bateman.

However, these people at Brentford paid promptly and regularly after a slow start and I forgot about Bateman. I wish I could remember the name of the kind managing clerk who threw these scraps to a very hungry bird. His name began with an S, and I won't mention his firm because some years later I was employed to bring a libel action against its principal.

My client was Mr Leopold Harris who had turned over a new leaf after receiving and undergoing a long sentence of imprisonment for fire-raising after what was then the longest case ever tried at the Old Bailey. He was very cross, for the solicitor had said, 'Harris is up to his tricks again.' I told him that I had the greatest sympathy with him, but that it was apparent that the solicitor had spoken to someone who had a genuine interest in the subject so that if only he could show that although the words were in fact false, he honestly believed them to be true, he would win, and Mr Harris would lose.

But Mr Harris would have none of that : costs did not matter to him; whoever won was of no importance; what must be shown in an English Court of Justice was that this was not a case of 'Alice is at it again', as the late Sir Noel Coward put it. He was insistent and we went to war. The solicitor didn't do particularly well, but well enough to win on the grounds set out above.

Then came the great moment that poor Mr Harris had been waiting for. I got to my feet and in my most soapy voice said that, whilst not quarelling with the verdict, my client was more than anxious that it should be made plain that there was no longer any blot on his escutcheon, and that he left the court proclaimed an honourable man.

The judge, who is still alive and I won't mention his name, said, 'Of course, of course, Mr Harris leaves the Court with the same reputation as he enjoyed when he entered it.'

That didn't help much.

My first resolve on coming back to the Bar was not to waste time on inessentials. That meant not to go out to tea at the Kardomah cafe in Fleet Street, and not do *The Times* crossword puzzle. I have only been in El Vino's once in my life so I didn't have to make a resolution about that. I had a cup of tea in my room and travelled to and from work with an emasculated *Times* after Papa came to live with us in 1950, he having cut the puzzle out. When I suggested that we might have two copies he, suspecting that he might be asked to pay for one, said that it was a wicked waste of money. I was allowed to help in the evening with the remaining two or three words, if he hadn't finished it, as he generally did.

As soon as I became a Judge, I ordered two copies and he didn't complain. I have never failed to finish it since : (not true – substitute 'What ! never ?' 'Well, hardly ever.' I did not get 'paedobaptist' or 'Sanditon') and I do it every day unless I am abroad. But I can't do it in record time like the winners of the competition. I must be getting too old. The first year I was all ready for the final, but I had to lead my step-daughter to the altar instead, and in the second year I was going to the Europa Hotel but Neil (now Mr Justice) Lawson and his charming wife asked us to Covent Garden instead, and in the third year they started publishing the puzzles for the finalists which would have taken me three hours instead of thirty minutes, and I gave up.

Let us return to 1946.

Things improved more rapidly than I deserved. Gerald got me into two cases each of which attracted a certain amount of publicity, and Edward Love, who was the clerk in the chambers, did me the best turn professionally that anyone could hope for.

He came into my room one Monday morning where I was sitting looking morose (I was sharing it with two others) and said two things. The first was, 'Frank's just said to me, "Miserable looking bugger, that Faulks of yours. I don't wonder no one sends him any work".' Frank was clerk to Sir Valentine Holmes, head of the rival chambers. I took this remark to heart, as it was merely that Bridget and I had had some silly little tiff about nothing that morning, and always after that I tried to avoid a hangdog look which clearly is not likely to attract clients. The second thing was what I believe is called a throw-away line, 'I played golf with Matthew Robinson on Saturday, and I think I may have got you a job at the Old Bailey. Should be worth about £250 a year,' and he walked out.

For the benefit of any young or non-legal reader, the great Matthew Robinson was clerk to the chambers which housed over the years Sir Patrick Hastings, Lord Shawcross, Lord Justice Winn, and Bill Fearnley-Whittingstall to name but a few.

The appointment was as Prosecuting Counsel to the Ministry of Food which in the few years of rationing was a lucrative position, and the Attorney-General also appointed me to perform the same function for the Board of Trade and the Ministry of Fuel and Power, neither of which was thought to be a post of importance.

£250 a year, indeed. By the time I took silk in 1959 it was worth £7,500!

And suddenly the room was empty and I was monarch of all I surveyed. For Charlie Cahn wisely took off for the Judge Advocate General's Department and Ronald Guest, who was a man of tremendous ability, decided to put in for a Metropolitan Police Magistrateship which was advertised in the Inner Temple Hall. He had a large practice on the Oxford Circuit (which then ran across the country from Birmingham, which was shared with the Midland Circuit, calling at Reading, Stafford, Stoke-on-Trent, Shrewsbury, Worcester, Gloucester and Newport (Mon.) on a somewhat devious route), was Recorder of Worcester in 1941, had won a first at Oxford and was an examiner for the Bar Final Exams.

I think he put in for the job in a moment of pique being fed up at all the travelling involved in his then practice, as W. H. Thompson, the solicitor to most of the trade unions, had realised his worth, but kept sending him to County Courts in East Anglia, which was wholly off his beat. I think with a little more patience he would have ended up on the High Court Bench. But it was not to be : Mr Chuter Ede or his advisers knew a good man when they saw one, and he was appointed in forty-eight hours. He always says that he has never regretted it, but I sometimes wonder. It is an odd profession, for only the other day (1974) George Baker, my boss, the President, and the man who gave me the chop at Caserta Palace, an Oxford circuiteer some six years younger than Ronald, said to me, 'You know the great thing for me when I came back from the war was Eric Guest (as he calls him) taking a job, for I got his bits and pieces on the circuit.'

No droppings came my way but I bought Ronald's Law Reports for £400 which somehow I raised, and I had the room to myself, rent free.

Very few defamation (a generic word including libel – on paper or what the law regards as permanent, such as a broadcast – and slander – by word of mouth – a ridiculous distinction today) cases are fought to the finish, and it is the brief fee and refreshers which make the work a paying business for, at any rate in those days, the preliminary paper work was by no means generously rewarded. Thus, if I had specialised in libel and slander alone, in defamation chambers, I doubt if I should have survived. But the advantage was that defamation was news, and that even the rather boring fact that A had apologised to B for having had said something about him and had paid him substantial damages was always good for a mention in the newspapers. Barristers are of course not allowed to advertise or tout for work, and I have always said that *The Times* newspaper in general, and Miss Hill its Queen's Bench Law Reporter in particular, have been the finest advertising agents I could ever have engaged. And I never paid a penny for their help. I have sometimes had my name in three cases on the same page in *The Times* in later years, two apologies, perhaps, and one fight, while the people in the real money, commercial cases, local government work, patent actions, and the like, would scarcely get a mention.

To illustrate this, the two cases to which I have just referred as getting a little publicity in a humble way, didn't bring me very much money but they produced a managing clerk who had instructed me at Bow County Court before the war. His name was Stanley Hart and he was very good to me getting his firm to put whatever they could in my way. And the first big one was, oddly enough, a libel action between two distinguished accountants, in which Gerald was against us, and I was led by Dick Levy who later became the second Chairman of the Monopolies Commission.

So by 1948 having now two children and a small practice which looked as if it might show promise, divided into three parts (a) defamation (b) Ministry of Food and Board of Trade at the Old Bailey (c) Capel-Cure Glynn Barton & Co., we decided to accept the offer of a short lease from the Prudential of a very large house at 28 Pembroke Gardens, W8, at a very reasonable rent. The Austrian Embassy was next door and we spent a lot a time in transforming the vast shrubbery at the back into an attractive garden. On the other side of us were employees of the Prudential in flats, who were no trouble at all.

I will explain how the Prudential came into it, after I have mentioned the two cases which Gerald got for me.

The first was a General Court Martial as opposed to my wartime Field General Courts Martial, which was held at a house in Curzon Street, Mayfair where our unfortunate client, Major X, who was forty-nine at the time having been commissioned into the RASC in 1918 and so would be eighty if he is still alive in 1977, had been Deputy Assistant Quartermaster General, China Command, in Hong Kong until the colony capitulated, when he was taken prisoner by the Japanese, and was appointed by them camp liaison officer at Shamshuipo by reason of his seniority.

The other prisoners of war took the view that he was too obsequious to them, that he was on their side, that he sneaked to them and helped them find wireless sets, heaters, and tunnels for escape.

Accordingly, upon the capitulation of the Japanese, the major, who was not a combatant officer, was placed under arrest by senior officers from the camp, and in the fulness of time stood his trial on eleven charges of assisting the Japanese while a prisoner of war in Hong Kong. A full colonel presided, with five other officers as members of the court, and with Oliver Barnett as Judge Advocate. He was then a Wing-Commander and afterwards became Judge Advocate General. Colonel 'Fat' Halse prosecuted vigorously but fairly, and the formidable Gerald defended.

The prosecution were to call no less than 44 witnesses and Major X had only himself. It didn't look too good, particularly when the court in rejecting, on the advice of the Judge Advocate, some technical submissions made by the defence, referred to the fact they had paid particular attention to the form of indictment in the case of Sir Roger Casement. So the press came in and took photographs and there was a scent of blood.

Major X was not exactly on the top of his form having been in close arrest since August 1945, and after a number of witnesses had been called, he was allowed out of Kensington Barracks to visit his wife and eighty-two year old mother.

But it soon became clear that although they had had a year's freedom, the three years' hell which the witnesses had undergone had made their memories unreliable and their testimony contradictory. Gerald was at his best and some of the witnesses whom I was allocated to cross-examine were easy meat.

I think that it does great credit to the Court Martial system and to the fairness and commonsense of the officers in that Court that, after I know not how many days of trial and after appalling initial prejudice against him, Major X was acquitted. We celebrated at the Savoy Grill, not uproariously, as the Slades were teetotal and poor old X was still half-stunned by the proceedings. I hope he didn't have to pay anything, and I fancy that we were the solicitor's guests. He, the solicitor, is dead now, and I can't ask him, but I shudder to think how much money – there was no legal aid – the poor innocent major, whose only crime had been that of being a little non-combatant officer, had to pay to clear his name.

The other case involved Mr Brendan Bracken, who, as Minister of Information, had been one of Churchill's more prominent lieutenants during the war, and was at the material time chairman of the Financial Times Ltd. and Chairman of the Union Corporation, a large mining concern in South Africa. Another newspaper and the editor of a periodical alleged that he had been up to some skulduggery on the Stock Exchange about mining shares, of which he was entirely innocent. The object of the exercise was to get publicity for the fact that the statements, which the Board of Trade were minded to take seriously, were entirely false, whereas damages were of no moment.

Writs had to be issued forthwith; by Bracken against the newspaper and the journalist and by the *Financial Times* itself against the journalist. It was, however the Long Vacation and Colin Duncan, to whom the *Daily Express* work was going in those days, (and the *Financial Times* used the same solicitors) must have been on holiday, and so Mr Hills of Shirley Woolmer & Co., who had heard me throwing my weight about in Major X's case, came to me.

I pointed out that for some inscrutable reason applications for an injunction (and it is still the practice) in the Queen's Bench Division, where the libel actions are heard, are heard in private, whereas they were heard in open court in the Chancery and Probate, Divorce and Admiralty Divisions, and I advised that the writs should be issued in the Chancery Division, and wondered if Gerald could hold my hand as I knew that the Chancery Vacation Judge would not be amused. Gerald did wonders, of course, when judicial astonishment was expressed, and we got our publicity. Eventually, one of the actions was settled before Mr Justice Evershed and two of them before Mr Justice Wynn-Parry which must have been the only time they had ever encountered this particular form of action, but as the only words they had to utter were 'So be it', they performed their judicial function to a turn.

The present Mr Justice Milmo apologised to Mr Bracken, and he and I went on apologising to each other for various clients for about a dozen years thereafter. He once gave me the intimidating advice, 'Never go to a public lavatory. It may end in trouble.'

It was round about this time when Gerald was at the peak of his career, shortly before he became a judge, that he led Sir Valentine Holmes on behalf of Harold Laski, a leading figure in the Labour Party and brother to Neville Laski QC, later Recorder of Liverpool, and was roundly defeated by Sir Patrick Hastings for the newspaper which was said to have libelled him, by accusing him of having advocated revolution. It was a very surprising result to me. I did a certain amount of humdrum paper work in the case but did not get a brief in it. Lord

Goddard used to say that Pat outgeneralled Gerald by keeping it short, while Gerald, as was his wont, went into every detail. But I think that Laski annoyed the special jury by using words like 'latifundia' and gave Pat a chance to tease him as a result. The Socialist Government abolished special juries in consequence and they have never reappeared.

Patrick Hastings and Norman Birkett were the household words of the Bar in the Thirties, although Wilfred Greene, afterwards Lord Greene, probably made as much money as the two of them put together, partly because they did their spectacular murders but more because of the tremendous amount of space that was accorded to their libel actions, particularly by any paper that they were defending. Norman Birkett, whose reputation unhappily was not improved by the publication of his diaries after his death, was unfailingly courteous and charming with a touch of the lay-reader. I was only led by him twice, and he would ask my opinion, which was of course valueless, as if he really thought it worthy of consideration. The Slades adored him and Phyllis in her widowhood has photographs of him in her flat.

Hastings was a different cup of tea. He was widely and rightly admired. He was the first Socialist Attorney-General but never got on to the Bench, whereas Birkett who espoused the unsuccessful Liberal party, eventually went to the Lords. But Pat was a pugnacious little man who never considered others very much. If you went to a consultation with him, either in your own right or devilling for someone else, you might as well have been part of the furniture, whereas Birkett or Walter Monckton would have said, 'Good afternoon' and even possibly, 'How good of you to come'. It means nothing, but it is very good for a young gentleman's morale.

I remember once soon after the War being at Bow Street Police Court in the committal proceedings of some Board of Trade matter in which Hastings was leading for the defendants. I had been given A. Aiken Watson QC who had been in my chambers before the war, to lead me. It wasn't really his scene, and I knew it, and the pugnacious old man knew it, and he could have sat back and chuckled. But he didn't. He turned to me, whom he obviously didn't remember from Adam from the odd consultation before the war, and hissed in an undertone, while my leader was speaking to Sir Laurence Dunne, the Chief Magistrate (who was a great respecter of persons, so that Sir Patrick started at plus thirty), 'Young man, you're going to regret that you ever started this prosecution.' I had too much respect for him to reply, but I thought that that was bullying.

After Brendan Bracken, kind Mr Hills did me another good turn. The Prudential were being sued for libel by one of their managers – I forget about what – and Mr Temple, their tame solicitor, asked the great Mr Hills, who acted for various newspapers, whom to instruct, and he recommended me. This was a turn up for the book because the Prudential not only had other work, but were able to let me lease my new home.

The case was heard at Norwich, where in later years I was to be the Recorder. It was the first time I had ever been to that city and I had the great advantage of being led by Gerald who was also on the South Eastern circuit. There was the inevitable jury, and Mr Justice Hallett. He was a very clever lawyer, opinionated, not liked, principally because he suffered severely from verbal diarrhoea. And eventually he had to resign because of it, before his time. I found him perfectly pleasant when I got to know him in his old age, provided of course that I realised that I was a feed, and that he wasn't in the least interested in anything that I was saying. It transpired unhappily that he and Gerald were not boon companions.

Gerald sniffed down, not up, his nose in frustrated fury when continually interrupted, and Hippy (H. I. P. Hallett) held forth incessantly in a sort of falsetto, and we lost.

We advised the Prudential to appeal, for we had advised them that we would win, but after a serious consultation it was decided not to do so lest the public image of the company be tarnished. Meanwhile, I had been instructed to appeal to the Court of Appeal for a stay of execution as to the damages pending a possible appeal. This was granted automatically for obviously the Prudential was good for the money if the appeal failed. Somehow news of this percolated to Hallett who was enraged.

Shortly after this, just as were moving to Pembroke Gardens, I got a set of papers which actually contained a point of law. When you are an undergraduate, you think that every case contains a fascinating point of law. This is not so : nine hundred and ninety-nine cases out of a thousand are questions of fact. Nobody appeals; nobody except the parties remember them, and it is only little Tommy, the one boy in a thousand, who finds a cosy little niche in the Law Reports, and then probably only because Mr Justice Buggins got it wrong and the Court of Appeal had to put him right.

I won't go into the point of law except to say this. A Gaming Act said that wagering was illegal so that bookies could not sue dishonest punters who refused to pay. So the bookies thought up a good one.

They wrote to the offender and said that if he didn't pay they would have to report him to Tattersall's and he would be warned off the turf. With any luck the punter would be mug enough to say, 'Oh! No! Not that! Not that! I'll pay, I'll pay.'

Then he would default and the bookies would sue him, not for failing to pay his gaming debts, which were unenforceable, but for breach of his contract to pay the correct sum provided the bookies didn't report him to Tattersall's. The bookie hadn't reported him to Tattersall's and so the money was due.

This argument had found favour with a majority in the Court of Appeal in 1906 or so, the dissenting judge being a man of great distinction. All the text-book writers including Professor Dicey the famous constitutional lawyer thought, as I did, that it was an illogical attempt to get round the law in order to achieve the desirable object of making the villain pay. After all, he'd have taken his winnings with alacrity had he succeeded. But it had stood as an authority for getting on for half a century, and there is a Latin tag about *stare decisis* which in effect means that if a decision is old enough, you don't upset it except for excellent reasons for fear of making it unduly difficult for lawyers to advise their clients, predictability being preferable to fluidity. That well-known case was called *Hyams* v *Stuart-King*.

My case was called *Hill* v *Hill*, William Hill Ltd. being the Plaintiffs. I explained to the defaulter that he'd either got to pay, the facts being the same as in *Hyams* v *Stuart-King*, or go to the House of Lords which, even if he won, would cost a bob or two. He was full of fight.

So in due course the late Bill Fearnley-Whittingstall the chain-smoker, appeared before Master Baker with an affidavit swearing that there was no possible answer to the claim and inviting judgment under what is called Order 14. Order 14, as you might expect, says that if the defendant on affidavit shows an arguable defence, why then, he must have his chance in Court, and there will be no judgment. If, on the other hand, the master, who is a minor functionary, thinks that there is no answer to the claim, he may save the time of a judge by authorising the Plaintiff to sign judgment forthwith. I said, 'Master, Master, (it was customary to evoke him twice, I don't know why) I shall be going to the Lords.' He looked at me as if I was demented, but gave me leave to defend.

Bill Whittingstall was a darling man and his brother painted my wife, Elizabeth, and also her late husband, the Bishop. Just as Annigoni seems to be better with women than with men, Fearnley-Whittingstall was the reverse and the Bishop is marvellous and Elizabeth is not done justice.

Well, the trial came on and I caught Hallett again. The event was really a farce because the facts were undisputed and he was bound by the previous decision to find against me. After he had given the decision that he was bound to do, I asked for a stay of execution as I was off to the Court of Appeal and then to the House of Lords. That brought an attack of fury, during which he referred to the trial at Norwich, and all his remarks appeared in the printed book when eventually we got to the House of Lords. Their Lordships may have smiled but they were much too dignified ever to have mentioned them.

How this defaulting gentleman was to afford two counsel, I didn't know, but when asked if I would like a leader in the Court of Appeal where the proceedings couldn't take five minutes, because in those days the Court of Appeal considered itself bound by its own decisions, I said, 'Yes'.

Asked to suggest one, I said Cyril Salmon, (now Lord Salmon) who was my second boy's godfather, and whom I thought to be a very talented and quiet advocate, just the man for the Lords.

We went through the formalities of the Court of Appeal and got our printed book ready for the Lords. When we got there we found that William Hill Ltd. who were not exactly without means, had taken in the great Sir Walter Monckton to lead Bill Whittingstall, and also that Lord Oaksey, a keen addict of the turf, was one of the seven Lords who had been selected to decide the matter. I told Cyril that we wouldn't get Lord Oaksey but that I thought the whole thing was so obvious that we ought to win 6–1.

I became ill, and arrived at the House of Lords, very selfishly, with a temperature of 101, thinking it more important to earn my brief fee for bread and boots for my children, than to infect the others. Nobody knew till it was all over : I did not make a speech, nor did I infect anyone.

Cyril held forth for about twenty minutes and that was about right, for it was only a short point, and, very politely, he turned to me, and said, 'Anything else?'

'What about the text-book writers?' I said, with my high temperature.

He obliged and my temperature went higher when, 'What', said Lord Jowitt on the woolsack, 'have the views of Professor Dicey to do with us? Is he an authority?'

Cyril got out of this very well, but not only had I obviously made an ass of myself, but also I began to wonder, as Walter Monckton's silken phrases fell upon an apparently sympathetic audience, whether we weren't going to go down the drain after all.

Their Lordships' house reserved judgment and months later we had a photo finish.

The Lord Chancellor, Lord Jowitt	against us
Viscount Simon, (ex Lord Chancellor)	for us
Lord Greene, (ex Master of the Rolls)	for us
Lord Oaksey, (Chairman at Nuremberg)	against us
Lord Normand, (Scotland)	for us
Lord McDermott, (L.C.J. of Ireland)	for us
Lord (later Viscount) Radcliffe, (Chancery)	against us

4 – 3 : it was really very exciting.

The brief had not come to me through any particular merit on my part. The London agents, madly respectable, were my brother-in-law's solicitors, while the country clients, I saw with horror, were, a few years later, struck off the Rolls.

Something that showed me how dispassionate the judiciary can and ought to be was when after the speeches had been read in the House of Lords itself and we had struggled out of the uncomfortable little box in which the advocates and their supporters had been confined, I stumbled across Lord Simon in a corridor. He, seeing that I had my wig on, realised where I had been and said, 'Fascinating case, wasn't it? For me, I thought Radcliffe's speech the best.'

I was a bit staggered as Lord Radcliffe had been against him, but managed to say, 'Oh! indeed', whereas perhaps I was expected to say, 'But not as good as yours.'

CHAPTER NINE

The Old Bailey and Other Early Cases

A corridor in the House of Lords recalls an anecdote that John Maude once told me many years ago before he had taken silk. There are always two and only two Scottish Law Lords. In 1974 we had Lord Reid and Lord Kilbrandon, now we have Lord Fraser of Tullybelton and Lord Keith. When I was a boy, the two were Lord Dunedin and Lord Shaw of Dunfermline – and they were there for a very, very long time. There was a very keen advocate from Scotland called Watson who wondered when his turn would come, and one day he encountered Lord Dunedin in a corridor.

'Ah! Good morning, Lord Dunedin. I hope you are very well.'

'Yes, I am, thank you – and so's Lord Shaw.'

John Maude, who has now retired from being a judge at the Old Bailey, became at one stage a bit worried about his figure, and we both went to the formidable Doctor Goller of Harley Street for our problems about which we shared notes. The diet was the usual keeping off sugar and obviously fattening things but the nub of it was 'four teacups full of liquid per day, and none of them must be alcoholic.' I did it for two months in 1951, lost two stone and collapsed and had to be revived with stoups of whisky. My face fell in, my buttocks disappeared, and my enormous paunch remained unhappily untouched. One day I was doing some case before John Maude which seemed to be going alone quite nicely (the Old Bailey juries used to convict in the fifties, unless there was a chance that the accused was not guilty: now the right to challenge is abused, so that anyone who appears faintly literate is removed with the object of getting a collarless dozen in the box, and you never know what may happen) when the Judge suddenly cried, 'Usher! Take this note to prosecuting counsel.'

He did so, and I opened it wondering what rebuke I was to find. It read, 'As much water as you like is all right. JCM.'

At the bar he had been the most marvellous mitigator, and I didn't have a great many battles against him, as his man would generally plead 'Guilty', after which we heard how excellent his character had been at Salonika in the First World War and how great was his respect for the Salvation Army, and a number of other fascinating and irrelevant matters. Irrelevant or not, they generally did the trick, and the villain was dealt with with much less severity than my ministry would have wished. If I were to rise to correct this expert piece of showmanship (his father was the great actor, Cyril Maude), the pained cry of, 'My Lord, this is persecution not prosecution' would be sure to follow.

We once had a matter at the Old Bailey when Cyril Salmon led me and the defendants, who were rich and important people and who didn't relish a conviction for an allegedly fraudulent prospectus, briefed four silks, Arthian (lately Lord Justice) Davies, Sir Edward Milner Holland, John Foster MP, and John Maude. The case went on for a very long time during which John Maude had great pleasure in referring to me as Mr Forks who had said this that and the other at the Police Court. On about the tenth day, a call of nature or some other excellent reason removed my leader and I was able to rise and protest about these incessant interruptions by my learned friend, Mr Mowed. I enjoyed that.

The case went on interminably and the final speeches for the defence were very long. My leader used an admirable economy of speech and finished at lunch time. It was Friday, and this was not what dear old Hugh Beazley, the Common Sergeant, had bargained for. He had intended to take home a transcript of the opening speech for the prosecution so that he could study it over the weekend and prepare a long and complicated summing-up with his facts correctly stated.

He came back at 2.15, rose at 4, and devoted the interim to telling the jury about the burden of proof upon the prosecution to satisfy them that they were certain, were sure, that the defendants were guilty. Unless they were so sure, it would be their duty and pleasure to acquit. If there was a reasonable doubt they would do the same and so on and so forth like a caged animal at the zoo pacing round and round to find an exit that was not there.

Then he went home to Hertfordshire to prepare his summing-up for Monday, having played out time.

But no: the jury thought that they had got the message. On the Monday morning, before the judge had time to arrange his notes, the foreman of the jury stood up and announced that they wished to hear no more, for they were unanimous that the verdict must be 'Not Guilty'.

The old man was flabbergasted, but retained his dignity, and refused an application by the Defendants for costs, which he would not have done today.

I should add that some judges prefer to direct the jury as to the 'onus' of proof rather than the 'burden', which is the same thing. Lord Justice Bridge tells me that this practice has recently led to a jury returning for further instructions about these 'owners of proof' they had heard so much about. John Meade used to have a similar anecdote about 'Mens rea' which needs no explanation.

Another similar occasion in the fifties was when I was against Gilbert Paull QC (later Mr Justice Paull). He took over the mantle of Gerald when Gerald became a judge, and was for some time the man whom the rich who were indicted at the Old Bailey wanted to defend them. When the Labour Government went out and Winston got in again, things became different for that meant that the great Hartley Shawcross, the finest advocate of my time, came back to the Bar, and provided competition.

The case was all about Boot and Shoe Regulations where some footwear manufacturers were accused of supplying shoes above the prices allowed in S.R. and O. 1413 and 1415 of 1946, and the Board of Trade said that £17,000 had been overcharged in nine months.

We had the usual cries of 'incomprehensible bureaucracy' in the lower court, but the tribunal understood what it was all about, and committed without any trouble. The case went on for a week or two, during which I wrote my only letter to *The Times* which was printed to my surprise (its inaccuracy and pomposity is incredible).

'Sir,

It was gratifying to read in your columns on Saturday the statement by the member for Brixton that the idea of having the National Theatre in Lambeth would not be criticized by any section of the local population. It was amusing also to note the mordant sally with which the Financial Secretary to the Treasury disposed of Mr Bernard Shaw's objection that the South Kensington site was more metropolitan than that chosen. Kensington, he said, amid laughter, had an aroma of early Victorian times and the memory of Prince Albert and all that he meant to this generation. The argument, if somewhat obscure, was clearly effective.

Mr Hall, however, conceded that, if the theatre had been built in Kensington, people no doubt would have learned to find their way there. In this he may have been right, as a number of people appear to have been able to find their way to the 'Britain Can Make It' exhibition and to the displays of foreign art treasures at the museums

immediately opposite the site. Meanwhile, the derided borough appears to fulfil a need at the hall with the unfortunate name, until the Queen's Hall is rebuilt in Lambeth or elsewhere.
Yours faithfully,
Neville Faulks,
28 Pembroke Gardens, W8.'

On the day after my birthday, 27th January, this appeared :

Sir,
    Many people besides Mr Neville Faulks appears to believe that the Albert Hall is in the Royal Borough of Kensington. It is, of course, in the City of Westminster.
Yours, etc.,
Francis N. Beaufort-Palmer,
2 Rosary Gardens, S.W.7.

and I was cut down to size.

When I got to the Old Bailey that morning, Gilbert Paull was very amused. 'Got your bottom smacked this morning, I see.' We went on and finished the evidence. I was feeling fairly fed up and during the luncheon adjournment where we sat beside each other either in the Bar Mess or being invited to luncheon with the Sheriff, I forget which, I suggested that the jury must have made up their minds by now one way or the other and we might as well forgo our final speeches. Gilbert, who was twelve years or so older than I was, and that much more experienced, said, 'Of course, dear boy, of course.' Again it was a Friday afternoon, again the Judge was looking forward to a weekend's preparation for his summing-up, and Judge George McClure said, and I quote from the evening paper, 'If you honestly feel when you consider this matter that you just can't grasp it, then the only thing to do is to say not guilty.'
    In those days the accused would say that the Board of Trade Regulations were incomprehensible bureaucracy while the restaurants who were caught red-handed in breach of the Food Regulations would cry 'agent provocateur,' at my witnesses, but of course there was no other way of proving your case than by planting a witness there. But it rubbed off on me for an old friend of mine, when running the Hyde Park Hotel without, I am sure, any breach of the Regulations, thought of cancelling a

Middlesex Yeomanry dinner when it was heard that the man Faulks was coming, no doubt with two civil servants dressed up as waiters with false moustaches. A lawyer would have understood that prosecution, not snooping for evidence, was my job, but then we are not all lawyers.

The first thing I ever learned by heart was;
    'Gentle Jesus [pronounced Gee-Gee] meek and mild,
    Look upon a little child,
    Pity my simplicity,
    Suffer me to come to thee.'
and the coda, 'God bless Mummy and Daddy, Grandpa and Grandma and all my kind friends and relations, and make me a good boy. Amen.'

And at a very early age, we were taught the Lord's Prayer before we could really understand it. My younger sister, Lorna, who sadly died of cancer of the lung just after Papa died – I didn't give up smoking until 1971 – thought until she was about eight that Thames Station must be a very dodgy place because she was always saying, 'Lead us not into Thames Station but deliver us from evil.'

But by 1949 the struggle to keep our heads above water financially had led me to concentrate upon temporal to the exclusion of spiritual matters. I recall with shame that in that year Bobby Milburn, who had accompanied me on my only visit to Great-Aunt Nellie, and whom I had not seen since he married us, came to call and I regaled him with sherry. He was then a Fellow of Worcester College, Oxford, and was on his way to deliver a sermon to the girls of St Felix at Felixstowe. I said, as was true, that I could not envisage any experience more terrifying than to have to instruct a congregation of any age on the basis of my infallibility and that I would consider it presumptuous so to do. I dare say that it was the sherry that was talking. But he didn't take me up on infallibility, a Papal concept, and merely said, quietly and sincerely, that it was no problem. He then asked me which was my parish church. Pembroke Gardens is off Edwardes Square, and I am ashamed to say that my answer was, 'I don't know'. This, after coming through the war unscathed.

By the beginning of 1950, Bridget wanted another child, and when she was pregnant announced that living in leasehold accommodation was economically absurd, that she must have her own little piece of England, and that to try and bring up two children in London was difficult enough, but that to try it with three of them was impossible.

Quite right, of course, but I have always been reluctant to leave anywhere, as I am easy to please, and I wasn't exactly rich.

I had thought that after our earlier problems with help, we were settled. Our first au pair girl came from Sweden. I paid her passage over and she stayed with us for a few months after which she deserted. She went to a colonel and wife, childless, whom I had known in the war, declaring that she would rather go to a family where there were no children. I was too proud to ask for her fare back, but I was not amused. She had taken the place of a Norland Nurse aged about seventy who was the only performer we were able to recruit during the frightening days when my second boy was continually upside down in his mother's womb. All went well in the end after a consultant had been called in, and all went well with the old lady for a bit. She was more keen on telling me about her distinguished brother in Hong Kong than on pushing the pram, itself a bit of a trial as we lived on the third floor.

The end came when one day we returned from shopping and found her with her head in between the shelves of the Welsh dresser, the dresser on top of her and the entire Copenhagen china set of dinner plates and so forth on the floor beneath her, in pieces. The china had been my mother-in-law's wedding present to us. It was a tearful occasion and I was not allowed to laugh. The old dear gave notice although the whole trouble was that she had pulled at a drawer which had slightly stuck; then I had to see what could be done with the pieces. My eldest son has the set now, but it is so heavily riveted that it is almost unrecognisable.

After the Swede had ratted on us, we had the most charming Italian girl of good family. 'Of good family' is of course disastrous, and we lived, apart from the children, in a *ménage à trois*, in the nicest possible way, of course. Poor Bridget seldom spoke to me alone except in the bedroom. The Italian duly went. We were sorry as she was very helpful and willing, if a bit of a mollusc. She was there when Aunt Win arrived for a long stay. Whether that led to her departure I can't say.

Then we had a cook, who was absolutely marvellous, with the inevitable daughter, and two young girls from Scotland who were moderately successful. They went but the cook remained. What we would have done without her, I don't know, but when I was faced with this desire for the country, I had thought that we were happily fixed for some time to come.

However, I looked in the newspapers and found a most attractive house which would obviously suit us splendidly. I went after it and to my surprise found my modest offer accepted. My stepson lives there today having paid about six times the amount that I paid for it. That is the inflation of a mere quarter of a century. I left 'to better myself' in 1954.

Bridget was surprised and thrilled, loved the place; she had the baby in St George's Hospital having moved to the country when she was eight months pregnant.

The very day that we arrived the local lieutenant-colonel, retired, who looked after the pigs at the East Surrey depot, came to ask for my subscription to the local Conservative Association. I thought this a bit much, so I said that I was a Liberal. The look on his face was one of amazement. He forgave me later. It was only half a lie, for although I wasn't a Liberal I had voted Liberal at the 1945 General Election.

We settled down happily with a superb Austrian au pair, now, alas, dead, and then I put Bridget to the supreme test. 'Do you think we could ask Papa to come and live with us? He is neither generous nor jolly, I know, and he never laughs, but after all, he is my father, and I can't have him living in a private hotel (a euphemism for a boarding house) at the age of 73. The other three will have him for three months of the year each I am sure.'

The old gentleman was still going up to London every day then but we didn't expect him to live until ninety-three and eleven months.

Bridget said, 'Of course' without any hesitation which was really very remarkable when you consider that her mother had been nothing but a nuisance to us throughout our marriage.

When Grandpa Ginner died, leaving infinitely less than was expected, he left his estate to Mummy for life and then to the four children in equal shares. He left nothing to Papa, and scored heavily from the grave by appointing me the senior executor, followed by Papa and a grey, faithful clerk.

We all got £500 as executors and I got his gold hunter thrown in with his personal effects. I have never worn a signet ring and I don't know what happened to the odd bits. Grandpa would have chuckled to know how very very offended Papa was at being the Number Two Executor who did all the work while the other two did nothing for the same remuneration. I think Grandpa was naughty about this, and I sympathised with Papa to whom my attitude was always one of filial affection rather than of the love which I bore towards Mummy.

So I bought the house in the country by selling everything that I had inherited from Grandpa after Mummy died in 1941.

Before we moved to Surrey, I had been involved in a case about overcharging for poultry, in which enormous sums were involved. There were four defendants, one of whom, the principal, had gone abroad and was never apprehended. His name was Isaac Cole. It was impossible to resist the obvious comment, and I referred to it as 'Operation Fiddler' with 'Old King Cole and his fiddlers three'.

Immediately Derek Curtis-Bennett KC, son of the man who had led me in Lord de Clifford's case, jumped to his feet in forensic indignation in protest against this dreadful piece of prejudice. Harold Sturge, the magistrate, and an old friend of mine, was reported as saying that the comment ought not to have been made, although in fact he smiled and said nothing. Nor did the present Lord Justice Sebag Shaw get to his feet.

In the end one of the other three defendants gave King's Evidence, one pleaded 'Guilty' and one was sent to prison, fined £10,000 and ordered to pay 300 guineas costs. Isaac Cole has not been heard of since, and when I made my pathetic little joke again at the Old Bailey no objection was taken.

Derek Curtis-Bennett's father, 'the governor' as he always called him affectionately, offered me a red bag before the war, or so I was told.

Perhaps, I should explain the blue bag to which I referred in my anecdote about the garden wall in case any non-legal person should attempt to read this book. When you are called to the Bar, as I was in 1930 by Lord Sumner (whose portrait in the Benchers' smoking room of the Inner Temple was pointed out to Bridget and myself by Lord Goddard with the comment, 'Benevolent malevolence'), you have to have a wig, bands, a gown and a butterfly collar, the basic necessities. But custom had decreed that you had to buy a blue bag with your initials on, a tin with your initials on for your wig, and, in the fullness of time, a silk might allow you the honour of buying a red bag with your initials on in order to sling it over your shoulder and show your juniors how experienced you were. Presumably all this started with circuiteers who before the days of the iron horse went about the countryside with their law libraries in these capacious bags.

Edward, our clerk, telling me of Sir Henry's honorific gesture, which flattered me, added that the clerk would expect three guineas. I suspected that Sir Henry knew nothing about the offer and I refused it, and struggled on with my blue bag until the war. After the war, I never used a bag or a wig tin again, but kept my things in an inconspicuous suitcase.

In 1948 or 1949 I took my first pupil. His father was the senior partner of a firm of solicitors who had never sent me a brief in my life. When approached, I said that I had no work and that the hundred guineas pupil fee would be better spent elsewhere. Mr Cecil, the partner sent to treat, said that they would see that there was plenty of work and the pupil arrived and helped greatly with the renovation of the shrubbery at Pembroke Gardens. Then he stayed on at the end of his year to devil for me, not that there was a great deal to do, but people began to send me undefended divorces so that there was usually a certain amount of paper work to be done.

I think that, because of the publicity in *The Times* and elsewhere for an apology in a libel action, for which I would get paid ten guineas in fact, people began to think that I had a much better practice than I really had, for there was a constant stream of applications for pupillage during the rest of my time as a junior. At first I welcomed them, for they could learn from my patchwork practice with the variety of courts visited, so different from that of Wilfrid Lewis, which gave you a glimpse of the heights without letting you know of the foothills where you would have to begin. After a time, however, I cut the number down, as the Bar was in my view becoming overcrowded, and I couldn't see how I could fulfil my moral obligation to find them a good home after their year of pupillage was over.

I told an applicant in 1948 that I was sorry but I could not take two pupils because my practice did not justify it; he is now a High Court Judge. Years later I told an applicant that if he was to be the fourth pupil, he would be unlikely to get the special attention that his academic and general record deserved. He agreed; he is now a member of the Shadow Cabinet.

Others who became pupils have taken silk in different parts of the world and half dozen or so in England. I used to come back from luncheon in Hall to find my desk slightly disturbed as the present Recorder of London and other miscreants had been playing some form of tennis across it, which involved the use of a golf-club. I was sent out for a walk round the Temple Gardens if they had not finished when I returned.

The solicitor who had instructed me in the Court Martial case of Major X later brought me another case which involved an interesting point of law which entertained me, and also involved the stepson of a duke and the daughter of an earl, which entertained the public.

My client was born in Germany in 1918 in conditions of luxury.

A pretty young girl of eighteen, she met the 'stepson' (I don't propose to mention any names as the other parties may be alive although I should think it unlikely) while he was studying for the diplomatic service in Germany. They fell in love and were engaged at Whitsun 1937, secretly.

Then she went to stay with her uncle in Los Angeles, where the stepson joined her in May 1938 and they slipped across the frontier to Mexico and were married in July. Shortly thereafter the husband returned to England where he joined the Auxiliary Air Force, and quite right too. She went home to Germany where she kept the marriage secret. On 10.1.39 her husband wrote to say that he didn't love her and did not want to marry her (but he already had). On the next day, *The Times* announced her husband's 'engagement' to a titled lady. My poor German girl wrote and protested, but the other two went through a form of marriage at Brompton Oratory on 11.2.39. The husband and his new 'wife' flew out to Bavaria to see her. It was the only time the two women met.

War broke out. My client was desperately anxious about her husband's well being. No doubt, she was told by the propaganda machine nightly that the war was all but over in Hitler's favour. At last, with the help of an Italian flying-officer, she managed to smuggle out a letter to her husband in a diplomatic bag via the Portuguese Embassy. My client's Christian name was Eleonora.

A reply back to a friend of hers in Switzerland signed by the new wife:

> Dear Therese, The news is very sad as Michael has been killed a year. I hope you are all well. Will you tell Lornie and friend? Yours sincerely . . .

My client had just passed her twenty-third birthday; she was not a child and was very much in love. She had a nervous breakdown and was treated by a doctor for eighteen months.

When the war ended in 1945 she went to a solicitor and found that the letter was a lie and that her husband was still alive. She realised that her marriage was over, and she did the decent thing. She came to this country and obtained an undefended divorce on the grounds of the adultery of the other two. They were legally married after the decree absolute.

She claimed (1) damages for pain and suffering and out-of-pocket expenses under the rather special principle of *Wilkinson* v *Downton*, the point which entertained me, of which lawyers will be aware and with which non-lawyers might be bored, and (2) exemplary and punitive damages if they decided that the female defendant had written the letter maliciously in order to keep the true wife silent.

Over the twenty-five years since, I have at last come to the conclusion that exemplary or punitive damages ought to be abolished for reasons which I will not set out here but which are to be found if anyone is interested in the Report of the Committee on Defamation, 1975, but that was not my view at the time.

I had to take on the present Lord Gardiner leading the present Lord Hailsham of St Marylebone for the Defendants. The titled lady did very well in the witness box on the basis that she wrote the letter out of kindness to put my client out of her misery.

I cross-examined her with great vigour but could feel that somehow my case, which I had thought cast-iron, was not going very well.

Eventually, Gerald Gardiner in his final speech suggested that there were plenty of other reasons why my client should have received shocks in Germany during the war years, apart from the anxiety of being secretly married to an Englishman. He concluded by saying that this was an action in which there were no merits at all.

The late Mr Justice Gorman, who was a great worrier, left three questions to the jury :

1.   Damages (for pain and suffering and out-of-pocket expenses,)
2.   Was Lady — malicious?
3.   If yes, damages?

What he was worrying about was, as he said to the jury, 'Counsel for Lady — argued that the case was not of the kind in which aggravated damages could, as a matter of law, be awarded, and that question may have to be subject to consideration later.' And he went away and worked on this point like a beaver.

He sent for Gerald Gardiner and myself and as we waited in the Judge's corridor, the late Mr Justice Hilbery emerged from his room, ignored my existence completely, and said, 'Ah! Gardiner, interesting case, that of yours; legal blackmail, of course', and he swept away. Like many Englishmen that really very good judge loved the aristocracy, but I must say that that took my breath away.

When we got into the Judge's room, he very courteously showed us a very long judgment which he had prepared concluding that if the jury found Lady — to have been malicious, as I, at any rate, expected, none theless aggravated damages were not permissible. He asked for our comments. It would have been discourteous to have argued with him. As the law then stood, I was satisfied that he was wrong. So I said nothing and nor did Gerald Gardiner, as inscrutable as ever. We should have to go to the Court of Appeal, if indeed my poor client could afford it.

But, as so often happens in the law, all the Judge's homework was in vain. The jury found that Lady — had *not* been malicious ,and gave me the comparatively small sum of £814 damages. I obtained an order for costs as the Defendants' advisers had only paid £500 into court.

This is one legal technicality which I ought to explain as it is really not difficult to do so. A says he is entitled to damages from B. B says, 'No, I'll fight.' But at the same time he may pay a sum into Court – let us say £500. It is a bet. 'You can have £500 and your costs up to date, if you like. I bet you don't get any more.' A says, 'No. I won't settle for that.' Battle is joined. Neither the Judge or the jury know that there is any money in Court.

1.　A gets £600. He gets it and costs and the £500 in Court is paid out 'in part satisfaction'; or

2.　A gets £450. He gets that, the odd £50 is paid back to B, and A gets the costs up to the date of payment-in, and B gets the much larger costs of the trial, so that after mutual set-off, A may get nothing.

3.　A gets nothing. He pays the costs, B gets his £500 back.

In 1950, the solicitor who had briefed me all those years before in Lord de Clifford's case, sent me a slander action which I only mention because this sort of thing goes on, regrettably, today.

I was for Chief Superintendent Charles F. Satterthwaite; and a very likeable and amiable man whom I haven't seen for a long time called Ralph Milner appeared for a Mr Philip Piratin, who had formerly been the Communist Member of Parliament for Mile End.

The issue was quite simple. Did the Defendant speak the words or not? If he did, how much? The jury found that he did and I forget how much they awarded.

The sadly up-to-date words complained of were, 'Police protection in the East End of London is given to Fascists and when the Police do take action against the Fascist thugs it is because they are forced to by public opinion. I don't blame the ordinary policeman : he carries out the instructions of his superiors. One in particular is the Chief of Police for Hackney – Satterthwaite – he is detested by his men and is one of the worst enemies of the working class. He should have been kicked out of the Police years ago.' And again, 'I wonder what instructions police received from their superior officers. I mean those at the top. There is one man who is not fit to be in charge of policemen: that man is Superintendent Satterthwaite of Hackney: he is a friend of the Fascists and is hated and despised on all sides, even by his own men. I have asked the Home Secretary several times to have him removed from his job – [N.B. the then Home Secretary in the Socialist Government was Mr Chuter Ede of whom everyone approved] – I am still trying and will mention his name at every street corner until I do.'

Poor Mr Piratin was not properly indoctrinated, for he mentioned Satterthwaite by name. His fellow travellers today know a trick worth two of that. Write to *The Times* with indiscriminate abuse of the police without giving any names . . .

CHAPTER TEN

The Press

I can't remember when it was that I got my first newspaper. In defamation, you have not really arrived until you act for a newspaper. I should probably never have had one at all, if my best friend had not been a great friend of a solicitor who had as a result given me work including a lot of small cases in the County Court for BASMA – the Boot and Shoe Manufacturers Association. (It always amused me that my step-daughter shared a room at Benenden with Princess Basma, sister of King Hussein.) He got Lord Rothermere's work, and influenced it in my direction under the no doubt mistaken impression that I was rather good. Now Lord Rothermere did not only mean the *Daily Mail* but the *Daily Sketch*, the *Evening News*, numerous provincial newspapers, the now defunct *Sunday Despatch* and, for a very short period, the *TV Times*.

I had a lovely time, advertised by *The Times*, apologising first to the great Madame Pommery, president of Champagne, Pommery et Greno Societe Anonyme, whom someone had associated with the unlamented Herr Ribbentrop, who had been a champagne salesman in his time, but of German wines.

No doubt there is a school of thought that holds that the number of German names in the champagne industry, such as Bollinger, Krug, Heidsieck and so forth, might lead the uninitiated to conclude that the Germans instructed the French after the battle of Sedan, but it is a subject of which I know nothing.

The solicitor for the newspaper group was Dennis Walsh whose father, Sir Cecil Walsh, had been a distinguished member of the Bar and a Chief Justice in India. At his orders I apologised concerning various matters to a gentleman called Franz Egon Count van Furstenberg, to the Royal College of Obstetricians and Gynaecologists, to Baron Leopold von Mildenstern, to Miss Olga Deterding, to the late Duke of Norfolk, to the Maharani of Baroda, and to innumerable others.

Sometimes, however, we fought and won. The first one that we won was rather amusing. Others that we won were rather dull, largely with silly plaintiffs, and I won't take up space by recounting them. Suffice it to say that I gather that Lord Rothermere was extremely generous, and word would go forth not to bother to enforce an order for costs against the defeated plaintiff.

Sometimes I would be asked if I wanted a leader. On the whole I was too fond of the sound of my own voice to welcome a leader but I thought that the amusing case referred to above merited one as I was told that Bill Whittingstall was to lead the other side. I cudgelled my brains and suggested Gilbert Beyfus QC, whom I had listened to and admired before the war but who was now considered to have missed the boat for a High Court Judgeship – (in fairness to his memory, the old boy told me on his deathbed that he would not have taken a Judgeship if it had been offered to him. 'Trying all those cases of buggery on Circuit,' he said, 'revolting.' He added, however, that he would have liked to have had a few years in the Court of Appeal towards the end of his life, but he agreed with me that that was just a day-dream as apart from political appointees like Slesser, Somervell and Scott, only Fletcher-Moulton that I could think of had dodged the first hurdle. Lord Radcliffe had by then gone straight to the Lords from the Chancery Bar but that is a different point) – he was much in demand for defended divorces, and expert in matters concerning gaming and wagering – but that was all.

Dennis Walsh's decision to brief Gilbert in the case of *X* v *Associated Newspapers* began his famous Indian Summer which lasted until he died for as he walked out of Court having won his last case against the Duchess of Argyll he turned and said, 'Not bad for a dying man.' He used old-fashioned but telling phrases and on that day he said to me, 'Neville, I'm a goner.' He was then seventy-five. I had to give up being a trustee of his will, being so often on Circuit and unable to sign documents conveniently and I don't know what has happened to his widow, his third wife, a charming young girl, much too young for him, but who obviously adored him and he her. I miss him very much.

In this case the alleged libel was in the *Daily Sketch*,

Mother takes nude's place in lion show. Mrs Y, a 22 year old mother, posed as a nude in a lion's cage in Southampton last night in place of Zelda Lamone who vanished two days ago after lion-tamer Nikolai was attacked during the show at Nottingham. Zelda turned up again yesterday – at the Law Courts to give evidence in a divorce case.

That was said to be very libellous and juries being what they are, Bill might have pulled it off. Gilbert did as later I learned that he almost always did when he was defending – and I didn't always agree with him – he decided to call no evidence in order to get the last word. In spite of my saying above 'juries being what they are', juries nowadays are a great deal more intelligent and better educated than they were when dear old Gilbert was a boy. But it is not because of Gilbert or Bill that I have chosen to include this little case.

It is because we had Mr Justice Hilbery in charge. And who better? Naked ladies in a lion's cage were scarcely his cup of tea. So I quote from his summing up; I can almost hear him as I write : 'Now, members of the jury, the first question you have to decide is whether the words in their natural meaning are defamatory of the Plaintiff, that is, whether they tend to lower her in the estimation of right-thinking people, or cause her to be shunned or avoided, or expose her to hatred or ridicule.

'As ordinary people, you will know the standards to be applied, whether a thing is immodest or not. It may be that we are in an age when immodesty is prevalent.

'For my part, I have not the least doubt that if I expressed a view on this matter, many young people would say things that were not complimentary to that view : they would attribute it to old age and all sorts of things. I can hear some of them almost saying, "Stuffy Victorianism". But, members of the jury, it is not my view that counts, but yours and you have to consider it against the whole background of the case. It is said, you know, that the Plaintiff has been injured in her professional reputation. I cannot for the life of me see how whether she chose to wear a bikini or not could damage her reputation as an inventor of dances.

'You may indeed wonder what was the point of exposing nudes in a lion's cage. Was it because the public would get a sadistic excitement out of the idea that a lion might maul one of the girls? If that was the idea, it was horrible.

'Now it has been said that a nude is a girl who wears a large hat and a G string. All I know about a G string is that it is the lowest note on a violin, as I believe.

'If, members of the jury, you are of the opinion that the words were not defamatory and conveyed no special meaning, why then, that is the end of the matter. If, of course, you think that they were defamatory, then there are other matters to consider.'

Faced with this summing up, the jury came back after one hour and twenty-five minutes (during which I suspect that they had been having luncheon) and found for the Defendants.

Lord Rothermere did not enforce his costs, and the lady was said to have received a quarter of a million pounds maintenance from her then husband, a quarter of a century later.

And Gilbert was in the centre of things again. It was as well that the case in question was of that particular nature, for Sir Malcolm (as he was known at the Bar) didn't greatly care for Gilbert. He always used to address him with dignified courtesy as 'Mr Beyefuss' whereas, as he knew perfectly well, Gilbert called himself 'Bayfuss'. I remember the late Rodger Winn telling me how he, against him as a Treasury Devil then, had joined in the hunt, and how the old gentleman had not enjoyed being baited. But that is inevitable if you have a difficult name.

I remember a dear old Chancery silk called Harold Christie asking me in some summons when I was the man in the middle for two guineas, while the other two contestants were the ones who mattered, how I pronounced my name. This in an undertone – so I wrote down $\phi \omega \xi$. He twigged, and rebuked his junior, who could not read Greek and who in his view had not been educated.

That was of course in the Thirties, when I used to spend a lot of time in Court listening and trying to imitate the style of the wizards. I don't know that I eventually imitated anyone in particular. I noticed that they all stood erect and made the most of what height they had in order to have a 'presence' while one dodge which I copied from Patrick Hastings, which served me in good stead, especially in crime, was to sit down immediately one's opponent rose to protest about something. If, as often was the case, he was protesting just to impress his client, he would be left standing alone looking rather silly.

Naturally, every keen young man tries to get experience by listening and learning and I was very flattered to be told by Jeremy Thorpe, recently the leader of the Liberal party, that he had sat through the case of *Tracy* v *Kemsley Press Ltd*. in which I appeared for the Plaintiff. That is, until he told me later that he was a captive audience as he was then a pupil of my opponent.

Others of my erstwhile clients have acquired greater political importance than they enjoyed when I appeared for them. I will be selective. Mr Clement Freud, the Liberal member for the Isle of Ely and one of his party's shadow cabinet, may smile when he recalls how I made a statement on his behalf and how Mr Helenus Milmo (as he then was) apologised publicly to him after he had been libelled in the now defunct

Empire News. There is no need to repeat the libel but I see that I addressed Mr Justice Pearce, as he then was, as follows :

'The Plaintiff is an accomplished cricketer who has played representative cricket, and still plays regularly. In 1955 the Plaintiff used to take exercise at the athletic track at the Duke of York's barracks in Chelsea where the well-known athletes Bannister, Chataway and Brasher, who were all personal friends of his, trained. After their training spells, these friends often went to the Royal Court Theatre Club of which he was the proprietor.'

It all seems a very long time ago. It wasn't a very serious libel although the event justified Mr Freud in suing.

It was also a very long time ago that I appeared in May 1957 before the Lord Chief Justice, Mr Justice Hilbery and Mr Justice Donovan on behalf of Mr Eldon Griffiths, recently the Shadow spokesman for Industry and Conservative Member of Parliament for a constituency in Suffolk.

The Attorney-General, now Viscount Dilhorne, and Mr Rodger Winn (later Lord Justice Winn, deceased) prosecuted. Rolls House Publishing Co. Ltd. were represented by Mr W. P. Grieve (now Percy Grieve QC, MP) and W. H. Smith and Sons Ltd, of course, by Mr Gerald Gardiner QC, and Mr Helenus Milmo.

It was all about the American magazine *Newsweek* which was printed in Amsterdam, imported into England by Rolls House, and sold on their bookstalls by W. H. Smith and Sons Ltd. Mr Griffiths was the London representative of *Newsweek* in those days. The offending issue of the paper was on sale while the trial for murder of Dr Bodkin Adams who was acquitted, was proceeding at the Central Criminal Court. It was gravely prejudicial to the case of the doctor. The case was a *cause célèbre* if ever there was one, and the court was clearly anxious to make plain that the law of contempt of court in England was one which was not to be flouted lightly.

Poor Mr Griffiths was first in the receiving line; the Court was a strong, tough, Court and it was plain that we were in for trouble, stemming largely from the American habit of hyperbole whereby my client was styled 'chief European correspondent in London of the magazine'. It was not surprising that he was prosecuted and it was going to be exciting, provided, and provided only, that we won.

We had had a conference at which I had been much impressed by this young man's insistence of innocence. But what of the great Lord Goddard, always ready to withdraw when he had been demonstrated to be wrong, but desperately difficult to dislodge from an entrenched position. Someone had to be punished and after all it was plain that the importers and distributors were morally blameless and entitled to talk about the doctrine of innocent dissemination.

The Attorney-General was kind and temperate. He ended up by saying that he did not contend that the contempt was of a serious character, but, at the same time, it was a contempt. The respondents, Rolls Publishing Co. Ltd. and W. H. Smith and Sons Ltd. had behaved with commendable promptitude, though he would not put it quite so high in the case of the respondent, Griffiths, who did not act until after consultation with America.

I rose to face three faces of stone in the large and crowded Lord Chief Justice's Court, a row behind Gerald Gardiner, as I was still only a junior. I was unusually nervous for I knew, as far as counsel can ever know, that my client was innocent and I knew that there was a real danger of his being convicted. Because of this I was very nearly impertinent to the Court.

I started by saying that Mr Griffiths had been brought before the Court on the grounds that he had

1. Published the words complained of
2. Caused them to be published.
3. Distributed the publication attacked.

My case, I said, was that I had done none of those things. (The first person singular is used when the advocate forensically identifies himself with his client. Good, because it saves unnecessary words, before judges; not good, as tending to muddle, before juries.) I argued that the position was as though the editor of *The Times* had written an article upon current events in America which gave rise to possible proceedings for contempt in America and it was there sought to attack the Washington correspondent of *The Times*.

I read Mr Griffith's affidavit in which he said that although his name appeared after the word 'editorial' the publication was written in American-English and that word did not mean editorial in the English sense, but the American 'reportorial'. It was used to distinguish his department from the other two independent departments into which *Newsweek* was divided, the advertising and circulation departments, which were quite separate and distinct. The European edition came under the editor in America and he, Mr Griffiths, had neither written the article complained of nor sent in the material. Nor had he written on or reported on or even attended the trial of Dr Adams.

If that were to be believed that would be enough, as there was no evidence that Mr Griffiths had distributed the magazine in this country.

But they were after me at once. Lord Goddard asked me, 'Who in this country is responsible for *Newsweek*, and who is the person responsible for its conduct in this country?'

I said that Mr Griffiths was not. He collected the information and sent it to America. The only person to whom liability might attach was a clerk who took an infinitesimal number of copies from Rolls House to the news stands; that was a technical publication. The people who decided what was to be in the paper were in America.

He said crustily, 'Then this paper could publish anything that they liked, and no one would be responsible?'

I said, 'Mr Griffiths is named as the chief European 'correspondent', that is all.'

Mr Justice Hilbery (Sir Malcolm) chipped in, 'But he is the person in charge of editorial matter from this country.'

I said boldly, and I meant it, 'It might be expedient to hold my client responsible, but it would not be justice.' I paused to be rebuked, but there was a silence. I went on, 'He sent cables to America telling them not to touch the trial, to play it down. Instead the paper published the article of which complaint is made. Had he attempted to interfere with what was published he would have been reprimanded and might have been dismissed.' It would, I added, be indefensible to extend the principles of vicarious liability to make a foreign correspondent here liable for the conduct of his editor in Washington. In the face of the affidavit it would manifestly be wrong to hold my client liable.

I was working pretty hard to compete with the Court but all the time this young man behind me was baying, 'Let me tell them, let me tell them.'

And when I saw old Doggie, as the Lord Chief Justice was affectionately (for he was much loved at the Bar) nicknamed, turn to Sir Malcolm and unmistakably growl, 'Don't believe a word of it.' I thought, well why not? and I said rather cheekily, 'I am afraid that inadvertently I heard what your Lordship said. I submit that it would be wholly wrong to disbelieve the contents of an affidavit when the deponent is in Court and ready to be cross-examined as to its contents. May I tender my client for cross-examination?'

'Never heard of such a thing.'

I was about to say, 'Well, there's always a first time,' which was all I could think of, when, unexpectedly, Sir Malcolm said, 'I don't see why not.'

This was really something, for Sir Malcolm was to Lord Goddard what Avory and Humphreys had been to Lord Hewart, the *eminence grise*. He said little but what he did say carried weight.

At once, 'Oh! very well then.'

It was all very dramatic, and I've seen as much forensic drama as the next man.

The young man went into the box. He was then thirty-two years of age. He gave a magnificent performance. He said exactly what had already been read to the Court but with obvious sincerity. It may not have sounded very impressive when read by a hired assassin, but from him it was most effective.

Even the Attorney-General could make nothing of him. He asked him, 'But you are the person in this country responsible for the extra European editorial text, are you not?'

Answer: 'A special person in New York does that. Many stories appear in the column "Britain" of which I know nothing.'

In re-examination I elicited from him the explanation of the matter of which complaint had been made by the Attorney-General in opening.

'Why did you take no immediate action to remove the magazine from the bookstalls?'

'I had no authority to do so. I had to get authority from New York.'

Then Mr Justice Terence (afterwards Lord) Donovan joined in the fray but scored no points. Doggie asked a few questions, but then Sir Malcolm turned to the Chief and said, 'Don't see how we can punish the agent for the crime of his master,' and I knew that we had won.

I wish I had thought of saying, as did Lord Justice Harman many years later in *Egger* v *Lord Chelmsford and others*, that I didn't know of the doctrine of *respondeat inferior*.

While I was standing talking to my client and telling him how well he had done, Gardiner stopped on his way across the Court and said, 'By your advocacy you have got your man off and my people will go down.' I was taken aback. Gerald Gardiner is no extrovert and it was a great compliment coming from him to a mere junior. And undeserved. All the credit was owed to that voice breathing loudly behind me, 'Let me tell them.'

Gerald Gardiner was right. A week later the Lord Chief Justice read the judgment of the Court, distinguished the law of innocent dissemination in cases of defamation from the law applicable to contempt of court and (in my view illogically) found the other respondents guilty, fined them £50 each and half the costs of the trial, but found that 'in the state of the evidence it did not seem that responsibility for the article on its publication could be imposed on the Respondent Griffiths'.

As we had persuaded these formidable gentlemen in effect to eat their words, I did not think that an application for Mr Griffiths' costs would be well received, particularly as I suspected that *Newsweek* were supporting him. He is now a very distinguished man and I hope he will forgive me.

I see that so far I have put in a Communist, a Liberal and a Tory. It would be churlish to leave out the Socialists but apart from the Bank Rate Tribunal where they did not distinguish themselves, I cannot recollect that I ever fought for or against them.

I see that the Co-operative Press Ltd. apologised to me on behalf of Mr Anthony Fell MP for Greater Yarmouth, for having said something beastly about him which I forget, and another case, which shows how important you can get after a slow start, is *Evans* v *Tribune Publications Ltd.* and another.

'Another' was Mr Michael Foot, then regarded as a wild man, now (1977) probably the most predominant of the 'Feet', (although his nephew, who not long ago was fined for contempt of court and is a somewhat revolutionary gentleman, may steal his thunder eventually), who made in *Tribune* – on 19th May 1953 – a strong attack upon a dear old man called Sir Lincoln Evans, who had been the General Secretary of the British Iron, Steel and Kindred Trades Association and had accepted a place on the Steel Board.

I won't set out the article. My client didn't want any damages, and accepted the apology, and his costs. The Defendants made an unqualified withdrawal of all the allegations made and wished to apologise. The apology was made by our present Attorney-General, Mr S. C. Silkin.

Griffiths' case was in May 1957, three years after we had moved again in February 1954. Bridget didn't like living in a village with people popping in unasked all the time and she wanted to move. I was strongly against it, but, as it turned out, she was absolutely right.

I was forty-six, she was thirty-two, and we had a boy at Uppingham, a boy at Cottesmore Preparatory School near Crawley, run by the Rogersons, and a little girl of three.

Michael and Marion Rogerson were two of my oldest friends, Michael having been at Cambridge with me. We used to enjoy enchanting holidays together at Deauville, one year in a very grand villa which he had hired from some chum of his, and another when he took over a pension filling it up with his friends.

We used to compete in the Coupe des Veterans. In France, you are a veteran at forty-five as far as lawn tennis is concerned, and ex-Davis cup players were liable to appear as soon as their birth certificates allowed, and sweep all before them. Michael was much better than I was but we used to play a goodish double together. One year we came up from 2-5 down to win the final set to be greeted with a cry from some old gentleman, *'Tenacité brittanique – Wellington!'* The 'W' was pronounced as a 'V' and it was great fun.

In the next round we got beaten by the same score of 7-5 in the final set, and one of our opponents, who spoke perfect English, put his arm round Michael and exclaimed, 'It is a shame : you were far the best player on the court.' I did not need to ask what he thought of me.

Corporal Hitler and the Inland Revenue had contrived to give me, in effect, three only children with five years between each other and no handing down of clothes. I had an overdraft and it was no use to tell the Bank Manager that the Board of Trade owed me over a thousand pounds, which was true. He merely looked sceptical and said, 'Even a barrister must learn to cut his coat according to his cloth.'

This enraged me although I said nothing, and it was a happy occasion for Bridget, for from then on I was determined to get June Farm with which she had already fallen in love. So I put in a bid which I never expected to be accepted, but it was. I think it was because kind Mrs Waley, who had been left a widow in a house which was much too big for her, and to whom money was not important, quite liked the look of us. And I told the house agent to ask a thousand pounds more than he suggested for Blatchcombe and I got that. So I exchanged the two properties for £500, plus the conveyancing and house agent's charges, which was incredible. Neither house was surveyed and I never had any trouble with either.

Blatchcombe was the name when I bought the house and I did not change the name. It was in a village called Blackheath in Surrey near Guildford, up the hill from Wonersh on one side and Chilworth on the other. One village shop. Plenty of heath if you could afford horses or ponies which I couldn't. It hasn't changed. Everyone was very hospitable. Naturally the people in the big houses, the Herberts, the Darwins, the Stewards and Pat Sandeman, were older than we were but it didn't seem to matter. Pat was a large man with enormous feet, dropsy I should think, and it was painful to watch him tottering up the platform at Waterloo. It was sad when he died, but his Port empire still flourishes.

The gallant Major Steward was Master, as was his father, of the Skinners Company to which I belong, and his wife, who is still alive, was I believe the daughter or granddaughter of the original Thomas Cook.

The name Darwin speaks for itself; the eldest son is called Erasmus, and Mona Darwin still lives on at Tangley Mere, a charming hostess, with $21\frac{1}{2}$ acres including the lake. How she does it, I don't know.

But the monarch of the glen was Edwin Herbert, later Lord Tangley, who was kindness itself to us and who let us play on his tennis-court, and asked us to recitals where Gwen, his talented wife, would play the piano. So much could be said about him : alas, he is now dead, and the last time I saw him was when he gallantly came to give evidence to my Committee on Defamation to support a view with which he knew that I was not in sympathy. I saw him to the lift and he confided, 'I'm afraid I wasn't at my best. You know, I had a little stroke last year.' I said that I couldn't believe it, and I was telling the truth. He had been President of the Law Society apart from being chairman of innumerable companies and doing so much work for the Government. He had come up the hard way having as he was wont to boast been born over his father's chemist's shop. A very remarkable man.

As far as I can remember, he only sent me one case, but, by George, what a case ! It came on in 1956 and *The Times* which naturally enough I have always found compulsive reading for the Law Reports apart from the crossword puzzle, headed it : 'Action for bonus by men who had gone on strike.' It was supported by the ETU which was then communist dominated under Mr Foulkes (not to be confused with Faulks). The details are of little importance, but the late Mr D. N. Pritt QC, the Wykehamist who worshipped Stalin – a sea-green incorruptible – was for the ETU, and Willie Wells MP and I had the honour, a very remunerative honour, of being led by Sir Hartley Shawcross QC, the undisputed king of the Bar. It went on for a long time before we won, and an envious old friend said to me one morning as we went up in the train together, 'And how are you getting on with your lawyer's dream?'

I walked with Pritt in Pump Court after the case and said that it had been a good fight. He said, 'Well what could you expect with the judge's conservative background?' The particular judge, Colin Pearson, now retired from the Lords, was the most impartial of men. Poor old Pritt, marvellous advocate and charming man, was just off-net when politics were in question.

In June 1973, Sir Henry Lawson wrote a piece about Edwin which I could not hope to emulate. Although it may be out of place in what is intended to be essentially a light-hearted book, I reproduce it here with his consent:

Edwin Lord Tangley of Blackheath
Chairman of the Industrial and General Trust Limited 1957–1972.

The passing of a great man always leaves a sense of desolation, but in the case of Edwin Tangley the occasion should be one of thanksgiving for he had given all that was in him to give and perhaps even more.

I still see him in my mind's eye rising at 4.30 a.m. on three mornings a week, sitting in his dressing gown with perhaps a pot of black coffee at his side, working not for aggrandisement or reward, but for us the men and women of contemporary society. He, himself, would have regarded his continuous intensity of labour not as an effort, but as using his versatile and extraordinary talents over innumerable fields merely in discharge of a duty or the performance of an obligation to his day and generation. In any company, to adopt Milton's words, he could have kindled an undazzled eye at the mid noon-day beam.

Few possibly in the City knew of the spiritual depth of his faith and source of spirit from which throughout his life flowed standards of conduct impeccable and of a quality an example to us all. He gave of himself to the limit of endurance; that for him was the purpose, meaning, and fulfilment of life.

Each year he withdrew for refurbishment of soul and spirit to the seas or to his beloved mountains because there enfolded amidst the magic stillness and silence of the hills and the mystery and power of encompassing nature, he found himself close to the eternal.

Some of us remember the exquisitely beautiful lines of Keats in his 'To Sleep', which Edwin may sometimes in moments of contemplation have just whispered to himself:
'O soft embalmer of the still midnight. . . .
Turn the key deftly in the oiled wards
And seal the hushed casket of my soul'.

There we leave him at rest in peace, our hearts full of gratitude for a life of splendour in its vision, service and accomplishment.

When we were at Pembroke Gardens we had, thanks to the Prudential, a tiny garage which on my departure I bequeathed to

Irene Scharrer, the pianist, who has by now, I imagine, joined the great majority. In Blackheath, we had a double garage but only one car which was a bore. I had got rid of the 1934 Humber, which had cost £350 in 1946 and for which Golly's Garage in the Earl's Court Road generously gave me £15, and bought a Jowett Javelin which was fun, although tiny.

Finally we persuaded Papa to buy a very very old Austin Ten called HVU 25 which indicated its age and we were able to go to and from the station without being dependent on lifts. By the time we went to June Farm, just south of Reigate Heath, I had my first Ford Zephyr and it and the Austin were the first incumbents.

June Farm was a marvellous house and I spent $16\frac{1}{2}$ years there. I have not the talent to describe it. I think, and I have lost the book, Sir Nikolaus Pevsner, when dealing with Surrey, says, 'Long, low, and comfortable, so heavily restored that it might be by Lutyens, this is a courtyard house'. When he went on to describe my brother-in-law's house not far away as having some of the finest pargetting south of the Thames we were delighted although we only had a vague idea as to what pargetting was.

CHAPTER ELEVEN

Litigation and Libel

Messrs Crane and Hawkins who had instructed me for *Newsweek* in the Eldon Griffiths case sent me another fascinating matter where I appeared for a Mr Dodge, a millionaire scion of the American motor car family. He had been persuaded to buy an old master, a Lawrence or a Romney, I forget which, for a lot of money, and it was a fake. Meanwhile, his cheque had been swiftly passed along the line until it came to rest with a fourth party who claimed to be a holder in due course and to know nothing of the terrible things that had preceded his innocent receipt of the cheque. The villain who was represented by Dick Levy KC, a marvellous performer who, like Sergeant Sullivan KC (who led me twice before the war), always seemed to be on the wrong side, wasn't worth powder and shot and the idea was to catch the 'holder in due course'. Arthian Davies KC (later Lord Justice Davies), who led me, managed in the end to catch him, owing largely to our solicitor who would come forward with some superb new piece of ammunition every time that we looked like being stumped. But the highlight of the case was during Mr Dodge's cross-examination. Lord Hailsham was giving him a fairly rough time on behalf of the holder in due course and Mr Dodge, almost in tears, turned to Lord Goddard, who was trying the case, to ask for protection.

This he received and the Judge said, 'Mr Dodge, may I give you a piece of advice?'

'Oh! yes, my Lord.'

'Have a non-alcoholic breakfast tomorrow. I shall rise now,' and with that he swept out of Court.

The Plaintiff was a new man in the morning.

The Board of Trade cases were remunerative but on the whole strictly for lawyers with very little general interest. In 1952, I had to prosecute the Rank Organisation for not showing the appropriate quota of British films in supporting programmes. The defence in effect admitted that 15.4 per cent had been shown instead of the 24 per cent recommended, and hinted that the British supporting films were not worth showing.

My recollection is that there was a conviction with a comparatively small fine, and the matter was by no means newsworthy. But the Defendants made it so. First, they briefed the acknowledged leader of the Bar, Sir Hartley Shawcross, and second the great man himself, later Lord Rank, went into the witness box, and third, he left his deaf-aid behind and was too proud to admit it. So that this distinguished charitable and religious man was not at his best in cross-examination. He became cross with me and said, 'If you want to buy the Gaumont, Haymarket to-morrow, you can have it. I am stuck with it.' He agreed that if the Gaumont had shown three more second feature films instead of three American, he could have complied with the quota with 200,000 feet of film to spare, and he agreed that in the relevant year the organisation had made a profit of £5,147,805. He said, however, that there was a loss on box office takings, although he had made a profit on the sale of ice-cream of £1,151,000. All this seemed somewhat strange, but when I cross-examined him about operatic films which had become popular – I think that this was the Deanna Durbin period – the answers became stranger. The demand for such films was not growing much he said, although he agreed that Mario Lanza's *The Great Caruso* had been a big box office success.

At this time Beniamino Gigli, who was sixty-two, was still in the first flight of operatic tenors, had been singing at La Scala since 1918, had made three films and as the *Daily Express* said next day 'his fame has swept the world', largely because of the gramophone records which he had made.

I cannot remember why I asked the question, but I said, 'Mr Rank, is not Signor Gigli the best known of the operatic tenors?'

'I don't know anything about him.'

'Have you heard of a man called Gigli?'

'No.'

Even Sir Laurence Dunne could not resist saying, 'He's a gentleman with a good voice.'

It may have been the lack of a deaf-aid but it looked as though this was a strange chairman of a chain of 541 cinemas, and the newspapers lost no time in announcing that Gigli had never heard of Mr Rank.

I made quite a lot of money round about 1950. The prospectus case where the jury wanted to hear no more on the Monday morning was remunerative, as was the 'pottery case'. I found myself sitting next to the late F. G. Miles, the principal defendant in the prospectus case at a Private Guest Night in the Inner Temple some years ago. I asked him if he remembered my prosecuting him and he said, 'Indeed I do', and we got along together like a house on fire. He was excellent company, and it was a very stupid question of mine. Such a man, who was not only highly intelligent and successful but had probably only been prosecuted once in his life for anything serious, would be much more likely to remember the case than Faulks who had done hundreds of these things.

The pottery case is of no interest except to students of the law of public mischief, the existence of which appears now to be in doubt. After twenty days before the first judge to try it, someone said that a juror had been on the top deck of the same bus as one of the witnesses or some rubbish of that kind. But that was good enough for the judge who could see that, with fourteen defendants, summing-up was going to be a very tricky business. He discharged the jury 'so that justice should be seen to be done'.

We had to start all over again. Doggie Goddard overtook me in the Temple and said, 'Didn't think much of that, Forks, I'm going to send you a proper judge this time, Glyn-Jones.'

What had happened was that Glyn, who I know won't mind my telling this story, had become the leader, through seniority, of the Welsh Circuit, but wasn't particularly busy. He had gone to war like a good man and, as he was too old to fight, had taken a job in the Judge Advocate's Department. He became Recorder of Cardiff, but he didn't get into the London work, which is what really matters, although he led me quite brilliantly in a medical negligence action which we would have won if my solicitor had listened to my advice to take the evidence of the principal witness before an examiner before the trial came on, because of her state of health. But no; he was busy with his conveyancing, and what have you, and the woman died, and all Glyn's Celtic fire could not get us a verdict from the jury.

So when Lord Goddard set out on a peregrination round the Welsh circuit in the course of duty as Lord Chief Justice, there came a day when the Circuit gave him a dinner, and of course the leader had to propose his health, and the leader was a very able and amusing man who had fortunately time on his hands to prepare the speech. And what a speech!

In 1963, at the Swansea Judges' Lodgings where I, as fourth judge, was occupying the maid's bedroom with an iron bedstead and performing my ablutions in the maids' bathroom at the top of the servants' staircase, I twitted him with the circumstances of his promotion, and, standing there before the drawing-room fireplace, he recited me the speech. Not bad. He was fifty-seven at the time of his appointment which followed shortly after the great speech, he had been on the bench for a month when he tried the pottery case. The content of the speech I have forgotten save that it was very entertaining and principally devoted to the various religious attitudes of the other leaders on the Circuit.

The second trial of the pottery case lasted 41 days and the prosecution called 150 witnesses. I was led by Eric Sachs QC, now retired as ex-Lord Justice Sachs, who really made a meal of it. There were all these defendants, two of whom were companies, and it was important to show the manner in which these vast quantities of brand new but allegedly 'reject' tea sets were exported contrary to the regulations. He took the view, rightly I think, that the only way to explain this to the jury was to use a blackboard showing diagrammatically how each defendant was involved and the journey of the materials. When he did it at the Magistrates' court, it took a very long time, and I was lost in admiration. When he did it at the Old Bailey again in exactly the same words, I was quite entertained for it was as predictable as Beethoven sometimes is. When he did it for the third time, after the Jungle Judge had discharged the jury, before Glyn-Jones, I could have written *déja vu* all over the blackboard. I had a certain amount of fun however because Eric was unwell for a week or so during the trial, and I was able to take charge. It is very boring sitting behind a leader, however eminent, and taking notes.

Glyn did it marvellously, and after giving a general summing up, he then proceeded to try all these characters separately in that he summed up the evidence against each man individually against the background of the general summing up, and took individual verdicts one after the other. It was brilliant.

There were lots of appeals, but Lord Goddard in the CCA as it was then called, said, 'The Court can see no objection in law to the course which the Judge took. It was no doubt unusual but so was the case.' And later his Lordship expressed the appreciation of the Court for the way in which Mr Justice Glyn-Jones dealt with a case of extraordinary length and complexity.

Not bad for a start. He did his fifteen years and retired on the dot, which is what I propose to do, if I last that long.

People used to apologise to my clients sometimes although by now I was mostly at the receiving end having more or less got the *Daily*

Mirror although it was not for many years that there was any question of a retainer from them. I apologised to Lester Piggott while he was still a minor, and in 1955 appeared in the Patino libel action, in which the millionaire Plaintiff employed Messrs Gordon Dadds & Co. and went to the rival chambers, instructing for a change, not Mr Helenus Milmo, but the Hon T. G. Roche who did not specialise in libel but had the largest all round common law practice at the junior bar. As he is a bachelor, I suppose he didn't mind – indeed he was extremely proud of – taking away a great suitcase full of briefs to work on over the weekend and over every weekend. It wouldn't have amused me. However, Sir William Charles Crocker who then did some of the *Mirror's* work told Mr Parsons his very distinguished-looking managing clerk to let me be the junior for the newspaper. Old Gilbert Beyfus was back into the public eye, and appeared for Mr Patino. The newspaper gave me George Baker, whom we have met in Caserta and walking across the Strand, to lead me. He had only just taken silk and libel was not his speciality. He did very well in disastrous circumstances for which I feel that I was at least in part responsible.

To begin with, the article was undeniably offensive, and I could not plead that the words were true. Mr Roche said in the statement of claim that the words meant that Mr Patino had insisted on his son-in-law being present when his grandchild was born, and promised him seventeen gold mines if he would agree to be present and had shown himself by his conduct to be an uncivilised person lacking in proper feelings of decency and propriety. A quite modest precis of what had been said. All I could do was to plead that the words didn't mean that. I suppose we paid a lot of money into Court, but that it was not enough for the outraged millionaire.

The only card we had to play was the argument that surely there was nothing strange in asking your son-in-law to be present when his child was born, and Sir William's lieutenants dug up a copy of *The Times* for 11th May 1907 which showed that King Alfonso of Spain, whose niece was the Plaintiff's wife, had been present at the birth of the royal baby. This was waved at Mr Patino who merely replied, 'It is the way it is said. Every man is entitled to be with his wife at the birth of a baby, but the way it is said makes one look ridiculous. I never asked my son-in-law to be present.'

Q. 'You say there is nothing wrong in a father being present at the birth of a child?'

A. 'No.'

Q.   'Does it make a difference that the word 'assist' is used?'
A.   'No.'
Q.   'What words do you complain about?'
A.   'You said that I insisted upon him being present and gave him seventeen beautiful gold mines.'

After that there was little to cross-examine about. The son-in-law whom he had described as 'a prince of the highest birth' gave corroborative evidence. We called no evidence and it was a case of 'how much?' and we settled down to listen to Gilbert's final speech. That is where I let my leader down. As the alleged expert in this type of litigation, I ought to have warned him that putting in that copy of *The Times* was the same, in those days, as calling evidence, and that he had thereby lost the last word.

Imagine the consternation on our faces when the old man sat still and said, 'Your turn. You put in the newspaper,' and I had to whisper, 'That's right.' My leader did remarkably well, caught off guard, with a hostile judge, and, although we did not know how hostile, a hostile jury. He pointed out that there was no evidence that this article had ever reached France where Mr Patino lived, Bolivia of which state he was a citizen, or the United States where he had lived for a while. They were a British jury, he added, and they had to consider the position in respect of the British Isles.

Good stuff, but the old man banged away about journalism which was a disgrace to the British press and how the only way to prevent the repetition of such a thing was by imposing such a deterrent as to show that it was just not worth while. And the learned judge, summing up correctly and with infinite fairness, could do nothing to bank down the fires which were burning in the jury's minds.

Twenty-five thousand pounds damages (free of tax to the millionaire). At current rates of inflation I wonder what that would be worth!

The largest fine I ever got in thirteen years of prosecuting at the Old Bailey was £27,500, with £1,050 costs. The defendants (father had fled to America or Israel, as usual, and we only caught the son) had hired all the available forensic talent, Sir Valentine Holmes for the company and Mr G. O. Slade KC for the son, and they said that father had had all the ill-gotten gains. £25,000 of the fine was imposed on the Company and £2,500 on the son who was to remain in custody until it was paid. Gerald, who appeared for him, said that that would be paid that day.

I was continually complaining that the fines imposed at the Old

Bailey were so small that it was clear that crime paid, even if you were caught, which was unusual.

Compare these facts with £25,000 for Mr Patino, £40,000 for Lord Keyes, and £217,000 or whatever it was for Mr Lewis and Rubber Improvement Ltd. against the *Mail* and the *Telegraph*. The tariff is altogether different. It is because an experienced judge imposes the fine in crime while an inexperienced jury puts its hands in other people's pockets in defamation.

I remember prosecuting a very well known company indeed for conspiring with another to contravene some order or other, before Mr Justice Parker, later Lord Chief Justice. Fifteen hundred dishonest and illegal agreements had been entered into. The companies pleaded 'Not Guilty' but were found guilty. The Judge said, 'This is a particularly bad case disclosing conspiracy amounting to barefaced contravention of the order, and I take a serious view of it.' Fine : £5,000 and £150 costs each. Peanuts! Even so it was a lot for those days and I said to Leslie Boyd, then the Clerk to the Central Criminal Court, 'I say, that was more than I had anticipated.'

'Well, what can you expect; the poor fellow's been down here for four weeks, and this is the first conviction he's had.'

Dear old Gilbert was like most of us, a better performer when he was for the Plaintiff in an easy case like Patino, than in a not-so-easy case such as Liberace, whom we shall meet later in my reminiscences, in a second volume. Although I never regretted having introduced Gilbert to the newspapers, I found him to be an incurable optimist when he defended, and to have an old-fashioned *idée fixe* about the value of the last word with the jury. That was why he was so pleased with his little piece of erudition in Patino, although I doubt if it made much difference.

I can think of two cases where this optimism caused us to come unstuck. One was where all we had done was to publish something inaccurate which the Press Association (the PA) had sent us. There were two witnesses from the PA – honest, respectable people whom the jury would have believed, and whose testimony would certainly have cut down the damages. But no. 'No, no Neville, (not Nanette!) we shan't call them. We want the last word with the jury.' We had a splendid summing up from Mr Justice Ashworth who said in effect that any sensible man would not consider the words in their context to be defamatory. And the famous last word landed us with £1,500 damages and costs. A lucky plaintiff, I thought.

The other case was where the then or ex-British Heavyweight boxing champion, Mr Don Cockell, who had been beaten in the second round of an important contest, was referred to on the front page of my newspaper as a 'fat and horizontal layabout'. The leader went on to say that he had not taken the trouble to train as he should, and that he was grossly overpaid for not doing his job properly. A writ was issued and all that we had was a photograph which made the Plaintiff look obese. I didn't think that that would do, and I think that if it had been left to me the solicitors, who normally took my advice, would have settled it. But Gilbert said that we must fight. Meanwhile, I kept Ian Percival (now the distinguished MP for Southport), as he will remember, on his toes, as we waltzed round the Bear Garden from Master to Judge in chambers and back again. But he didn't give in, although he had some costs against him, and eventually the case came on.

Cockell called Henry Cooper and his brother to say that he had trained incessantly, Lord Goddard called them 'Castor and Pollux' which may or may not have meant anything to them (he ought to have done the job properly and called them 'the Dioskouri' which Jo Stephenson and Bazil Wingate-Saul, had they been in court, would have understood), and said that they were 'two of the finest young men I have seen in the box for some time'. We called the late Len Harvey, former British Heavyweight champion, Harry Carpenter, who is now a great TV pundit on Wimbledon, and poor George Murray, who had based his leader on Carpenter's article, and who was the nicest man you could possibly meet. All to no avail. The Lord Chief Justice whipped up the damages, and half an hour later the jury gave Mr Cockell £7,500.

Perhaps Patino's case did not show the press at its best. But I have absolutely no complaint of them. They have been uniformly kind to me over the years. I have never been addicted to the carefully considered word and have often strayed when seeking for the mot juste, only to end in an indiscretion. This applied much more when I was a Judge than when I was at the Bar, but throughout they have protected me, glossed over my more idiotic remarks and have refrained from destroying my image, if I had one. Except once. But that comes in the next volume.

One, and it is the only one that comes to mind, example of lamentable taste was the publication in *Picture Post*, which I had thought to be a very good periodical and to which I subscribed, of an article about the 'Monkey Club' as it was popularly known and which may well continue to exist. It was a finishing school in Pont Street to which parents sent their little darling after she had finished her schooling in this country instead of sending her to Madame whoever-it-might-be, (they change so often in fashion, and I mention no names), in Paris.

Two elderly maiden ladies were ushered into my room, full of righteous indignation, determined to have their reputations vindicated, but adamant that they would not sully their hands with one pennyworth of damages from what, I am afraid, they called the 'gutter press'.

I had every sympathy with them, but when I read the article complained of, it was so awful that it was hard to restrain a smile. My clients were really tremendously respectable, Miss Marion Ellison and Miss (I think she was the Honourable Miss, being Lord Brentford's daughter) Helen Grizelda Joynson-Hicks, and I know that when I was a boy a lot of girls I knew had gone to this establishment, to do which was considered to be one of the done things. I need not repeat the article, but I will repeat what I said, and it was to Mr Justice Hilbery, known as 'Sir Malcolm' which made it hilarious :

'The Plaintiffs are the proprietresses of the Club of the Three Wise Monkeys, the well-known educational establishment at Pont Street, Knightsbridge.

'In the issue of the *Picture Post* for March 14th last the defendants published an offensive article entitled "How to grow up gracefully", relating to the Plaintiff's establishment.

'As to one photograph accompanying the article, P.T. was not taught at the Monkey Club, the young woman in the "very unusual" position had no connection with it, and instructresses at the Club were not permitted to smoke while giving instruction.

'The picture of the young girl in a bar full of bottles of alcohol over the heading "Final Exams; How to pass out at a party" was not taken at the Club.

'A suggestion that girls were taught to smoke at the age of sixteen was remote from the truth as in fact they were discouraged from smoking before the age of eighteen.

'Finally, particular offence had been given by the suggestion that the most important part of the curriculum was how to attract the right type of nice young man, and by the further suggestion that pupils were taught to "throw a cocktail party" at the age of sixteen.'

I added that the newspaper had apologised, undertaken to indemnify the ladies as to their costs, while the Plaintiffs had adopted a dignified attitude and had made no demands for damages. The defendants had published an apology in the current issue under the heading 'Readers Letters'.

And then the old ladies had their moment; for Sir Malcolm intervened, looking down his nose, 'Is that regarded by your clients as a sufficient apology?' They were delighted, and all was forgiven and forgotten.

It isn't everyone who is so easily pleased. One day I had Field Marshal Lord Alanbrooke and Sir Arthur Bryant about whom Lord Beaverbrook's newspaper had been beastly. They were quite properly incensed. Mr Helenus Milmo, I need hardly say, apologised.

The nature of the libel, about *The Turn of the Tide* which was written by Sir Arthur based on the war diaries of Lord Alanbrooke, doesn't matter. What amused me was that Lord Alanbrooke was adamant that he would not demean himself by touching a penny from Lord Beaverbrook, whereas Sir Arthur, with whom I sympathised, took, possibly not having a pension, a more realistic point of view, and concurred reluctantly.

I never dreamed that I could ever take silk. I was no longer young and I had a wife and three children. Silk was, in London, for people with independent means or for bachelors. Bachelors of course are in an extremely strong position and the number of bachelor judges we have had in my time is quite astonishing. Looking at it from the outside you would be tempted to say that a bachelor is not a suitable man to be appointed to deal with sexual offences, certainly not to be a judge in the Family Division; and one might think that a married man without children was scarcely the man for custody cases. But it is not so : a bad judge is a bad judge, and a good judge is a good judge, regardless of these matters. The late Mr Justice Finnemore was a bachelor who knew very little about the world but was a wonderful judge in civil, crime and divorce.

And I greatly doubt if I should ever have applied for silk had I not had four or five cases all of which gave me some publicity. It never for a moment occurred to me that one day the Lord Chancellor might send for me to tell me that he intended to recommend me for a judgeship. This came a long time later on, and by then I had got so above myself that, unless commonsense had prevailed – and Bridget was absolutely against it – I would have turned it down.

To continue to anticipate – when I thought for applying for silk at the mature age of fifty-one, I told Edward Love, my ex-clerk, to whom I owe so much, and he charmingly said, 'Don't be so bloody silly. You're much too old.'

It wasn't all libel and crime. Messrs Capel-Cure, Glyn Barton and Co. began to drop out but by now I had a certain amount of general common law work and divorce to take their place and make the third part of my practice. I was beginning to think it beneath me to go into County Courts and when I was invited to go to the Watford County Court in September 1956, I only went because I was instructed on behalf of a doctor by Messrs Hempsons, the solicitors for the Medical Defence Association, who had a great deal of medical negligence work which was both interesting and remunerative but which I never managed to get. I think somehow that my brother Cumming-Bruce – may his shadow never grow less – got in first.

I was to deal with the case of a doctor who had arrived back at the hostel where the conditions of his employment obliged him to live, only to find that his personal belongings had been stolen. So he sued the Hospital Management Committee, saying that they ought to have taken care of his bedroom, his personal clothes and effects and keys to the door and so forth. I'd looked up the law and saw that Lord Justice Du Parcq had made some remarks about ten years before which weren't very helpful to my theme, but I thought that we might side-step them on the facts. When I went into the robing room I found that the local firm of solicitors in Watford had briefed a charming character with a moustache whom I had never seen before in my life and of whom I felt satisfied that I could make mincemeat. But not at all. He made mincemeat of me, and, although I poured out the charm in all directions, the Judge, who looked like a basset-hound, was absolutely on the ball, and down I went. Off to the Court of Appeal with the same result and leave to appeal to the House of Lords refused.

The Times headed its report 'Master not liable for theft of servant's goods : hospital not liable to house-physician'. Of course, if you put it like that, perhaps we were wrong, after all. My opponent is now the Lord Chief Justice of England.

The crime rolled on, and the Board of Trade, under Morland Parsey, prepared their cases so well that everyone seemed to be convicted. We had 'Deals in Roller bearings; Despatch behind Iron Curtain alleged', '£50,000 Vanished Export Nylons Story', and a villain called Owen whose case very remuneratively went to the House of Lords on a technicality. Then there was a gentleman known to schoolboys at Eton College as 'Rosie'. His stamp frauds which involved all sorts of titled and distinguished people who looked pretty silly in the witness box netted £250,000 in four years. He went to prison for six years, knowing that £135,000 had not been traced. Whilst he was a clever villain, I did not care for him. If he is alive he will only be seventy-one, and I dare say he has turned over a new leaf. I do hope that with a lot of money to hand when he came out, he hasn't started on the game again.

While I was a junior, I was involved in the case where the chairman of Whitehead Industrial Trust and a number of other persons were charged with having taken part in share-pushing transactions. Mr Whitehead and a number of others were acquitted. So was my client, for I was defending this time which was unusual for me.

I got him off simply and solely through the fact that my man who was a reporter on one of Lord Rothermere's newspapers was represented by Mr Philip Kimber, a solicitor to whom Dennis Walsh trusted the defence. He was good enough to let me get my toe into some of the ETU litigation years afterwards.

P. R. Kimber, knowing that it was the law that there is no property in a witness, went and interviewed the very nice secretary and director of the particular gold field company and got a signed statement from him. I was able to sit up late during the weekend preparing a cross-examination where I knew the answers and even preparing an alternative assault if the wrong answer were given (as Sir Leslie Scott was always said to do).

The cross-examination sounded much better than it really was and I enjoyed every moment of it enormously.

I do not propose to say much more about the Old Bailey. I made a lot of friends there and I am sad never to have been there officially as a judge.

CHAPTER TWELVE

Miss Honor Tracy and The Sunday Times

Miss Honor Tracy is a very determined lady who will not be put upon. She had a good war and afterwards found herself covering the Korean war as a special correspondent for *The Observer*. This involved a lot of flying and other tiring activities which she took in her stride. In those years, she spent a period in Japan and wrote *Kakemono* which is in some ways the best of all her books. Christmas Humphreys was the senior junior prosecuting counsel at the trial of the Japanese war criminals and one day, as we travelled together in the train towards Grimsby where we were to occupy ourselves gainfully in the defence of various gentlemen or companies who were being prosecuted for publishing pornographic picture postcards – the jury I seem to remember, loved it, and everybody was acquitted – he referred to *Kakemono* and said, 'Once she had said that, there was nothing left to say.' I think that possibly he had contemplated painting a literary picture of Japan at that time.

Then she published a deliciously witty book about Ireland and the Irish called *Mind you, I said nothing*. I had read and enjoyed that before she came to me as a client. She is a Roman Catholic with a very marked sense of humour, who was accustomed to move in the circles of the Protestant ascendancy, and the book was a tender and graceful leg-pull of Eire and the Church. It was not meant to be taken seriously and, when eventually Gilbert Paull QC came to cross-examine her rather heavily about it, she scored very fast all round the wicket.

She became the correspondent on Irish affairs for *The Sunday Times* whom she eventually sued. A brave thing to do, for if a journalist sues a newspaper, it is reasonable to expect Fleet Street to become closed thereafter. Indeed, as far as I know, she only writes in English newspapers today for *The Daily* and *Sunday Telegraph*. And very amusingly too. Fortunately, after the case, she has written a number of successful books of two kinds, travel and fiction – the fiction being the more successful in the United States and the travel in this country. And she received the accolade of having a quotation from her novel *The Straight and Narrow Path* in the preface to *Present at the Creation* the autobiography of somebody really important, the late Dean Acheson, Secretary of State to President Truman.

The passage in *The Sunday Times* which caused all the disturbance was about an article which she had written called 'Great Days in the Village'. It was the fourth article she had written for the newspaper.

She had gone to stay with a friend at the village of Doneraile in the South, which had a population of 700, the parish including 2,700 souls, and found that the principal topic of conversation was the great new house going up for Canon X, the parish priest. The money came from parishioners of the class of agricultural labourer and their average wage was £3 to £4 per week. For the most part they lived in cottages without light, water or sewage. They had already subscribed £7,000 for the building of a new church at Shanballymore, a hamlet of eighty souls. Miss Tracy did not complain of that, as to subscribe £7,000 to the glory of God for a church, is one thing, but to subscribe £7,000 for a house for the canon to live in was another. £1,000 of this sum had been lent to the congregation by the Bishop of Cloyne at 1% or 2% interest. She took the view, rightly or wrongly, that a parish priest ought to live in a similar style to that of his parishioners rather than as the local aristocrat of whom his parishioners were expected to be proud. The canon depended for his livelihood upon 'dues' collected in this particular parish four times yearly. Just before the article was written there had been a fifth collection solely for the house. And there were jumble sales, concerts and raffles to raise the money for the house and the furniture and to stock the garden.

She saw that here was the raw material for an entertaining article which she wrote and *The Sunday Times* published, and which naturally included some of the comments made to her, behind the hand, when the villagers knew that they could not be overheard. I will not set it out *in extenso* here for some of it will emerge from the evidence, but it was a riot of fun enjoyed by all except the Canon who, despite that the village was not named in the article, knew that his parishioners recognised him.

Miss Tracy was told that the Canon had been given leave in December 1950 to serve a writ, on *The Sunday Times* and on her, out of the jurisdiction. She telephoned the newspaper and was told that if a writ was served on her, they would defend themselves and her. (This was of course long before Lord Thomson took over *The Sunday Times*.)

This satisfied her, although she had naturally expected to hear such an answer, which was in accordance with the great tradition of newspapers to stand up for their reporters and correspondents. She wasn't out of the jurisdiction, and she went off to Kerry, was not served with any writ, and concluded that the Canon had got cold feet and dropped the matter.

As well he might, she thought. After all there was a beautiful old fourteen-roomed Georgian house which had been good enough for his predecessors, and here was he getting the parishioners to pay for a new house with a view. It was only later that she learned that the reason for the new residence was apparently that the fourteen-roomed house was required for two curates, who by an immemorial custom of diocesan discipline should live separately from the parish priest.

Her conclusion was wrong. While she was sitting quietly in Kerry without a care, the newspaper had accepted service of the writ on her behalf, the Canon was asking for £5,000 damages, and negotiations for settling the matter were in progress. She wasn't consulted about this, any more than the Canon's parishioners had been consulted before it was decided to build the house with a view. The newspaper, perhaps understandably, wanted to get out of the impasse as cheaply as they could. And impasse it was; they were advised by senior counsel in Ireland that with a Catholic jury and a Catholic Canon, they would have no hope of succeeding. Counsel didn't find it necessary to inquire of Miss Tracy whether or not she could prove the article to be true.

So they wrote a letter to the Canon's solicitors, apologising for the article and saying that any imputations on the Canon in it were wholly unfounded; and without any authority from Honor Tracy, they actually filed a defence on her behalf admitting liability, apologising, and paying money into Court by way of amends.

Miss Tracy found this out and was enraged. Many journalists in her position would have accepted this as an occupational hazard, and have been glad not to have to pay anything. But she was made of sterner stuff and, satisfied that what she had written was correct, she complained.

She then received the most astonishing letter from the editor, a gentleman of great distinction, who is very much alive and whose name, accordingly, I shall not mention. After saying that there was no question of any personal apology from her, it continued that it was 'not a matter of the justice of our cause but of the probable views of the jury' which made him take the course he had taken. That wasn't good enough and she instructed solicitors to fight the action, if necessary alone, stating that she wasn't associated with the apology, and didn't admit that any of the article was untrue or defamatory.

But the newspaper and the Canon knew a trick worth two of that, agreed to Miss Tracy's name being struck out as a defendant, and announced a settlement in the High Court in Dublin, again without consulting her.

The newspaper got away with paying £750 to a charity nominated by the Canon, and also published in *The Sunday Times*, for all the world to see and to read, an apology admitting that the article constituted an unjustifiable attack on the character and position of the Canon.

It was a very angry lady who came to see me about that.

We agreed that the letter and the apology both meant that she was an irresponsible journalist prepared to write articles recklessly, not caring whether they were true or not, and was a person whom no newspaper or broadcasting corporation should employ, and we further agreed that, ideally, Lord Kemsley and his minions ought to pay. We also agreed that there wasn't a dog's chance of getting any of the villagers to testify in her favour, whatever they may have said to her in secret. In short, she would have to take on the newspaper single-handed with some possible support from the lady with whom she had stayed, but who hadn't heard the earthy comments of the peasants. It was risking a lot of money in costs and the result might be disastrous financially.

'True', she said, 'but we press on.'

So I pressed on.

As a practising Catholic she took the view *magna est veritas, et praevalebit*. I was somewhat more cynical, and understood the views, although not the conduct, of the newspaper, with regard to the probable outcome of the case in Dublin.

However, in England where *The Sunday Times* principally circulates, we should have an impartial jury in due course.

The newspaper seemed to have changed its mind about the 'justice of our cause' and pleaded in their defence that, yes, they had written the letter and printed the apology, and, by George, what they had said was true in substance and in fact.

So battle was joined. I began to worry. The newspaper obtained an order for the evidence of their two principal witnesses, the Canon and the Bishop of Cloyne, to be taken in Ireland, as, being eighty-two and eighty-four respectively, they could not be expected to come to London for the trial.

I couldn't very well resist that – but the expense! We had to have an Irish solicitor, and the English solicitor came along too. We had a distinguished Queen's Counsel to act as examiner, and the Hon. T. G.

Roche, who was against me, was not exactly cheap. What on earth was going to happen if we lost this fascinating case? It was no business of mine what private means Miss Tracy had; all I knew was that her brother-in-law was an Ambassador; but that didn't necessarily mean anything, and I was worried.

We flew to Dublin, and I was driven down through Ireland, and arrived at Limerick for the night where I discussed some splendid bottles of Pommard with my client, the Irish solicitor, and a great literary figure called Sean O'Failoin (whose name I may have spelt wrongly as I only remember how to pronounce it). We didn't discuss the case at all, which was very civilised of them. Next day to Mallow, where the examination was to take place, and where rooms had been booked in an hotel which was comfortable, although there was a great deal of ringing of bells.

Up in the morning and everyone except Roche and myself appeared to have gone to Mass. Roche was a bit touchy about the fact that the Bishop of Cloyne was Dr James Joseph Roche, and pointed out that he himself was not of Irish extraction. I, of course, accepted that. As if it mattered!

The Canon turned out to be a dear old gentleman and it may have been just as well that the jury didn't see him. He had won the DSO in the First World War which would have counted a lot with me, albeit illogically, (indeed the Plaintiff in cross-examination said that she couldn't see what his record had to do with the building of the house – which was right) and he genuinely thought that there was nothing wrong in putting up the 'dues' and extracting the money from the poor for his new house. He said with apparent sincerity that he knew from personal experience that money was plentiful among the poorer people and that the dues were not beyond their ability to pay. Even when I mentioned a parishioner – oddly enough named Roche – who gave £3 a year when earning £3 to £4 weekly and keeping a wife and four children, he said blandly that it was rather a lot, but that he had not asked that person to pay that amount.

Desultory cross-examination for half a day, and I had not got much further.

Then, just before I finished, I said, expecting once more a straight bat pushing the ball slowly down the wicket towards the bowler,

Q. Would it not have been desirable to consult your parishioners, who were going to have to pay, about the building of the house?

A.   Ordinary people know very little about building or designing houses.

Q.   But it was their money.

A.   Yes, but you could not depend on labouring men to tell you exactly what style of house to build – not half-educated men.

Q.   Are most of your parishioners half-educated?

A.   Barely able to read or write.

Q.   What percentage are half-educated?

A.   Ninety-eight per cent are able to read and write, but they could not do much more.

I thought that an English jury might think that the Canon had let the cat out of the bag.

Then we had the large, aged, dignified and very formidable Bishop whom no one could have believed to have been as old as eighty-four. He told us that in his own parish five priests lived side by side, each having his own house (and, presumably, housekeeper; it sounded very expensive for the parishioners), and that he had approved of the fourteen roomed Georgian house being occupied by the two curates, and that the new house was very suitable and of average size, modern without being luxurious. It was desirable, he said, that a priest's house should be approached by parishioners without their being observed by the neighbours.

I had been advised by the Irish solicitor to 'pitch into him' and I 'pitched' as best I could with only moderate effect, for all the things that seemed strange to me, he, like the Canon, thought quite natural. He said that he knew of and approved the practice of reading out the dues with the name of the donor and the amount given, beginning with the largest and ending with the smallest. The object was to express thanks to the people for their contributions, and people rather expected it. He did agree with me that if a man, who had not given as much as was expected of him, had his name read out, he might not like it, but he didn't think the dues would fall much if the practice were to be abandoned. The people contributed their dues very generously as a duty.

When I thought that the fourteen roomed house had been renewed out of parish funds, and that the Canon had increased the dues with the peremptory words, 'Those who now give four shillings, will give five shillings', I found this difficult to swallow, and I continued to 'pitch in'. When I had finished, he rose from the large round table, at which we were all seated (not as large as that in the Canon's house at which there were ten of us and there was plenty of room) and made past me to the

Beirut 1943

The author by Pietro Annigoni – Florence 1944

Romain, Faulks and Peter Wood – Italy 1944

door. There was a scuffing sound behind me and there was my Irish
solicitor ('pitch in') down on his knees, kissing the witness' ring. A very
remarkable people, the Irish !

Eventually the case came on in the High Court before Mr Justice
Glyn-Jones (of 'pottery case' fame) and a jury, Mr Gilbert Paull QC
and Mr Roche for the newspaper.

It was clear to us that all was going to turn on the Plaintiff's evidence
as to the facts, which was going to be uncorroborated, together with
such forensic help as I could give her. So I spent the entire day making
my opening speech to the jury, telling them that the newspaper had
sold my unfortunate client 'down the river' in order to get away with a
payment of £750 to charity, and so forth. You never can tell with a
jury, but they seemed to be listening, and the Judge made occasional
noises which I judged to be sympathetic. I was heartened, too, when I
walked across the road to the Temple to hear Gilbert say, 'My dear
Neville, do you think that you really had to make such a very long
speech about such a very short case ?' I felt like saying, 'Thrice armed is
he that hath his quarrel just, but five times he that gets his blow in first.'
After all, if there was to be no corroboration, the only way to rub it in
was to let the jury hear it all from me, and all over again from the
Plaintiff in the witness box. I'd done my home work, she was obviously
very able, and I felt that she would corroborate me.

She did, and all went magnificently to start with. She was very enter-
taining and gave the sources of the quotations in the article. On 4th May
1950 she had gone to the old fourteen roomed parish priest's house in
Doneraile, and an elderly woman had come up to her and said, 'The
Canon has got a fine new house up the street. Oh Lord, it's the size of a
ship. Oh Lord, you'll never forget it.' She made a note of those words.
Then on Sunday she heard the Canon give a sermon about the Stock
Exchange. The poor parishioners were told 'not to mind the Stock
Exchange and things of that sort, but to lay up for yourselves the un-
speakable joys of Heaven'.

The newspaper's great point was that the house had cost £7,000 and
not £9,000, as was stated in the article. Personally, I thought that one
sum called for comment as much as the other in the circumstances and
the article said, 'price of it all is said to be £9,000, which strikes on their
ear as devoid of real significance as nine million, or the Wealth of Araby'.
She added that she didn't call on the Canon to ask if the villagers'
figure was correct, for if she had done, she would have been thrown
out.

When I asked her about the passage which had said that everyone was selling raffle tickets to everyone else and that the winner would hand back the prize as soon as received, she said that that was quite a normal practice, and added that she had been told that the nuns were inclined to be severe, if children went back with the tickets unsold.

Again I asked her about the statement 'the collections multiplied' and 'the Canon's voice, so tired and confused at times, rises clear as the Shandon bells from the steps of the altar as he pricks the faithful on to fresh endeavours'. And she replied, 'During one particular Sunday nine o'clock mass which I attended, there were four collections.'

I wondered if we were in for a *bonne bouche*, so just before I sat down I chanced my arm.

Q.   What other comments did you hear from the villagers about the house?

A.   Well, they said, 'All he's a-needing now is a swimming pool.'

Up got Gilbert Paull and we had what *The Times* called 'Another Apology'. 'On behalf of *The Sunday Times* I wish to apologise to you for the fact that your name was taken in vain in the proceedings.' (Very surprising. They had had years to say that, and had not done so.) He continued by making a point that the Plaintiff (who knew no law) could have brought an action for breach of warranty of authority. The Judge with some ferocity said that she couldn't. I was full of glee, and my opponent changed his tactics.

Q.   Do you think that *The Sunday Times* would have published this article if you had said it was about a true place and the priest in that place?

A.   It was perfectly obvious what the article was about, without any explanation from me. It must have been about a real village and a real priest, because I was employed by *The Sunday Times* to write about real places and people. What else could it have been? A prose poem?

Q.   This is a serious matter. It is the first libel action *The Sunday Times* had had to face for many years.

A.   I told them I was sorry to involve them. But I think that with a little firmness on their part, nothing more would have been heard about it. I know Doneraile and what is going on.

Q.   Why did you not mention the Canon by name?

A.   I was not interested in individual shortcomings. This was something that can be found in almost every county and parish in Ireland. I was discussing an abuse and something that everybody in

Ireland knows is an abuse and is heartily sick of. Do you understand?

Q. You must not ask me questions. Do you want to attack the priests in Ireland?

A. Not all of them.

Q. What about your statement that he wanted a view?

A. He admitted that he wanted a view.

Q. What other reason have you given for the Canon's new house?

A. Well, the noise of the children, the shaggy donkey; he wanted to get out of Main Street, Doneraile and all that went with it.

Q. What about the passage concerning the Canon's voice. What do you say about that?

A. Well, I was present myself and able to contrast his voice when soliciting and when exhorting.

And so on, until the end of what seemed to me to be a perfect day. Next day, undaunted, Gilbert returned to the charge.

Q. Did you hear Mr O'Brien, a solicitor, say that the article was a disgraceful attack on the Canon?

A. I did. But I also heard him say that he knew nothing about the matter.

Q. Did you know that the house has three bedrooms, two reception rooms and a parish room?

A. I should think that would be average. Some of the priests in Ireland live in mansions.

Q. Some of them 'the size of a ship'?

A. Which ship, Mr Paull?

(I thought that a gem, I was glad I didn't have to cross-examine her.)

Q. You say in the article, 'Ah he's a queer old fellow altogether – mind, there's no harm in him'. Has the word queer any sinister meaning in Ireland?

A. Not at all. You have taken it out of its context. In its context in the article it might have been said affectionately.

Then the Judge stepped in. It was splendid.

'Mr Paull, are you seeking to suggest that the word 'queer' was used in the connotation it sometimes has in this country of homosexual?'

Mr Paull: Oh no! no! Only that it would tend to make people think that the Canon was not fit to be a priest.

Miss Tracy: I deny that absolutely.

Later on an amusing passage occurred.

Mr Paull: Is it usual that a newspaper will fight on behalf of its contributors?

His Lordship: Fight, Mr Paull?

Mr Paull: I use the word advisedly, my Lord.

His Lordship: Then the only answer you can have to that question is that they do not seem to have done so in this case.

Mr Paull: I accept that.

The Judge interrupted the cross-examination again later and I thought, and I am sure the jury thought, that his sympathies lay with the Plaintiff. I called a couple of witnesses who didn't say anything very much.

Then my opponent addressed the jury saying that the Plaintiff had 'stabbed the editor in the back' by not mentioning the Canon by name (I am not mentioning him by name, for although he would be one hundred and four, if alive, and was a bachelor, he might have some relatives to whom this recital would not be amusing). Then he freely admitted that the newspaper had no right to join her in the defence in Ireland without her consent, and said that the apology to her was left until the parties were in Court for reasons which he would explain later. (He never did.)

He said that no more serious libel on the Canon could be imagined, and he called the editor of *The Sunday Times* as a witness. I had not expected this, but assumed that he was being called to give some explanation about the delayed apology and about the letter concerning 'the justice of our cause'.

He wasn't asked about either of these matters by my opponent. In fact, all he said was that when he saw the article before publication he thought that it was a vignette of village life based on a patchwork of facts about a village which on the whole was imaginary. (Whatever that may have meant to the jury.) He complained that as it referred to a particular Canon, Miss Tracy ought to have told him so. And that was all.

(The question was whether the newspaper could prove to the satisfaction of the jury that there was no excuse for what Miss Tracy had written. If she had told the truth in the witness box, there were plenty of excuses.)

So there he was, having said nothing which had anything to do with the question which the jury had to try, standing like Aunt Sally in the witness box.

I asked him first why the apology to Miss Tracy was left until the hearing of the action. He said that it was because she appeared to be hostile to the newspaper and likely to bring an action against it. This seemed so unsatisfactory an answer for having failed to apologise for misbehaviour that I judged it wise to leave it there.

I asked : 'Did you employ the Plaintiff to write fiction ?'

He said : 'No.'

Q. Is a vignette of village life fact or fiction ?

A. It is based on fact.

Q. You agree that whether or not the Canon's name was mentioned, people in that part of Ireland would have recognised him ?

A. That is what is said.

Q. You regard this article as 'a stab in the back', as your counsel has described it. Whose back ?

A. The Canon's.

(That surprised me. I was pretty sure counsel had indicated that it was the editor who had suffered this serious attack. But they were only words and it didn't matter.)

Q. But why if everyone would have recognised him ? Did it never occur to you to inquire from her, the writer of the article, whether it was true ?

A. I assumed she believed it to be true. She had told me so at a cocktail party. I have always held that she believed it to be true.

Q. You didn't care whether it was true or not, so long as you got out of it cheaply, did you ?

A. That is not true.

Q. You know enough about the law of defamation to know that in deciding whether a defamatory allegation could be justified, the first duty is to ascertain the facts from which justification can be shown ?

A. Oh ! Yes.

Q. Would you agree with me that the best source from which to elicit whether such facts exist, is from the person whose pen is responsible for the allegation of which complaint is made ?

A. It would be a source.

Q. It would be the best source ?

A. I think not. She would be an interested party.

The Judge chipped in, 'Anyway, it would be a fairly good point to begin.'

Q. But you didn't begin there. Tell me. Did you begin anywhere ?

A. I instructed my legal advisers.

I thought that those answers might be found unsatisfactory by the Jury, and left the point. He then agreed that it was a great tradition of journalism for a newspaper to stand up for its reporters, but, not, although Mr Paull had cross-examined the Plaintiff to the contrary, with the same conclusive effect for their correspondents.

Q.   How did you stand up to that great tradition? You didn't ask her whether what she wrote was true or not, but just handed the papers to the lawyers.

A.   She had told me it was true.

He agreed that the apology was written without Miss Tracy's authority. He agreed that so far as he knew no inquiries were made as to whether the allegations were true. And he said that the letter of apology was written in the belief that it was true.

The Judge, not surprisingly, asked, 'What satisfied you of that?'

A.   'It was the Canon's denial with some detail that satisfied us that the imputations were unfounded.'

He said that it was his case that everything in the article which constituted an attack on the Canon was untrue. He said it was reckless of Miss Tracy to publish a figure of £9,000 which she did not know, but had only been told, to be true. He then agreed that he thought he would get out of the action as cheaply and quickly as possible, having been advised that it was indefensible.

Having had a certain amount of fun about the fact that neither counsel, solicitors, nor he himself had inquired about the facts from the Plaintiff, truth being, after all, a defence, I turned to the famous letter.

'I suppose,' I said, 'that in writing that " it was not a matter of the justice of our cause but of the probable views of the jury that made us take the course we had taken," you were writing something diplomatic, if not strictly true, in order to placate a woman who showed every sign of becoming tiresome?'

That, I thought then and think now, was the explanation, and if he had accepted it he would have admitted something perhaps somewhat discreditable, but the jury would have understood, and I could have made no more play with it. I wasn't laying a trap but was merely trying to get at the truth. He is a very clever man, and I think that he must have credited me with intelligence of his own calibre, and with cunning which is not part of my armoury. There was a pause and the silly fellow said, 'Not at all; I meant exactly what I said.'

Then he really was in a pickle, and I had rather a jolly time urging him to explain how it was that the newspaper and the Plaintiff together had a just cause against the Canon, while at the same time her attack on the Canon was inexcusable.

I had a good dinner at home at June Farm and went to sleep soundly and happily.

The fourth day was taken up with reading to the jury the evidence by the Canon in Ireland. It had all been taken down in shorthand and transcribed at heaven knows what expense. We could not afford to have a transcript of the evidence, but when it came to the cross-examination of the Canon, Gilbert very kindly lent me a copy so that I could read it to the jury extempore.

The Judge kept his hand in satisfactorily.

Judge : Is there an explanation for the suggestion in the evidence that some collections are more voluntary than others? Your witness is drawing a distinction between contributions called 'dues', which seem to suggest some sense of obligation, and contributions to the parish fund, which are voluntary in the true sense of the word?

Mr. Roche : I think that is correct. Dues are paid four times a year. Each person fixes an amount for himself and pays it in Church at Christmas and Easter and the amounts are read out in church.

His Lordship : So the reading out in public would perhaps constitute a little element of coercion or sanction, since the priest at least would know the amount of the dues; but there would be no knowledge by anyone of what was put in the collection : it might even be a trouser button?

Mr Roche : Yes.

Later when I was reading, the Judge interrupted to emphasise that the cost of the house was £7,000.

And again, when we read that the Canon objected not to Miss Tracy's saying that the dues had been increased but that they had been multiplied, the Judge interrupted, I thought, scornfully : 'The difference between addition and multiplication.'

I slept well that night.

Next day, however, the wind changed. The Bishop's evidence was read with no interruptions from the Bench. My cross-examination was received without comment, and Gilbert was permitted to submit that in the context of 'they admit that the imputations constituted an unjustifiable attack' the word 'unjustifiable' meant 'that which cannot be justified in a Court of law'.

That struck me as nonsensical, but the Judge did not comment, and I began to feel cold shivers down my back.

I merely said that a person reading *The Sunday Times* and seeing that the words were 'unjustified' would not immediately pick up his bed-side books, *Gatley on Libel* to the right and *Fraser on Libel* to the left of the bed, and turn to the chapters marked 'Justification'. What he or she would do would be to conclude that it was said that the attack by the author on the Canon was inexcusable, was without foundation.

All that could be said against Miss Tracy was that the gossip she retailed of £9,000 instead of £7,000 was inaccurate (but £7,000 was as bad as £9,000 in the circumstances) and that she had not reported that the Bishop had approved of the building of a new house in 1940 (a fact which she did not know). If that was all that could be put against her, it could not be proved that her article was inexcusable.

No comment from the Bench.

I did not sleep well that night.

On the sixth day, we each made our final speeches to the jury. My opponent's passed without interruption. But I *was* interrupted, a very unusual event. Normally the Judge allows the advocate to say what he likes in his final speech, and then tears him to pieces in the nicest pos-sible way in his summing up to the jury. For, after all, he has the last word.

But no, the storm cones were out.

I was saying that, with regard to the statement that the house cost £9,000, the jury would have to consider whether it meant that the Plaintiff said that it cost £9,000 or that the villagers told her that it cost £9,000. If it were the former, well, the Plaintiff was wrong, when the Judge interrupted : 'Am I not bound as a matter of law to say that in that sentence Miss Tracy was putting into circulation a statement that the price was £9,000 ? Surely that is a matter of law ?'

I answered, I think correctly, that it was a matter for the jury, and didn't matter very much anyhow. The effect was that the price was something which the villagers considered to be fabulous.

Then came the summing up which was a complete *volte face*. I can only assume that the Judge had read his notes late into the night before, and had decided that he had leaned too far in favour of the Plaintiff, and that it was now the time to redress the balance.

Why, I shall never know.

His summing up could not have been faulted. It was, of course, as was inevitable, very complicated, and the day ended with his telling the jury that if they thought that the article contained nasty remarks about the Canon which were wholly unfounded, and for which Miss Tracy ought to have apologised, it couldn't have hurt her reputation to say, wrongly, that she had apologised.

That didn't seem to me to be a point that Gilbert had even thought of.

A sleepless night.

The seventh day should have been one of rest. But it was one of the longest and most burdensome in my life. The summing up, hostile throughout, went on until noon. It was brilliant and I could not have complained of its terms, but its nuances left the Judge's view quite plain.

The jury came back at ten minutes past two for further instructions. They got them. Again in terms of which I could not complain. Again, I thought, unhelpful to my cause.

So much so that I made certain propositions to the other side which were rejected with contumely. After biting my nails in Court for what seemed an indefinite period, I went down to the Crypt for a cup of tea, where I was joined by my client, and by a friend of hers who turned out to be the famous Miss E. Arnot Robertson who had lost her case against Metro-Goldwyn-Mayer in the House of Lords. Not a very good omen, and the dreariest tea that I can ever remember.

At ten minutes past five we were recalled into Court, whither we walked in near despair.

However, the jury gave my client £3,000 damages in all. Why that sum, I know not. I have often wondered. I think possibly it was four years' salary, for she had £750 p.a. from the newspaper, which was not too bad in those days. Indeed, dear old Beyfus told the jury in Patino that the Prince was probably better off than most of us, drawing a salary of £1,100 a year from a travel agency . . . etc., etc.

But, however the jury arrived at the figure, the Judge was visibly upset. And he suggested to the unfortunate Paull that he should apply that Miss Tracy should be deprived of the general costs of the action. Gilbert, knowing that this was a hopeless application (for the winner always gets the costs except in the most extreme circumstances) muttered a few words and sat down.

Then the Judge said, without giving me a chance to answer, 'I have to take into consideration whether the litigation has been caused by one or other of two false statements in the Plaintiff's article, the result of which would have been a libel action by the Canon to which *The Sunday Times* would have had no answer; namely, that the price of the house was £9,000 and that the Canon built it because he wanted a view, both of which were damaging and untrue.'

By now it was a quarter to six, and I was somewhat elated by our unexpected victory. I said impertinently, 'To deprive the Plaintiff of costs would be expressing a judicial view in flagrant contradiction of the views expressed by the jury, who are the judges of fact, and the judicial view must be governed thereby.'

It may have hurt, but this very good judge said, 'I think that is right.' And we got £3,000 and costs.

The newspaper did not appeal.

A lot of judges might have retired to their tents to lick their wounds. Not so, this splendid man. I treasure a letter dated 9th April 1954, and headed Royal Courts of Justice, London WC2.

Dear Neville,

I must congratulate you on a marvellous win. You did that case jolly well. The verdict didn't do my migraine any good! But I'm all right today.

Regards,
Yours,
Glyn.

CHAPTER THIRTEEN

Evelyn Waugh

I appeared only three times before my favourite tribunal: Mr Justice Stable. Twice in London and once on Circuit. It was not surprising; I never went on Circuit if I could help it, being a family man, and he never came to London if he could help it, being a family man. Indeed so rarely was he in London that when in 1968 I showed a coloured photograph of his eightieth birthday breakfast, which I have already described, to Reggie Dilhorne, who as Lord Chancellor had had Owlie Stable as his senior puisne* he said, 'Who's that?'

And Owlie had been a judge for thirty years and Reggie had been Attorney-General or Solicitor-General for fourteen as well as Lord Chancellor. It was a good likeness taken by Owlie's clerk, and I was amazed.

He used to say, 'London, my dear Neville. I hate the place, and where am I to stay? There's only Boodles and that's so expensive.' If I suggested that he might stay with his children, that was waved aside.

The first case was madly technical, all about the liability at common law of a husband for the costs of a divorce suit against him, properly incurred by the wife as an agent of necessity. My clients were then called J. N. Nabarro & Sons, although I think that they are now Nabarro Nathanson & Co. We won the case which pleased me because I did down poor Harry, the late and much lamented Lord Justice Phillimore, with whom, as a leader, was Harold Brown QC.

Harry Phillimore had beaten me in a Chancery case before Mr Justice Vaisey when I was appearing for a husband called Reed against a wife who was professionally known as 'Dorothy Squires'. She has been in the public eye consistently over the ensuing years, and I will say no more about the case than that he had put a very expensive house in his wife's name, and that was that: it was hers.

In order to get a little sympathy from this rather erudite and elderly

---

* puisne – born later – is to be distinguished from 'aisne' – 'older' which – although now in desuetude – applies to judges in the Court of Appeal.

judge, I told him that my case was that the wife's family, sisters, cousins and aunts (as in *HMS Pinafore*) used to batten on my generous client whom I described as a 'human cornucopia'. The Judge understood me and I thought no more about it. When my man went into the witness box, the first question he was asked in cross-examination was:

Q.   Do you know what a cornucopia is?

A.   No.

Roars of laughter and I was discomfited. But, after all these years, I still can't understand why.

The second case seemed to go on for ever. We started in Norwich in a very, very cold January, and finally after we had exhausted the whole of the time allotted to the Norwich Assizes we had to go on to Chelmsford, the learned Judge's next port of call.

I remember lying shivering in bed at Norwich, and saying over and over again to myself on the night before the case opened,

> 'St Agnes Eve, ah! bitter chill it was,
> The owl for all his feathers was a-cold'

but I didn't see how I could fit it in, and I feared that Owlie might think it cheeky.

We had no jury, but the witnesses had come by charabanc early in the morning from Norfolk to get to Chelmsford by the time the Court opened. And who do you think was against me? Mr Helenus Milmo, who caught his train at Horsham, while I caught mine, the 7.43 from Earlswood. By the time we got to Chelmsford, we were exhausted, and it was on our way back that he warned me at Victoria Station of the ruin that could attend an appearance in a public lavatory.

I appeared for the Borough Surveyor, against whom the council had passed a vote of 'no confidence'. It was really Tracy all over again. He had no supporters and there were all the Council (and the Town Clerk, who got off) to be cross-examined.

At the end of the lengthy matter, Buster Milmo and his then henchman, Stephen Terrell, who is now very important in the Liberal party, taught me something about British Railways Beaune, which really was astonishingly good. I won hands down, and got £1,500 damages for my man. There was no appeal against the judgment, for a jury would have given him £15,000.

Auntie *Times*, however, thought it right to weigh in with a leading article, which was very sensible:

The quarrel at East Dereham in Norfolk between the electors' association and their urban district council has entered a new phase of financial argument, but no new point of principle is likely to emerge. The point that has been argued for nineteen months is of constitutional importance. It arises from a case heard by Mr Justice Stable at Chelmsford Assizes in February last year. The council's surveyor, Mr C. D. O'Donnell, against whom they had passed a vote of no confidence, sued them for libel. His case was found to be overwhelming. Rarely do any set of men hear their conduct described in more blistering language than the Judge applied to nine of the defendant councillors. They 'were actuated by malice from start to finish' in a 'pernicious combination to destroy Mr O'Donnell'.

'The councillors,' the Judge added, 'knew perfectly well they had a competent surveyor. It was simply a question of personal malice, spite and dislike.' Mr O'Donnell was awarded £1,500 damages against the council and against the nine individually.

A successful litigant in these circumstances may recover from any of the defendants he pleases, leaving them to settle accounts with their fellow tortfeasors. In the Dereham case the intention appears to have been to find the whole £1,500 from the rate fund; but after protest the council decided that the nine members concerned should contribute between them a nominal £50; and this arrangement the auditor passed in July 1956. There is now a further but similar dispute about the allocation of the liability for costs, which amount to double the damages, and again the electors' association object to payment from the rates. No one will deny that the ratepayers have a grievance. But the principle involved is operating everywhere and all the time, on the largest and on the smallest scale, wherever delegated authority is entrusted with the care of public funds. The remedy is only at the polls. No doubt if the delegate purports to exercise powers that have not been conferred upon him – for example, by spending the education fund on his own riotous living – different considerations apply. But where he has exercised lawful authority in a reprehensible way, the fact of his representative character has to be faced. It is no bad thing that the voters should sometimes be reminded that they have a responsibility for the consequences of drawing an anonymous cross upon the ballot paper, even to the point of having to pay up for it. It may well make them reflect in future on the powers they are delegating to the men of their choice.

It was a pity that the newspaper left out Owlie's best bit :— 'They did not come to try him : they came to crucify him,' he thundered.

These were days when I was making in theory a great deal of money but somehow the fees didn't seem to come in quickly enough, and I was very pushed to deal with the ordinary bills. And I used to sing to myself, the pupils being absent, for I would not wish to lose face – to the tune of Pomp and Circumstance No. 2 – or at least I hope that I have got it right :

> Eland, Nettleship and Butt
> Langford, Borrodaile and Thain
> Swepstone, Walsh and Co.
> Gordon Dadds and Co.
> Will they come again ?

They did, in fact, but where I would have been without them, I don't know.

The third case concerned Evelyn Waugh.

He was an absolutely charming man, but I could not bear his smoking his confounded cigars in my room. I was in those days a compulsive cigar smoker also, but I left it for after dinner.

After our first case, he sent me a couple of jeroboams of champagne, which I thought typical of him.

It was in May of 1959 that I climbed out of the aeroplane at Dar-es-Salaam, put my foot to the ground, and found myself in great pain. The Attorney-General of Tanganyika, who had been kind enough to meet the plane, whipped me off to the hospital, where the diagnosis was that I had gout. I had never had it before, and I certainly had not been drinking vast quantities of vintage port. But I suppose there always has to be a first time.

I had come from London with Geoffrey Cross QC, now Lord Cross of Chelsea, to deal with a claim by a widow for one million pounds.

The husband had been a sisal millionaire, Greek by birth, a Mr Galanos. I appeared for a chartered accountant and for an advocate, who were said to have used undue influence on the deceased. The advocate was one of the two executors, and the Standard Bank of South Africa, for whom Geoffrey Cross appeared, was the other.

We travelled out first class which was very agreeable, and were stranded at Rome Airport for some hours, during which Geoffrey kindly expressed his admiration for my conversation with the waiter, who thought highly of 'State Express Cinque Cinque Cinque'.

After I was released from hospital, we attended the High Court, which had only recently been opened by Lord Kilmuir, the then Lord Chancellor, and agreed that, as he (Geoffrey) was the clever boy and I was the offensive old cross-examiner, he would make the final speech and I would cross-examine the Plaintiff. This was not difficult because the poor old Greek had taken out a summons (successfully) in a Police Court in Nairobi, asking for help in view of his wife's cruelty towards him.

We had a lot of fun, much hospitality, and we won without difficulty.

The only point in mentioning this particular case is that we were billeted in what was known generally as the 'German Club', because it had been so in the 1914-18 War, and officially as 'The Club' as we were now under British authority.

One ate out in the open owing to the extremely muggy heat – in December – and I looked across the tables and said to Geoffrey, 'You see that little fat man there. That's Evelyn Waugh.' And I went over to him; he was glad of companionship, and Geoffrey Cross is very, very bright, and I acted as a feed and said very, very little and we had a high old time for ten days or so. It transpired that he was out there because, 'At the end of the year, you know, one cannot bear one's wife and family, and I go away for a month or two and write a pot-boiler. They understand.' And a pot-boiler it was; I bought it; I don't know how many others did.

He had come to see me a year or two before on the instructions of Messrs Rubinstein, Nash and Co., experts in the field of defamation and copyright.

When he first came he was full of fire, demanding an apology, unwilling to sully his hands, in spite of the expensive messy cigar that he was smoking, with a penny of Lord Beaverbrook's 'ill-gotten' fortune. I smiled and agreed.

A week later he wrote to say that he had had second thoughts and an expensive family, this that and the other, and he would like some damages. I smiled and agreed.

This was the third case before Mr Justice Stable. I had two more for Evelyn Waugh with which I shall deal later. But this was rather fun.

Miss Nancy Spain was a well-known journalist. I wasn't particularly partial towards her, because she had been educated at Roedean where my niece was at the time, and earned money by being beastly about her old school. Which I, at any rate, think is 'not on'. I didn't mean to be beastly about Uppingham which is nowadays an absolutely first-rate public school, with an excellent academic record.

In June 1955, Miss Spain decided that it would be rather a good wrinkle to visit and interview a number of distinguished literary characters, no doubt, as was the fashion at that time, to denigrate them. So she went off with a chum, whose name I won't mention because his children went to school with mine, and they called on the unfortunate Poet Laureate, John Masefield, and all they got there was an oatcake and a cup of tea. So they motored on hopefully into Gloucestershire to see Mr Evelyn Waugh.

On the Waugh gate was a notice, 'No admittance on business', possibly an antithesis to the notice 'No admittance *except* on business' which Adam encounters in *Vile Bodies* when visiting Colonel Blount at Aylesbury. Miss Spain had rung up some days before to say that she was coming to interview Mr Waugh and would be bringing Lord X. Mrs Waugh, like a sensible woman, said that her husband, didn't see anyone at home, and there was no point in them coming.

Miss Spain didn't care. When asked in cross-examination, 'Is it your view that a *Daily Express* reporter can go on anyone else's property whether he has a right to or not?' she replied, 'A reporter's function is to do his best to get a story.'

And she decided to come to Piers Court, although she had been told quite clearly that she would not be welcome. But she got a story of being ejected, which her newspaper published two days later under the heading 'My pilgrimage to see Mr Waugh, by Nancy Spain'.

When the case eventually came on in February 1957 I had the advantage of being led by Gerald Gardiner who conducted the case with vitriolic brilliance. Not a laugh from start to finish; it was all very serious stuff. Indeed, I had always said that a jury would lap up 'an Englishman's home is his castle', even if it had very little to do with the case. Any comedy element that was required was supplied by the little Plaintiff himself who sat in front of us, beautifully dressed, plethoric in countenance, and wielding an immense ear trumpet which he placed in his right ear at strategic moments, whether to enable him to hear the better or to distract the attention of the jury, I cannot say.

I would like to go about this engaging character, but, as Lady Donaldson has already written a very readable book about him, and any-

one who attempts to read my book will presumably be literate ,and therefore have read most, if not all, of his output, I do not propose to do so.

A further reason could be that my spies tell me that his son Auberon
has recently referred to me as 'Nosey' in a review thus revealing that his
father-in-law, Arthur Onslow, had made him aware of my existence.
Although I would never write anything in criticism of E. W., I should
be foolish to take the risk of offending any journalist of importance.

I have not yet come to the libels – and I use the plural because Miss
Spain retorted that Mr Waugh had libelled her – but I am sure that
Gerald Gardiner put it better in his opening address than I could from
recollection many years later.

In the pre-trial consultation, as was his custom, he more or less de-
spaired of our cause, lamented the fact that we had got the wrong
judge (and how right he was about that), and generally produced an
atmosphere of gloom.

I told the Plaintiff as we walked down about seventy steps into King's
Bench Walk, while he puffed away at his cigar, so that I wondered if
he would survive the ordeal, not to worry. 'This is an act', I said, 'and
you will see the most superb performance tomorrow.' He was an emo-
tional man, but he was kind enough to believe me, and fortunately I
was right.

'Members of the Jury', Gerald Gardiner said, after introducing the
various counsel, Sir Hartley Shawcross and Mr Milmo appearing for
the newspaper, 'the Plaintiff lives in Gloucestershire with his wife and
children and has one or two old-fashioned ideas, one of which is that
an Englishman's home is his castle, and although he writes books at
home, he does not bring his professional life into his home life.

'He does not read the *Daily Express* and that he had not heard of
Nancy Spain, I must, on his behalf, confess. Since her rude incursion I
understand that she has taken part in panel games on television and is
therefore today as well known as the Prime Minister. (I can hear him
saying this, dead pan, with his right hand rolling the ribbon of his silk's
gown up and down all the time, as if it were the day before yesterday.)

'Refusing to see a *Daily Express* reporter was a very serious thing and
about 7.45 one evening Mrs Waugh found on the front door-step a lady
– Miss Spain – and a man whom Miss Spain said was Lord X. She asked
if Mr Waugh could persuade her husband to see her. Mrs Waugh saw
her husband who asked her to tell them to go away. They would not go,
and the Plaintiff told them to go away, and shut the door.'

(In fact he used a well-justified four letter word, followed them out, and secured an iron gate to prevent their return.)

Evelyn Waugh made no complaint about the 'pilgrimage' article and the whole affair seemed to have died down.

Much later, in February, 1956, he read an article in *The Observer* called 'A Book Sales Enquiry' summarising an investigation into the sales of books, and he also read a hostile criticism of the late Sir Pelham Grenville Wodehouse by a Mr Wain, which he thought was unjustified. So he wrote an article in *The Spectator* in the great man's defence called 'Mr Wodehouse and Mr Wain'.

Three weeks later the *Daily Express* published an article by Nancy Spain entitled 'Does a Good Word from Me Sell a Good Book?' It read:

> *There is a war* between Evelyn Waugh and me. He said some weeks ago, in a literary weekly, that the *Express* had no influence on the book trade. The *Express*, he complains, sold only 300 of *his* novels. He once had a book chosen by the Book Society, so that sold well. But the total first edition sales of all his other titles are dwarfed by brother Alec. *Island in the Sun* (Cassells 16s) foretold by me as this year's runaway Best Seller has now topped 60,000 copies as a direct result of my *Daily Express* notice. [Cocky little piece – my comment. N.F.] so the publishers told me yesterday. [How could the publishers have been certain of the reason for these great sales!! – my comment again.]

As Gerald Gardiner said, every sentence was untrue. There was no war between Evelyn Waugh and the Defendant unless she was still smarting because he would not see a *Daily Express* reporter. In his article he had not said that the *Daily Express* had no influence in the book trade, nor had he said that the newspaper had sold only 300 of his novels.

Her article had made it look as if the Plaintiff's books had only sold about 40,000 copies, whereas in fact his sales were about 4,280,125. First edition sales amounted to 180,000.

Miss Spain for her part said that she ought to have lots and lots of lovely lolly because Evelyn Waugh had written in *The Spectator:* 'Mr Wodehouse and Mr Wain'
(at the end of his article after smartening up Mr Wain)

> An investigation has lately been made in the book trade to determine which literary critics have most influence on sales.

I remember the time when the *Evening Standard* was undisputed leader. A good review there by Arnold Bennett was believed to sell an edition in 24 hours. The claim was exaggerated as I learned to my disappointment when he kindly noticed my first novel. The ensuing demand was, I think, something between two and three hundred, but I wonder whether any critic today has so large and immediate an influence. At the same period his colleague on the *Daily Express* was D. H. Lawrence, then at the height of his powers.

Times have changed. The Beaverbrook press is no longer listed as having any influence at all.

Those words were said to imply that Miss Spain was no good as a journalist or a literary critic, because she was the leading literary critic of the Beaverbrook newspapers.

Gerald Gardiner ended up his speech by asking the jury to tell the Defendants that they could not tell damaging lies about a person just because he had shown the door to *Daily Express* reporters trespassing on his property. As for Miss Spain's counterclaim, all that Mr Waugh's article meant was that people who read books tended to read book reviews in the more serious papers.

He added for good measure that in the twelve months before the article no less than twenty-two people, apart from Miss Spain, had reviewed books in the *Daily Express*.

The Plaintiff gave his evidence and was cross-examined by Sir Hartley Shawcross, Chairman of the Bar Council, ex-Attorney-General, ex-President of the Board of Trade, today as Lord Shawcross, Chairman of the Press Council as well as holding many important commercial and other appointments. He was the finest advocate I have ever heard.

But Evelyn Waugh was very good, using a paucity of words. I remember his being cross-examined (although they called it interviewed) on television on one of a set of programmes which began with Lord Birkett who told us that he was a Christian agnostic, which I thought to be a contradiction in terms, and continued with the massacre of the late Tony Hancock. The interviewer asked Waugh what he was doing on a programme of that kind. Instead of flaring up, as he was no doubt intended to do, he replied quietly, 'Poverty'.

So here he gave the advocate little room to display his powers: so different from Harold, voluble Laski, with Sir Patrick Hastings.

Mrs Waugh gave evidence as did Alec Waugh, who had jumped into fame with *The Loom of Youth* and only rediscovered it after a number of years of supporting himself by his pen, with *Island in the Sun*. He is now seventy-seven and will forgive me if I say that I remember little of his evidence, but recollect most clearly his telling me that he lived in Tangier because of tax, but managed to spend much of the summer at Lords to watch the cricket.

I envied him, for although I have been a member of the MCC since 1940, I don't think that I have ever been to Lords more than twice a year, and often not at all. It was the same with Wimbledon. I was probably the worst playing member of the All-England Lawn Tennis and Croquet Club, but I shouldn't have resigned if I had not had to spend so much of the year on circuit, keeping out some keen young man who could make much better use of the Club's amenities.

Miss Spain had bad luck, for, just as we finished calling our evidence, it transpired that there had been a dreadful motor accident in which Sir Hartley's family was involved, and the case was left to Milmo. It must have been a terrifying moment for him, but he rose to the occasion and made a beautiful opening speech.

He told the jury that they were there about precious little and that the whole matter was very much a storm in a teacup.

And it was clear enough to me that the Judge agreed with him. Would the jury? Gardiner's very solemn and bitter approach was obviously more than justified. The jury must not be allowed to treat the case lightly.

Miss Spain had to admit, when my leader set about her, that there were 'discrepancies' in the article Mr Waugh complained of. She said that she now knew that he had had four, not one, books chosen by the Book Society, and she said that she was delighted about it. And, significantly, she agreed that she had not taken any steps, before the article was published, to ascertain whether it was true or not.

It began to look as though Gardiner had been right in saying that the article had been written in a flaming temper because she fancied herself humiliated in 'Mr Wodehouse and Mr Wain'.

Next day – no Shawcross. Lord Beaverbrook was not pleased, but surely the health of one's family must come first, and again his junior did very well. So, of course, did Gardiner, but my eye was on the figure on the Bench who, as usual, didn't appear to have made many notes, but had obviously been listening carefully, as he made one or two entertaining interruptions. With nineteen years on the Bench, principally in crime, there was nothing he didn't know about handling a jury, and I wondered what lay ahead. I had confidently predicted £2,000, yet it seemed that the Milmo theme of 40/- for each party and no costs, might have found favour.

The summing up was superb, if not exactly what we wanted.

'Now, members of the jury, most of the things that you have heard during the last two days have nothing to do with the case at all, and are matters which it is not for you to decide. On 22nd June Miss Spain paid a visit to Mr Masefield, and then went on to talk to Mr Waugh : she said that they had driven a long way and had only had a cup of tea, and an oatcake, and that Mr Waugh might have asked them in for a drink. You, members of the jury, are not here to decide whether Miss Spain was ill-mannered or impudent, or whether Mr Waugh was inhospitable or ill-tempered.

'The subject matter of this case is two publications. Mr Waugh wrote the article complained of in *The Spectator* of which Miss Spain says that anyone 'in the know' would realise that she is the principal literary critic of *The Daily Express* and think that she is a critic of no consequence at all.

'Of course, if you come to the conclusion that the article did not reflect discreditably on Miss Spain, you will dismiss the counterclaim; on the other hand [pianissimo] if you think that it did, you will compensate her accordingly.

'Now, that article appeared in February 1956, Miss Spain read it, and on March 17th the article was published in *The Daily Express* of which Mr Waugh complains.

'Now let us look at the facts as compared with the statements in Miss Spain's article.

'When she said that the sale of 60,000 copies of Alec Waugh's book *Island in the Sun* was the direct result of the article she published, she was rather overstating the case. It seems that she had scampered through it somewhat rapidly in the cocktail bar at the Ritz, and that the rather cursory notice of the book was by no means the most important factor in stepping up the sales of the book. But, you know, that is not what you have to decide : you have to decide whether the article is defamatory of Mr Evelyn Waugh.

'The article says that he has had one book chosen by the Book Society : 'in fact he has had four. The article says that all his sales were 'dwarfed by brother Alec'. You know that was a hopelessly inaccurate account.

'The question really is : Ought any intelligent person, picking up that paragraph, to form an adverse opinion of Mr Evelyn Waugh's books?

If you come to that conclusion, then he is entitled to such compensation as you think appropriate.

'It may be, however,' (leaning forward in a confidential manner, and putting on a very husky voice to emphasise his words) 'members of the jury, that in this literary atmosphere you may recall one of Shakespeare's earlier works – *Much Ado About Nothing*.

'But whether that expression applies here is exclusively a matter for you to decide.'

And he sent them out to consider their verdict.

However, he lost them; two hours later they came back and we got £2,000 damages and they found against Miss Spain on the counter claim.

And the Beaverbrook organisation did it again soon after. Dame Rebecca West, who is still with us, writing very entertainingly in *The Sunday Telegraph*, decided to make some alterations in a new edition of her very successful book, *The Meaning of Treason*, which was to be published by Pan Books Ltd.

The alterations were grossly defamatory of Evelyn Waugh and I won't set them out here as there is no point in hurting anyone's feelings, and *The Daily Express* lifted them from the book and put them in the newspaper. How silly can you be?

The case against *The Express* never came to Court. I don't suppose Hartley Shawcross will remember it, but he accosted me outside the Middle Temple Hall as I was on my way to luncheon in the Inner, and asked me how much I wanted. I felt rather important at being thus approached, mentioned a substantial sum, not, if I remember correctly, in five figures, and it was paid.

The Express were very realistic in those days: they thought it wise to pay rather than to grovel publicly in Court, and I always used to read 'Crossbencher' in bed on Sunday morning, to see who might be coming to see me for damages for libel on Monday.

One Monday three distinguished Members of Parliament came and they all got damages out of Court. In case it sounds as though I am boasting, I can remember the names of two of them; they were the present Lord Aldington – whom I can remember vaguely as G2 Chemical Warfare, 8th Army – and Sir Fitzroy Maclean.

After *The Express* had paid up, the action against Pan Books proceeded to Court, and the Plaintiff recognised that the Defendants, who had apologised very profusely, had been caused acute financial loss by the sudden withdrawal of the book. Accordingly he pressed no claim for damages against the Defendants, who had of course indemnified him as to his costs. So we got substantial damages and at the same time looked extremely respectable. Very satisfactory.

The subject of treason seems to be the Dame's Achilles heel for not long afterwards she was sent out by *The Sunday Times* to cover some treason trial taking place before three Judges of the Supreme Court of South Africa. She made some remarks about one of the Judges, no doubt by mistake, or owing to mishearing or something of that kind, which depicted him as grossly biassed. The Judge behaved with dignity and said that he would take an editorial correction and an apology, only to be met with the answer that the article was accurate. I am not for a moment suggesting that Dame Rebecca West was responsible for that silly slip. The result was that the Judge had to issue a writ and the newspaper paid up and apologised.

It was almost a family party. The Judge's solicitors briefed me to lead the late Dudley Collard, the newspaper briefed Mr Helenus Milmo, and Dame Rebecca West went to the ultra-respectable Charles Russell and Co., who never demeaned themselves by giving me a brief, although I was against them often enough, and they showed excellent taste by briefing my devil, David Hirst.

A newspaper is always at risk to attacks about defamation, however innocent they may be. And this is one of the matters with which we have become very concerned in the Committee on Defamation over which I have recently presided.

CHAPTER FOURTEEN

Far Above Rubies

In the late forties when I had time on my hands, I thought that I would pull the leg of a newspaper to see what would happen.

I had my opportunity when *The Daily Express* wrote that following Annigoni's triumphant portrait of the Queen, he was about to portray the Duke of Edinburgh, also for the Fishmongers' Company. The columnist added that this would be the first portrait of a man that the maestro had attempted.

Tongue in cheek, a letter was sent from 1 Brick Court, Temple, EC4 on behalf of Mr Neville Faulks who was said to be greatly incensed because he was male and had in fact been painted by Annigoni, had so stated to his relatives and friends, and now was held up by *The Daily Express* as a boastful liar. This was a very serious matter.

I got back almost by return of post a tremendous grovel from a dear old man called Critchley who was the legal adviser to Beaverbrook Newspapers Ltd. We all laughed, and I did no more about it, but that could have been worth a lot of money with a jury had I had an eye to the main chance. A judge, alone, would have made short work of it, I am sure.

When a middle-aged junior is certain that he cannot afford the risk of applying for silk, but also feels that, if something doesn't happen, his juniors in age will overtake him, the Government sometimes appears as the good fairy.

Not only had she helped me from destitution in 1947 with her job at the Old Bailey, but now she created a Restrictive Practices Court and a Monopolies Commission, just designed for me. Under the Registrar, the man in charge of the attacking side in the Restrictive Practices Court was the late Bunny Stephenson, one of the splendid men who had been accustomed to briefing me for the Crown in Ministry of Food cases at the Old Bailey. And, as he knew that I knew something about balance sheets, he gave me a lot of remunerative work in that field. The remuneration was fascinating : the work was not.

In the Monopolies Commission, it was another story. There I was always at the receiving end. My first case was for Dunlop's led by the late John Bussé QC, then for Fisons led by Gerald Gardiner, and then for the Imperial Tobacco Company led by Brian MacKenna, now Mr Justice MacKenna.

This last was murder. Mr (now Sir John – and I should think hereafter Lord) Partridge was in charge of the operation. He made me more than earn my fee by going down to Bristol and rehearsing.

I acted as the Monopolies Commission, ready to fire off any painful question, and to probe any weakness in that very large organisation. It was very hard work for me for I had to attempt to understand every possible defect in an industry to which I was a stranger, and to put aggressive questions designed to expose them.

In the event, John Partridge was such a wonderful witness that there was very little for us to do, and when we walked back from the Tribunal (MacKenna is crazy about walking and would never think about public transport) my leader said, reasonably, that he had never been paid so much with such a marvellous leader for doing so little.

There was also something called, I think, the Industrial Disputes Tribunal, presided over by Lord Terrington who welcomed brevity, which was more or less my middle name, and we got on very well.

The American Express Company is the only client that I can remember, but there were a number of them.

I had two interesting cases about jewellery. The earlier was for a young and pretty girl who had been a ballet dancer of distinction. She was engaged to be married to a handsome young man, who was living beyond his means. He pawned all her jewellery and sold her car which she had on hire purchase.

She sued the pawnbrokers and also a man who had possession of a £480 diamond ring of hers which the fiancé had pawned, later handing the pawn ticket to the other man, in order to redeem a gambling debt. The girl gave her evidence most convincingly.

The defence of the pawnbrokers was that she had consented to the pawning by the fiancé, or, if that weren't so, she had approved of what he had done. The other man said that she had no legal right to the ring. The fiancé was not in Court and his whereabouts were unknown.

Not unnaturally, I had called him the 'villain of the piece' in opening, and the judge, who was my benefactor, Gerald Slade, said, 'Perhaps this lady has at last realised what was the true value of Mr X.'

She was subjected to an interminable, cruel, and repetitive cross-examination by two counsel, about the fact that she had had intercourse with the fiancé during the engagement. Gerald was sniffing away down his nose, and I saw red, and protested repeatedly. But in vain. I suppose counsel were doing their duty, as perhaps a girl would be more likely to let her fiancé pawn all her possessions if she had been in bed with him the night before, than if she had not; but, with no fiancé in sight, it seemed to me unnecessarily unkind. She wept and finally left the box in a very unhappy state.

Throughout the case, the question was posed on all sides : 'Which of three innocent persons should suffer for the dishonesty of another?'

By the end of the second day, the Defendants had closed their case, and final speeches were being made. I couldn't lose : she was a decent girl and no one had contradicted her evidence. She had incurred substantial costs.

On the third morning, however, the fiancé appeared in Court with his new six foot American blonde wife, who wore a full length mink stole round her shoulders. He was dressed with great elegance, told the Judge that he had only been in England for a week, and was allowed to give evidence although the Defendant's counsel had closed his case.

My poor girl had to go back into the box to have her arm twisted all over again. The fiancé gave evidence and I cross-examined him. He looked at the dishonoured cheques, solicitors' letters, and an unpaid IOU for £200, and said, 'I have not denied that I was often short of money.'

I said, 'Dishonestly and deliberately you fobbed off your creditors by offering them cheques which you knew would not be met?' After a pause, he answered, 'I hoped to be able to settle. There was £8 a month allowance from my stepfather. The bank manager asked me to close the account because it was becoming a headache to him.'

And so it went on. It was apparent to the meanest comprehension that his word was valueless. And I waited to hear judgment for my client, after all that she had endured.

But I didn't get my judgment.

At the end of the man's evidence the Judge said that he doubted whether he should continue with the case, as he had expressed an opinion before hearing the fresh evidence. Counsel for the Defendants, of course, agreed with him.

I held forth to the contrary, saying that I could not imagine how it would be difficult for a Judge having expressed one view, to change his mind and express another view later.

(Lord Goddard, who used to jump forwards and backwards with engaging candour and who was always prepared to eat his own words, told me later that he had never heard such nonsense in his life – but that didn't help my poor client.)

It was a disaster. We had to listen to a judgment of some length in which Gerald said that, if he was erring, he decided to err on the side of punctiliousness. He felt that the fiancé would leave the Court thinking that justice had not been done if the Judge were heard to say that, having considered the fresh evidence, he was still of opinion that the girl had told the truth. Why, heaven knows!

And he ordered the case to be tried all over again before another Judge to whom he reserved the costs.

Some young man was then given leave – the proceedings being completely out of hand by this time – to say something on behalf of the fiancé, who was not even a party to the action.

He said that Mr X was anxious to make restitution to the parties concerned (presumably by selling his new wife's mink stole). I interrupted, 'Is he going to pay the costs?'

'I have no instructions as to that.'

I felt like saying that if he didn't, no doubt the Judge would, but sanity fortunately prevailed.

The poor girl wouldn't face all the filth in cross-examination again, and had to settle on the Defendant's terms. They didn't pay all her costs, but she did get her jewellery back. I forget about the car. It was a case of a very high-minded and honourable Judge doing a grave injustice. Down-to-earth characters like myself would never have decided as he did.

Roddy Romain had been in the JAG's department in Italy while I was having my tour of that country in 1944-45. His father was a well-known solicitor practising in or around Marylebone Police Court, and after the war Roddy persuaded his father to send me a brief on behalf of Crockford's to advise as to the legality of gaming. Father candidly told me that he had sent it to me because he understood that I had plenty of time for research. I gave him two months of research for twenty-five guineas and was glad to do so. But he never sent me any more work. After he died, Roddy, who is now a metropolitan stipendiary magistrate, left the Bar and went into the family firm, and appeared one day in my chambers with Mrs Shapiro, an old lady living in Oakwood Court, Kensington, which means that she was not without means.

She said that she had been compelled to sell her valuables to a couple of villains, for £90, when in fact they were worth £1,000. She said that she had been threatened with an open penknife. She asked for the contract to be set aside, for damages for trespass, for assault, and for conversion or detinue.

She was an elderly and ailing widow of sixty-five with a son who was a lecturer in Russian at London University. Again there was no corroboration of her evidence. She had a maid who was not there at the material time. She was frightened of the possibility of burglars and had arranged for the maid to give a sharp double knock when she wanted to enter.

The double knock came, but there were two men there who came in and remained for two hours. She had a nervous shock and a stutter as a result of that experience.

Two of them and only one of my client. Who was going to be believed? We had Mr Justice McNair and no jury. He will not mind if I say that he had the reputation, like Sir Malcolm, of being a Defendant's judge, although I never found it so, and have no complaint against him as a tribunal.

And I decided to try the Tracy treatment on him and deliver a long opening which would be corroborated by my client thereafter. After I had been going for some time, he said, 'You know, I have read the Statement of Claim. Have we got past the first sitting-room yet?' I said there was some way to go in order to paint the picture properly. He let me go on.

I don't hold with these judges who read the papers beforehand. Mine may be an unusual view but I think that it is important to go into Court with an open mind. I am not talking about crime or indeed anything where a jury is involved. There it is important to be master of all the details *ab initio* as any trivial slip on your part may result in some villain, who would have been convicted but for your incompetence, getting off in the Appellate Court. But in civil and family cases, I have always thought it fairer, and, of course, much easier from the Judge's point of view, to bring a completely unbiassed approach to bear on the matters I have to try.

One of my brethren said to me once, 'I haven't tried a defended divorce before, but I suppose I can try it on the pleadings, as I do in industrial injury cases?' I merely said that I didn't think that it was a very good idea and that it would be better to go to bed early. The case took him about three weeks to try and I have no idea what happened.

Willie McNair seemed to be a bit sceptical of my woman's evidence. I don't know why. She was a dear old lady who, after the case, sent me a silver flask with my initials on it and a covering letter saying that she felt sure that I worked so hard that it would be a good idea if at 12 noon daily I had a small glass of sherry out of it, together, of course, with a biscuit.

My examination-in-chief was designedly prolonged, in the hope of letting the Judge see how genuine my client was. She was cross-examined by Victor Durand, who had not yet taken silk, but who was in my view the best of all the criminal advocates I used to compete with at the Old Bailey. Perhaps 'best' is going a bit far but I would bracket him with Fred Lawton and Sebag Shaw (now both Lords Justice). He had a habit of standing absolutely erect all the time and he had an enormous head, even larger than mine, and was a most formidable adversary.

The case obtained a certain amount of publicity, and I received a letter or telephone call from someone else who had been subjected to the same treatment.

I had finished my side's evidence by this time and I decided to resort to an old dodge. My solicitors persuaded her to come to Court – for some reason or other we had transferred into the Lord Chief Justice's Court which is a large court, and we hid her out of sight. After the first villain had been saying 'No' to every question I asked, I said, 'Step forward, Mrs Z' and she emerged and the villain recognised her, admitted that he had been to see her in the Isle of Wight, and that the police had visited him about it.

After a little more, he started to weep, and agreed that he had a conviction relating to jewellery. He had not done very well, but all was not lost, and the Judge and I awaited the testimony of the second Defendant.

Victor did not call him. Afterwards, he told me he couldn't, as he had a conviction for just this sort of thing. As I had no idea of this, I thought it might have been an act of Providence. The Judge still wanted time to think about it and reserved his judgment.

Some days later, my old lady got judgment for £910 and the Judge said that he believed her, and had formed a most unfavourable view of the first villain by the end of his evidence, and had waited in vain for the testimony of the second man.

So all was well in the end !

CHAPTER FIFTEEN

A Case of Harbouring

I hope that it is clear that a successful barrister has a number of interesting consultations the nature of which it would be improper to reveal in an autobiography. I have had a number of clients from the Duke of Windsor downwards, in relation to whom my lips are sealed. I am only at liberty to write about cases that have in fact entertained the public in their time.

Of such, that of the Marchioness of Winchester against Mrs Fleming, was one. It only came to me by good luck, in 1957. Colin Duncan in my chambers threw it over at the last moment as he had a very important case for the Queen's Proctor which clashed with it, so that little Faulks collected the brief to argue it by himself, as the Marchioness thought it a waste of money to employ a silk. For Mrs Fleming, inevitably at that time, were Mr Gilbert Beyfus QC and Mr Helenus Milmo.

As I rose to open the case, claiming damages for breach of contract and for the ancient tort of harbouring, which means detaining a husband or wife against the will his or her spouse who is thereby deprived of his or her company, Mr Justice Devlin rather unnerved me by smiling pleasantly and saying, 'Yes, Mr Milmo.'

Lady Winchester was a Parsee lady whose maiden name was Bapsy Pavry, was of ample means and who lived at the Mayfair Hotel. Mrs Fleming was the widow of a member of Parliament and the mother of a very distinguished family; Peter, the author, and husband of Celia Johnson, the actress; Ian, the creator of James Bond and husband of Lady Rothermere – (I appeared for Lord Rothermere in the divorce); Richard, the merchant banker, chairman of Robert Fleming and Company and of the Pilgrim Trust; and Amaryllis, the well-known cellist. Mr Fleming, her late husband, had been a very large landowner in the North West of Scotland. From time to time various members of the family used to pop into Court and sit behind my opponents but as I knew none of them by sight, I didn't know which was which.

Both women had obviously been very beautiful in their time and both had an air of distinction at the date of the trial. My client, who wore a different and increasingly beautiful sari each day, was hopelessly excitable, smarting as she was under a sense of injustice, and, although she told the truth, was a very unsatisfactory witness. Mrs Fleming who was, I am afraid, a stranger to the truth, gave her evidence with great dignity even when she was obviously defeated. At one stage I tried to sit down and conclude my cross-examination, which was like hitting a defenceless child, but the Judge bade me continue. He was right and I was wrong, for she seemed unaware of the impression she was creating, and there was never a sign of a tear.

At the date of the trial my client was fifty-four, Mrs Fleming was seventy-three, and England's premier Marquess, the sixteenth Lord Winchester was ninety-five. He was Henry William Montagu Paulet and my client called him 'Henry' and Mrs Fleming called him 'Monty'. He was penniless. He had at one stage been the 'guinea pig' chairman of a number of Clarence Hatry's companies but, when the latter went to gaol for a long time, Lord Winchester went bankrupt and was undischarged at the time of this trial.

Although very old, he was very astute. He had been twice married and there was no son and heir. His nearest relation, he said, lived in County Wexford, and never answered his letters, and he was determined to live out the rest of his life in comfort, come what may.

Before he married my client, he had been 'unofficially engaged' to Mrs Fleming, and between October 1951 and May 1952 he lived in a separate part of her premises at Emerald Wave, Nassau. During 1951 she gave him money gifts amounting to £1,100.

In May 1952, they came to England together. In June, her doctor said that her heart was not very good, and that she was acutely exhausted. He advised her that Lord Winchester was too old for her to take care of him. And she broke the engagement off.

The old gentleman was not amused. He wrote to my client whom he had not seen since 1929, and she asked him to tea at her hotel. She walked back to his hotel with him and he proposed marriage. She did not accept him at once, but she did so next day at 6 o'clock in the afternoon. He had told her that he had an income of £500 a year, and had asked if she could support herself. She said that she could very well do so. That was good enough for his Lordship and the parties were married on 2nd July 1952, my client becoming the Marchioness of Winchester.

Mrs Fleming was not amused.

My client believed that this old ruffian really loved her. There was some correspondence between him and Mrs Fleming which made it clear, at any rate to me, that money was all that concerned him.

The question which took days to resolve was whether I was entitled in law to read the letters. Eventually, thanks to tremendous research by David Hirst (now QC and the leading advocate at the defamation bar), the Judge said, 'I didn't realise that you put it like that', (which wasn't surprising because, with a returned brief, I hadn't had time to do my homework on the law – it was quite enough to master the facts over-night – and I hadn't originally put it like that) and allowed me read them. Dear old Gilbert was furious, because they really were dynamite.

The Marquess wrote three days after the wedding :

Eve dearest, I am sorry you are shocked at my marrying a Parsee. If I had got engaged to a Jewess you would not have noticed it so acutely. [This was before the Race Relations Act.] As to her having no money, you cannot be painted by Augustus John, and live in expensive hotels, without substantial resources. She has one trait like you – she is careful but generous.

Mrs Fleming to Lord Winchester :

Dearest Monty, Of course I am terribly shocked over your Parsee. Who in England is not shocked? – and I am very apprehensive. I understand now the reason for the indecent haste and secrecy. For heaven's sake be careful and don't be persuaded to go to India. I am finding out about ships. If you need me I am always your friend.

Lord Winchester to Mrs Fleming :

Eve, beloved, I got your cable and I wonder who told you I was here alone. I don't intend to go to the Coronation, though she will. I used to indulge in dreams of planting your coronet on, but I am sure it will give someone more pleasure than it would you.

The month after the marriage, Mrs Fleming was writing :

Dear Monty, I have your lovely letter. I am off to Canada. I really don't want to go. The garden is so lovely. The Garden of Eden with-out Adam, and the sea is perfect.

And he answered :

The family 1950

Papa 1959

Esmond, Nigel and Neville, 1952

Eve dearest, . . . of course I miss much which life in Nassau brought to me – your lovely companionship, the scent of the jasmin and the sound of the mocking bird. Your ever devoted Monty.

Mrs Fleming to Lord Winchester :

Don't be downhearted. Something will happen to save you, to save us both.

Lady Winchester did not know about all this at the time, as her husband had removed to Monte Carlo shortly after the marriage, leaving her in London to deal with a reversion, to which he said that he was entitled, but which in fact came to nothing.

She thought that the marriage was happy, and the only disagreement between them was when she told him that she didn't like his corresponding with the other woman. He rebuked her for that, saying that Mrs Fleming was trying to help him as a friend and wanted to give him £100,000. He was clearly trying to keep both ladies sweet by denigrating each to the other. In January 1953, my client was persuaded to pay for her husband's journey from England to Nassau. She did not know that he had had a letter from Mrs Fleming :

Dearest Monty, I simply cannot understand why you have not told me of your divorce, arranged in August. . . . Why don't you have an annulment ? It would be quicker, easier, and cheaper, surely ?

Nor did she know then that her husband had replied, denying that there was to be a divorce but asking Mrs Fleming for 400,000 francs. Or that Mrs Fleming had said that he could not have the money until he was divorced and free to marry again.

Arrived in Nassau, he ceased to correspond with his wife after a month or so. In February, all was sweetness and light. But in March he began to demand money from his wife and continued to do so throughout the summer. Eventually on 12th August 1953 he wrote to say that he was determined never to live with her again.

She sent him a cake with ninety-one candles on his ninety-first birthday. But it was no good. She got a cable saying :

I am not resuming married life with you. My London solicitors are in touch with yours. Winchester.

In February 1954 she went to Nassau, and met her husband in a car park where she saw Mrs Fleming for the first time. They drove off, leaving her stranded.

In May 1954, she began proceedings in the Bahamas claiming damages for libel and for enticement of her husband by Mrs Fleming, who in turn counter-claimed damages for libel in a document which my client had circulated, in her fury.

Not very edifying: and the solicitors persuaded the two ladies to settle the matter. Attached to the memorandum of settlement was a letter from my client to her husband saying that she wished it to be made abundantly clear that the agreement should not be construed as giving her consent to his continuing to live apart from her with anybody, or by himself. She said that although his conduct had been reprehensible, 'I always have been and am willing to resume married life with you at any time you may request me to do so, your loving wife, Bapsy.'

By the memorandum of settlement Mrs Fleming for her part undertook that she would not thereafter in any manner directly or indirectly disturb or *interfere* with the Plaintiff. The agreement was dated 19th July 1956, *and this was the vital date*. Had she 'interfered' thereafter? Had she 'interfered' before 8th August 1956 (the date of the writ)?

Seven days after the agreement Lord Winchester filed a petition for nullity against my client in the Bahamas. Mrs Fleming's solicitors acted for Lord Winchester.

Where did the money come from to finance these proceedings?

Lady Winchester was sure that Mrs Fleming had provided it, and on 8th August 1956 issued a writ claiming that Mrs Fleming had persuaded the Marquess to start the proceedings and to live separate and apart from his wife. At the date of the trial, the Marquess and Mrs Fleming were living in the Metropole Hotel, Monte Carlo, occupying different rooms at the end of the same corridor. She was acting towards him as a nurse to a patient, or as Joan to Darby according to the way that you looked at it. My client had her suspicions, but I do not for a moment believe that there was any adulterous association.

The Chief Justice of the Bahamas dismissed the nullity petition on the ground that Lord Winchester was not domiciled there. My client had incurred a lot of expense in travelling there for the hearing. She was entitled to £500 deposited in Court as security for costs by the Marquess (and where did that come from?) and she claimed the balance from Mrs Fleming and also damages for harbouring and for loss of consortium.

The case was bitterly contested. Gilbert's ferocious cross-examination of my client didn't make things any easier. They shouted at each other for a long time until she was threatened with Brixton Prison and ordered out of the box, which didn't please her and infuriated Gilbert, who thought that he still had some good stuff up his sleeve.

When finally she was allowed to return to the witness box Gilbert was quite piano and the Marchioness turned to the Judge as she left and said, 'Please forgive me if I was impatient yesterday and today.'

So ended the lengthy cross-examination which had only served to reveal (1) that Gilbert had some personal dislike of my client, as a result of which he was continually pulled up by the Judge for asking her whether she was ashamed of herself and similar irrelevancies, (2) that, rather than saving his client from paying damages, he regarded his principal duty as that of preserving Mrs Fleming from any imputation against her character; He kept on saying this. (3) that my client, when she considered herself betrayed, was as full of fight and venom as the proverbial woman spurned; (4) that both women wanted the devious old man who was playing one off against the other for money; (5) that both denied that they wanted the title; (which might or might not be true), and (6) that my wily old friend Gilbert was going to dodge putting Mrs Fleming in the witness box if he could, hoping that my Parsee lady would have infuriated the Judge so much that he would decide that she had produced no evidence fit for Mrs Fleming to answer.

This last matter he had indicated when resisting the Judge's decision to remove my client from the witness box. He said that for technical reasons he would like her to remain there, (until she was punch drunk?) as at the end of her case he might wish to submit that there was no case to answer.

Counsel should never identify himself with his client. He should try to be as dispassionate as the Judge, and he will then know better how to tread safely. But I must confess that I had every sympathy with my client, who, I was sure, would have lived quietly and happily with the Marquess, who only wanted comfort and money, both of which she could provide. She would never have behaved badly had the other woman not interfered immediately after the marriage. But that she had behaved badly, indeed maddeningly, in the witness-box was undeniable, and although I underestimated the Judge, and need not have worried, I was terrified lest it might be held that there was no case to answer.

I had to think quickly and, without giving Gilbert a chance to speak, I said that the evidence of the Marchioness concluded my case, and that, if my learned friend was going to submit that there was no case to answer, he should be put to his election as to whether to call evidence, on the basis of the well-known decision in *Alexander* v *Raison, 1936 1KB169*. (In other words, he couldn't have his cake and eat it: he couldn't call evidence against the Plaintiff if he had unsuccessfully submitted that there was no case to answer, for by so submitting he took a final decision). ('Elect' is legal gobble-de-gook for 'choose'.)

This did the trick, for it was unexpected, and my opponent was enraged. He said it was possible that he would make the submission, but that, if he did, it would be wrong for the Judge to consider that he was bound to treat him as having elected to call no evidence. He raised his voice and shouted that it was a matter which he would take to the House of Lords with the purpose of undoing all the evil which the decision in *Alexander* v *Raison* had done.

He raised his voice still further, 'I shall refuse to elect.'

In a silken but dangerously soft voice the Judge said, 'No advocate so far has been courageous enough to refuse to elect. Have I not a discretion to put you to your election?'

'Your Lordship has.'

'In that case is it still your intention to refuse to elect?'

'I should like to think it over.'

And the case was adjourned with the enemy on the defensive.

The next day the Judge said, 'Supposing that the evidence falls short of a procuring, but nevertheless there is evidence from which I ought to infer that your client financed the petition of nullity, is financing by itself enough to constitute a breach of contract?' Mr Beyfus submitted not.

The argument went on for a long time. I was only once called upon to speak when I said that financing a petition for nullity against my client was obviously 'interfering' with her. And so it was. (But the bull point was 'when had Mrs Fleming interfered? If she had interfered earlier than 19th July, the date of the agreement, then it could not have been a breach of the agreement'. But Gilbert hadn't thought of that one, mercifully.)

Eventually, the Judge stated that he thought there was evidence – which might be rebutted – that the petition for annulment was financed by Mrs Fleming, and I was entitled to argue that that, without more, was itself an interference and thus a breach of contract. Gilbert's argument collapsed and we heard no more bravura about the House of Lords, and a refusal to elect. He said that he would call his client.

Mrs Fleming told us how she first met the Marquess in 1950 and how she had paid his debts when he came to live in a cottage on her premises at Emerald Wave, Nassau in 1951. He had proposed in a letter in which he had said that companionship was all that he wanted and they became unofficially engaged. Then we had the breaking of the engagement and the new marriage which she thought 'not suitable at all'.

She said that Lord Winchester had asked her for £1,000 so that he could get his marriage annulled but that she had refused to lend it to him. She admitted that since the agreement of 19th July 1956 the Marquess had been living on her estate although not as man and wife.

Then she said (and I was sure that she lied) that she had never persuaded Lord Winchester to file the nullity suit or to remain apart from his wife. She denied that she had lent the £500 which the old gentleman had paid into court in respect of costs for the nullity suit. She said to Mr Beyfus that Lord Winchester had been saving money, and had been lent some by a friend in South Africa, and by a nephew in London !

This all sounded wildly improbable, and I cross-examined with an easy heart, reminding myself not to be too unkind to a defenceless old lady, however untruthful she might have been.

She agreed that it was she who first went to see the solicitor whom Lord Winchester later talked to about the annulment. (This she denied on the following day.) She agreed that if there was an annulment she wanted to marry Lord Winchester but only in order to take care of him. She agreed that she knew that my client wanted her husband back. She agreed that she made it possible for him not to return to my client. She agreed that had it not been for the doctor's mistake in July 1952, she would have been Lady Winchester by now. She complained that my Parsee was not of the same religion as her husband, and I said, 'You would not have objected if he had married a member of the Church of England ?'

'Not if she was nice and would take care of him. I had looked after him for nine months before.'

At this time we were sparring at the end of a long day, and I knew, although she didn't seem to appreciate the position, that the massacre would take place in the morning when we turned to the correspondence.

Then the Judge, who had kept admirably silent hitherto, leaned across his chair towards the witness box, and in those silken, charming, and extremely dangerous tones, enquired, 'Is Lord Winchester a very religious man ?'

Answer : 'He was not until I took care of him, and now he very much enjoys going to church.'

I shall never forget that. My revulsion against this hypocrisy was such that I felt it must be shared by the Judge, and I believed that I had a leader up on the Bench.

Next day, after she had agreed that she was a wealthy woman, she said that there was no significance in her writing to the old man as 'my beloved', for a great many people wrote to her in that manner.

Asked about the words of the Marquess 'the flutter of your kiss on my lips which was the token of the perfection of our relationship' she said, 'We were informally engaged and it was the very least I could allow.' She added, 'I was not in love with him in the very least.' (That I believed.)

Then her answers became more and more improbable.

Q.   In your letter you say 'something will happen to save us both'. What did that mean?

A.   I hoped Lord Winchester would get enough money to pay his hotel bill and would get enough food.

Q.   In another letter you say, 'you must have prayed hard night and day as I have done'. What did you pray for?

A.   Again that he would have enough food. (Laughter).

The Judge : If there are any more of these silly gusts of laughter, I shall clear the well of the Court. The public in the gallery are behaving perfectly well. This is not a place of public entertainment.

Q.   'The Garden of Eden without Adam'. What does that man?

A.   Why, my name is Eve. It was just a joke.

She then said that the Marquess was always in a state of chronic impecuniosity and that she thought that a Swedish friend of his was paying for the annulment.

Q.   If there was to be an annulment the Plaintiff would cease to be Lady Winchester because the marriage had never been. If there was a divorce, she would be the ex-Lady Winchester and you would not like this Parsee getting your title?

A.   I did not know that I was going to marry him. I might have. I did tell him that if I married him, she should not be able to use his name.

Q.   It was one of the big things in your life that this woman should be stopped calling herself Lady Winchester?

A.   I thought it would be very confusing if we both got letters. I should not like my letters to go astray. (No laughter!)

I am afraid that the old lady was in the witness box for eleven hours. It hurt me, obviously not as much as it ought to have hurt her, but it could not be avoided.

Yet another day and the learned Judge decided that the tort of harbouring had disappeared with the welfare state. It is all in the Law Reports, if any reader should be interested. I was left with two alleged breaches of the agreement (1) persuading or inducing Lord Winchester to file his petition for nullity and (2) financing the petition.

We made final speeches with which I will not bore the reader. I talked about Jezebel, Sapphira, Mrs Malaprop and Dido – (but then I was young and keen.) On 26th November 1957 we had our judgment which had been written.

> The events leading to the writ which initiated the action by the Plaintiff on the 2nd May 1954 showed that neither Lord Winchester nor the Defendant entertained those notions about the responsibilities and obligations of marriage which are commonly approved. That action was compromised in the terms of a settlement now alleged to have been broken.

This passage came early in the judgment which I shall try to summarise.

The Judge carefully considered all that the Defendant had said and having said everything that could be said for Mrs Fleming, concluded that her evidence had not been candid.

'I reject her evidence', he said dramatically. He found that the Marquess required no persuasion or inducement to file the petition beyond the provision of money. As to that the natural inference was that Mrs Fleming had found the whole or at least a part of the finance and accordingly the Plaintiff had proved her point. There would therefore be judgment for Lady Winchester for a sum to be ascertained after an inquiry as to damages.

We were all wildly excited, but the point remained as to whether Gilbert would appeal on the question as to the date of Mrs Fleming's 'interference'.

Well, he did appeal. Somebody told me that his client, who could well afford to pay the costs and damages, didn't want to appeal, but that Gilbert was insistent. I should think that this was so, for he indicated as much on his death-bed. There he declared that he wanted his ashes to be fed to the fishes in the water nearby, and that his mantle would fall upon me. He had given up shaving by this time and with his beard and his poor sunken face looked like a Hebrew prophet, and I was ashamed to think that I had forgotten all that I ever knew about Elisha.

He addressed the Court for six whole days on how wrong the Judge was to reject Mrs Fleming's evidence, and how incomprehensible it was that a lady of very considerable wealth should commit perjury. In his excitement, he continually referred to my client as 'Lady Windermere'. Eventually, I was tempted to rise to my feet and say, 'My Lords, I can understand that my learned friend is not Lady Winchester's fan, but at least he might refer to her by her correct name.' I thought this to be a piece of deathless wit, but there was not a smile, even from Lord Pearce, who is the wittiest after dinner speaker I have ever heard, and I have heard very many. Lord Justice Jenkins merely said, 'Yes, Mr Beyfus' and I sat down deflated. Literary jokes generally fall flat although Lord Darling was constantly responsible for 'laughter in Court in which his Lordship joined' when displaying his erudition. But that was a long time ago, and by all accounts he was not a good judge.

At last Gilbert finished his address, and I said, 'My friends have laboured for six days. Today being the seventh day they can rest, and it is for me to endeavour to persuade your Lordships that, looking upon their handiwork, it is not very good.' This sally also fell upon stony ground, although I don't suppose they thought it was blasphemous. I think that they were bored after so long a speech which their natural good manners did not allow them to cut short in view of the seniority of the speaker.

However, they brightened up appreciably when I said that there were only two points in the case, (1) whether there was evidence that Mrs Fleming financed the petition and (2) whether there was a breach of agreement by her between 19th July and 8th August 1956, and sat down. I suppose I took about an hour, during which I likened my opponent to 'the wise thrush : he sings his song twice over, lest you think he never could recapture the first fine careless rapture'. 'Or perhaps I should have said thrice', I added.

Dear old Gilbert roared with laughter at this, in spite of the fact that it was aimed at his deaf ear and I was in the row behind him. He had a habit of turning round to look at you, however, when he wanted to hear you particularly, and he must have been doing this at the time. Usually, of course, my eyes would be on the tribunal, or the jury as the case might be, but if you happened to turn and see this face looking round at you it could be a daunting sight, as he had a nervous tic below the eye, caused by an accident in the hunting field. Not a smile, however, disturbed the judicial faces.

It really is not done to try and enliven the tedium of a trial, unless you are as old as Beyfus, who could be very amusing, particularly with a jury. Indeed, during his speech, he contended that the truth of the matter was that the Judge, when he thought of the point of the financing of the petition on the sixth day of the trial, became so bewitched by the hare that he had raised that thereafter counsel had no chance. Nobody smiled at this astonishing mixture of metaphors, and I had to suppress the desire to point out that hares were not known to ride on broomsticks. It did not however escape *The Times* reporter who had a heading next day : 'Judge bewitched by own hare'. I also had to suppress the fact that in my very opening address at the trial I had referred to the £500 deposited by the Marquess as security for costs and had said, 'He had not 500 pennies. I ask your Lordship to infer the source of the money.' So much for the hare on the sixth day.

The next day Gilbert was off again and took the whole morning to reply with no interruptions from anyone. At two o'clock Hubert Parker (later Lord Chief Justice) read the judgment of the Court, which he must have written the night before and had had typed during Gilbert's reply in the morning.

The judgment went against us on the question of dates, but all Gilbert's efforts to whitewash the character of his client were in vain.

As to that, the Court said that the Judge had formed a view that Mrs Fleming was not being candid. How could their Lordships differ? Indeed, were they at liberty to do so, they would not, from a reading of the transcript, feel so inclined. They thought that the only fair approach was to reject the whole of Mrs Fleming's evidence on the initiation and prosecution of the petition.

Approaching the matter in that way, they continued, the position appeared to be as follows :

(1) there was at all material times, except for a period of coolness at the end of 1952 and the beginning of 1953, a strong attachment between Lord Winchester and the Defendant. The Defendant had a strong incentive to help him to obtain his freedom.

(2) Mrs Fleming had adequate means to help him financially.

(3) Lord Winchester was by his standards impecunious. There was no acceptable evidence that he had saved money to prosecute the petition (i.e., they did not accept what Mrs Fleming had said about this).

(4) Lord Winchester had other wealthy friends, but he had not been in contact with them for nearly three years.

(5) Five hundred pounds had undoubtedly been found and paid into Court early in 1957 as security for the wife's costs.

On the other hand (6) the wife could never get to the point of showing some unexplained payment by Mrs Fleming and inviting the Court to infer that such payment was referable to financing the petition. It was for the wife to raise, on a balance of probabilities, an inference not merely that Mrs Fleming financed the petition, but that she did so within the critical period of 19th July to 8th August 1956.

They saw no grounds for inferring that any actual payments were made by Mrs Fleming during the critical period. Indeed it was, in their view, if anything more probable that she would have refused to commit herself by promising to pay the costs of the nullity proceedings. She would have confined any assistance she gave to the payment, if she thought fit, to Lord Winchester or his lawyers of sums required in respect of costs as and when necessity arose.

So there it was. We had lost, and Gilbert had gained a Pyrrhic victory, and failed to exculpate his client. I thought that we were unlucky, as it seemed to me the obvious inference that, when Lord Winchester went to his solicitor in Nassau about the proposed petition for nullity, the solicitor must have said, 'Who is going to pay for all this?' and the Marquess must have said, 'Mrs Fleming' and the solicitor must have satisfied himself by enquiring from Mrs Fleming if that was so. Otherwise there would have been no petition : for solicitors do not take speculative work for a bankrupt which is almost bound to be unsuccessful on the ground that he was not even domiciled in the relevant jurisdiction.

Lady Winchester was ordered to pay all the costs of the action and half the costs of the appeal. This latter was presumably because Gilbert had taken up so much time defending his client's character unsuccessfully.

I was refused leave to go to the House of Lords. I would have called it a day, but Lady Winchester instructed me to go to the Appeals Committee of the House of Lords. I did that : they were very patient, but refused to allow me to appeal. I still think however that Lord Devlin was correct in finding for my client, and that she did not receive justice.

The Marquess died either at ninety-nine or a hundred; I think the former. Mrs Fleming I believe to be dead; the Marchioness is still alive. I have never spoken to her since the case but I have several times seen her in a magnificent sari in Westminster Abbey as I walked in procession after the service on 1st October out into the open air and over to the Lord Chancellor's 'breakfast' in the House of Lords. I am told that she paid all the costs which must have been very substantial. She is said to have announced that she had 'made' me. She certainly provided a case the advertisement from which brought me a lot of work, and I am very grateful for that.

In fact, by this time I was Recorder of Deal, an appointment which I didn't want and for which I didn't apply. But when a ghostly and un-identified voice from the Lord Chancellor's Department told me by telephone that it had been asked to find out why I hadn't applied, I surrendered and did so. Bridget was quite pleased because I got into *Who's Who* for the first time. But I refused to buy it saying that it was a 'wicked waste of money'.

Once, it is generally believed, you flout the Lord Chancellor's Depart-ment, you have 'had it', and although I had not thought of the Bench, I didn't want to be foolish. It was while the Winchester case was going on that I had to go to Deal on a Saturday in my official capacity to watch Prince Philip open a new pier, and I was very flattered when Lord Cornwallis, the Lord Lieutenant of Kent, came into the robing room while I was putting on my robes and medals. I had read of him, as a small boy and devout Kent cricket supporter, as Captain the Hon W. S. Cornwallis, the opening fast bowler for the County. He knew all about the case and asked me what I thought about the prospects. I was full of it, and unloaded the point about the dates upon him, which was both technical and complicated. But he got it at once and actually seemed interested. Then we formed up at attention to await the arrival of the Duke. We faced the civic dignitaries and I had Lord Cornwallis on one side and an Admiral who had materialised from nowhere, covered in gongs, on the other. Later I was presented with a photograph of the occasion, and thirteen years later still it fell out of some book or other. Elizabeth picked it up and said, 'That's Uncle Gorgeous', (the children's name for Admiral Sir Frederick Parham, my stepdaughter's godfather, who was then Commander-in-Chief at the Nore and had commanded the *Belfast*, now in London River, and had been the first to open fire in the Normandy landings). On that day in Deal we were unaware of each other's existence.

CHAPTER SIXTEEN

Taking Silk

The Bank Rate tribunal was a political affair, which aroused enormous public interest, in which I played a very small part. The suggestion had been made that highly placed people in the Tory party had revealed the fact that here was to be an increase in the Bank Rate to a select few; an improper leak, to use an unattractive modern expression. I appeared for the late Donald Maclachlan, the deputy Managing Editor, and Francis Whitmore, then City Editor, of the *Daily Telegraph* who were said to have received the information. I had to cross-examine Sir Leslie Plummer, a Labour MP, whose name was always associated with Mr Attlee's government's ill-fated African ground nuts scheme, which was bad luck. He stubbornly refused to apologise however and did not cut much of a figure. My people, of course, had done nothing wrong at all, and were exculpated by the Tribunal presided over by Lord Justice Parker, later Lord Chief Justice. *The Daily Telegraph* gave me a dinner at Brooks's afterwards which I thought was very kind of them.

The highlight of the proceedings was the cross-examination of Mr Harold Wilson MP, as he then was, by the present Lord Russell of Killowen, and the most amusing, for me, was when I cross-examined Mr (now Sir) Gordon Newton, the editor of *The Financial Times* who had been up at Sidney with me and was once engaged to my sister. We had to appear strangers. On the third day of the hearing, *The Daily Mail* received a summons to attend and I went down there with the editor and the late Dennis Walsh, the newspaper's solicitor, thinking that the holding of two good briefs simultaneously was not to be despised. When we arrived, however, Reggie Manningham-Buller, the Attorney-General, (now Viscount Dilhorne), who was leading for the Crown, came over to us, asked to be introduced, and apologised for a mistake in the Treasury Solicitor's office, saying that *The Daily Mail* ought never to have been bothered. The editor was delighted, but I was perhaps a tiny little bit disappointed.

There were a number of counsel employed in this matter, of whom no less than fourteen have attained 'high judicial office' (which means the

High Court or higher still). One of them, like all three members of the Tribunal, is dead already, and one has moved away to another profession. The Tribunal is something for the rest of us to look back upon with pleasure. Especially Charles Russell's final address. He practised at the Chancery Bar, and I was of the opinion that the boredom of conducting Chancery work was only exceeded by the boredom of listening to Chancery leaders. How wrong I was was plain, when I listened to this gem, like the most superb of after dinner speeches, and with the inevitable effect of such a speech, that I cannot remember a word that he said.

My practice had now become exciting and fun. All big practices of course involve hard work, but not all involve fun. I remember a man with a much larger practice than I ever attained, and who went to the Bench before I did, saying to me once, 'I'm tired of my work. I've done it all before'. Lucrative it undoubtedly was, but dull, and I did not envy him. And those practitioners who spend their lives defending crime must, unless they are wholly insensitive, live on their nerves and eventually get ulcers. Poor Bill Fearnley-Whittingstall, pacing up and down the corridor at the Old Bailey, chain-smoking cigarettes endlessly, while the jury was out, comes immediately to mind. I was like Sergeant Sullivan who is said to have remarked, 'A wonderful profession : to do what you most want to do all the time, and then to get paid for it as well.'

Soon after Lady Winchester's case, I found that solicitors began to brief me with a junior quite frequently, presumably on the basis that they were in effect briefing leading counsel without having to pay him as such, and with the added security that he probably wouldn't run away to another court, leaving a small boy to carry on.

I was earning about £10,000 a year, gross, of course, which in those days was a lot of money for a junior, and I toyed with the idea of taking silk, in the hope of getting the big defamation work. It was true that Gerald Gardiner was there, and looked as though he would be there for ever. He would obviously be the first choice of any litigant but I thought that, as he couldn't be on both sides at once, I might be number two. On the other hand, I was over fifty, which is generally much too old to take silk if you are serious about it, for solicitors are likely to think that the old man is tired after his strenuous life at the junior bar, and has taken silk in order to retire.

Bridget, of course, thought that they would offer to make me Lord Chancellor as soon as I took silk, but that I must take silk all the same and show poor Gilbert where he got off. I pointed out that I was devoted to Gilbert, that there was not the slightest chance of anybody offering me anything, and that 'taking silk' was a misleading expression for one generally had to apply for three years running before being accepted. I tried it out on my ex-clerk who said 'You're much too bloody old' rather brusquely. Then I tried it out on my then clerk, Lionel Hawkins. He had an unparalleled experience of the big guns in advocacy. He had been clerk to Mr Justice Croom-Johnson, to Lord Jowitt, Lord Devlin and Lord Pearson, to give them their final titles, except that Bill Jowitt became an Earl. To my surprise he said that he wondered why I hadn't applied before. Now this was a splendid gesture. Clerks in the days when I started were paid on an antiquated scale, the result of which was that a junior with lots of tiny little briefs was much better for the clerk than a leader with a few big briefs. When we came back from the war we found that all that had changed and the clerks were demanding 'bobs on the guineas' or in some cases 'ten per cent'. That at least is what I was told.

But with Edward Love and with Lionel Hawkins, his successor, it was 'old scale' and you could never find a less greedy man than Lionel. It was typical that he should urge me into silk at an almost certain financial loss to himself, and I shall never forget that. I knew that if I was refused silk I was too old to apply again, and I wrote to five judges asking them to act as referees for me. They all said that they would. Actually, I couldn't read Owlie's letter, but there was such a lot of it that I considered it was favourable. All the same, I didn't know the Lord Chancellor, and he might think that I did nothing but libel, which was far from the truth, and I told Bridget to keep her fingers crossed.

I knew that if Lord Kilmuir granted me a silk gown, I should be faced with financial problems. I had a very expensive house to maintain and a wife to provide for as well as a boy at Cambridge, a boy at Uppingham, and a girl at a day-school. I should, as is usually the case, earn very little for my first year in silk, and be lumbered with surtax demands from my more profitable years as an elderly junior. I didn't want to have to borrow money from Papa who by this time had been living with us, inexpensively for him, for nineteen years, but I knew that he would help me if it became necessary.

One of the rules which is designed to help people with family responsibilities to take the plunge is that a new silk is allowed, for the period of one year only, to conduct his junior practice, dressed as a silk, but without his client having to pay a junior counsel to appear with him.

After that the new silk is in the swimming bath at the deep end, and it is a help to be able to swim, or to be a bachelor, or to have some private means.

And so, hoping for silk, and praying for luck thereafter, I decided to hedge my bets by arranging for a 'caravan holiday' in a field in Cornwall near a village called Gorran. The holiday which, had I known what the future was to hold, I should have cancelled, was an unmitigated disaster.

But what did that matter? In April I took silk : in the summer we had the Liberace case : in September I was appointed to look into the 'Jasper Affair' concerning the Star Building Society : in November I had the brief for Lord Keyes in which I cross-examined Zena Daniels, and the flood of exciting work never stopped until I found myself a High Court Judge on 11th January 1963.

Enough to fill a volume? Indeed : and that's what I hope it will do next year.

Index

Index